Handwriting Analysis
Putting It to Work for You

"Handwriting analysis was once sneeringly labeled a pseudoscience, but is now gaining acceptance as a useful diagnostic tool in business, criminology, medicine, and psychology. . . . McNichol's commonsense explanations are salted with wry humor and ironic observations on the handwriting of the famous as well as the infamous. No one, including the reader, is safe from her barbs. This is an excellent introduction to graphology . . . and an incentive to type all correspondence!"
—Library Journal

"I am a skeptic whose wife brought home your book. I found myself starting to read it and then couldn't put it down. Now I find that I use what you've taught me in every aspect of my life. Thank you for your excellent book."
—Dr. Joseph Walken
Madison, WI

"I am astounded by how easy you have made it for anyone to understand the connection between people's handwriting and the way they behave. You have a real gift for teaching."
—Susan Rosenberg
Teacher, Atlanta, GA

"Not only was your book the most fascinating, informative, and thorough I've read on the subject—it was very difficult to put down!"
—Constance Masters
Sales Rep., Dayton, OH

"After reading your book I will never look at handwriting the same way. I will be able to use what I have learned almost every day, at work and in my personal life."—John Shortell
Coventry, CT

"Thank you for writing such a delightful book. Your skill in graphology is high, but your skill as a teacher is superlative. I enjoyed greatly your sense of humor, wit, and development of topics."
—Cliff Farris
Engineer, Cypress, TX

"Thank you for your outstanding book. I think it is the best book yet that helps the uninitiated understand our profession."
—Marcel B. Matley
Graphologist, San Francisco, CA

"I enjoyed your book immensely, and ever since I've been busy analyzing everybody I know."
—Douglas Hoffmire, M.D.
Long Beach, NY

Sample A

IF RELATED TO ANYONE IN OUR EMPLOY
STATE NAME AND DEPARTMENT
(OMIT NAME OF SPOUSE)

(ACCOUNTING)

SUSAN LITTLE   REFERRED BY   SUSAN   FIRST

EMPLOYMENT DESIRED

POSITION SYSTEMS ENGINEER   DATE YOU CAN START Now   SALARY DESIRED 30,000

ARE YOU EMPLOYED NOW? YES   IF SO MAY WE INQUIRE OF YOUR PRESENT EMPLOYER? IT'S OKAY   MIDDLE

Sample B

IF RELATED TO ANYONE IN OUR EMPLOY
STATE NAME AND DEPARTMENT
(OMIT NAME OF SPOUSE)

Nobody   REFERRED BY   Jerry   FIRST

EMPLOYMENT DESIRED

POSITION Computer operating   DATE YOU CAN START May 1, 1986   SALARY DESIRED 2400/month

ARE YOU EMPLOYED NOW? Yes   IF SO MAY WE INQUIRE OF YOUR PRESENT EMPLOYER? NO. I don't want them to.   MIDDLE

Sample C

IF RELATED TO ANYONE IN OUR EMPLOY
STATE NAME AND DEPARTMENT
(OMIT NAME OF SPOUSE)

No   REFERRED BY   Sandra Lisbon   FIRST

EMPLOYMENT DESIRED

POSITION Data Entry   DATE YOU CAN START July   SALARY DESIRED 25,000 a year

ARE YOU EMPLOYED NOW? Yes I an   IF SO MAY WE INQUIRE OF YOUR PRESENT EMPLOYER? I would rather you didn't   MIDDLE

Sample D

IF RELATED TO ANYONE IN OUR EMPLOY
STATE NAME AND DEPARTMENT
(OMIT NAME OF SPOUSE)

Fred Conad   REFERRED BY   FIRST

EMPLOYMENT DESIRED

POSITION Regional Sales   DATE YOU CAN START Now   SALARY DESIRED #32,500 ∞

ARE YOU EMPLOYED NOW? Yes   IF SO MAY WE INQUIRE OF YOUR PRESENT EMPLOYER? No   MIDDLE

CAUGHT RED-HANDED

Who Murdered the Secretary's Boss?

A secretary who was responsible for throwing a surprise party for her boss drove to work the night before the party to secretly decorate his office.

She used her key to enter the building. As she approached her desk, she heard the voices of two men engaged in a heated argument inside her boss's office farther down the hall. She recognized her boss's voice but not the other man's. She stopped and decided she should probably leave and come back later.

Just then the argument grew louder and more furious, and the unidentified man began screaming and threatening her boss, saying, "You used to tell me you love me. You used to give me compliments and show me your feelings! And now you don't and I can't stand it! I sit at home alone, day after day. And now you're spending all your time with Boomer! Don't lie to me! I know you are! And I'm going to get rid of him. Boomer is history tonight!" Frozen, the secretary listened to the man grow angrier and angrier, until suddenly a gunshot rang out!

Shocked and not wanting to be seen when the killer emerged from the office, the secretary dove under a desk. She watched a man's feet dash past her and out the door. Paralyzed for a few moments, she finally got up and slowly entered her boss's office. She found his bloody, lifeless body slumped over his desk. She called 911.

That night, you, the graphologist, are called in to examine the handwriting of a pool of suspects. On the opposite page are four of those writing samples, one of which was produced by the killer. Can you spot the killer before he strikes again?

———— ◆ ————

This is an actual case for which Andrea McNichol was called in to help find the murderer. After reading this book, you too will know enough about graphology to be able to pick out the killer by his handwriting. You will be able to do it not only for this crime but for the many other real-life cases described throughout *Handwriting Analysis*.

For a full discussion of and the solution to this case, see page 284.

Handwriting Analysis
Putting It to Work for You

Andrea McNichol
with Jeffrey A. Nelson

CONTEMPORARY BOOKS

Library of Congress Cataloging-in-Publication Data

McNichol, Andrea.
    Handwriting analysis : putting it to work for you : a practical
step-by-step approach / Andrea McNichol with Jeffrey A. Nelson;
illustrations by John McNichol.
        p.   cm.
    Includes bibliographical references.
    ISBN 0-8092-4023-8 (pbk.)
    1. Graphology.   2. Writing—Identification.   I. Nelson, Jeffrey
A., 1956–   .   II. Title.
BF891.M36   1991
155.2′82—dc20   90-28404
                                      CIP

ACKNOWLEDGMENT OF PERMISSIONS

The authors would like to thank Kathi de Sainte Colombe for her generous permission to reprint certain handwriting specimens from her late husband's book, *Grapho-Therapeutics: Pen & Pencil Therapy*. The same appreciation is due to Melvin Powers at Wilshire Books for permitting us to reprint some samples from two of Nadya Olyanova's books, *Handwriting Tells* and *The Psychology of Handwriting: Secrets of Handwriting Analysis*.

Finally, a few other samples come from *Handwriting: A Key to Personality* by Klara G. Roman, copyright 1952 by Pantheon Books, Inc. These samples are reprinted by permission of Pantheon Books, a division of Random House, Inc. A special thanks to Gordon Gushee of Scriptorium and to Todd Gold of *People* magazine.

The rest of the handwriting samples in this book have been drawn from the collection of Andrea McNichol. The only exceptions relate to those cases where it was necessary to protect privacy and other rights of individuals. In those cases, substitute handwriting samples, which display the same traits as the originals, have been used.

Note: Throughout the book, for simplicity and brevity, the authors have used the personal pronouns *he*, *his*, *him*, and *himself* to refer to both males and females.

CONTENTS

ACKNOWLEDGMENTS

The authors would like to offer their heartfelt thanks to the many friends and associates who've lent a hand along the way.

Thanks are due to John McNichol for his time and energy drawing the superb characters and illustrations that are sprinkled throughout the book.

Much appreciation is due to all those who read drafts of the book and gave us valued, constructive criticism and other help (in alphabetical order): Jean Abenader, Michael Barnathan, Mitch Engel, David Gale, Judy and Stu Hagmann, Udi and Dorit Harpaz, Kevin Marks, Dr. Byron Newman, Peter Noerdlinger, Leslie Petrovich, Fred Porter, Jeff Schaffer, Rajeev Vaidanathan, and Sylvia Zaslove.

Thanks also to a generous friend, Dr. Jeff Giannini, whose computer expertise allowed us to pull the work back from oblivion on a number of occasions when we thought all was lost.

Much appreciation to our wonderful agent, Susan Cohen, who helped open a number of doors for us, and then made sure we went through the right one.

Ed Molyneaux deserves very special thanks for wise suggestions, opinions, and ideas too numerous to list here.

To Jason and Ariel McNichol, many thanks for being the most brilliant and wonderful kids anyone could hope to work with, and for helping make this book possible.

It would be difficult to overestimate the contributions made by Jim and Mary-Armour Nelson. Their support, judgment, and enthusiasm were key factors in making this book a reality.

Finally, special thanks to Harvey Plotnick, Stacy Prince, and J. D. Fairbanks whose vision, enthusiasm, and warmth have made working with Contemporary Books a rare pleasure.

INTRODUCTION

Handwriting was my worst subject in school. My mother was always yelling at me about my handwriting. It never got hung on the walls like the other kids'. It was messy, ugly, and nothing like my mother's—she used to win penmanship awards for hers. I was not a chip off the old block; I was an embarrassment.

Now, some twenty-plus years after graduating from college, I am on the witness stand in L.A. Superior Court, and the examining attorney is asking me, "Would you state your profession for the record, Ms. McNichol?" I respond, "I am a handwriting expert."

Yes, as ironic as it may sound, I now make a living using my knowledge of handwriting to help "finger" forgers, thieves, arsonists, rapists, spies, murderers, and your everyday rogues and crooks. I specialize in personality assessment via handwriting, and in authenticating handwriting on questioned documents.

I guess you could say that the handwriting really was on the wall for me. I just didn't know it at the time. Now my mother sends me typed birthday cards!

My interest in graphology actually began way back when I first tried to improve my handwriting. At that time I began to notice a definite connection between how I was feeling at the moment and what my handwriting looked like. Then I began to observe that other people's handwriting seemed to reflect directly the way they were behaving. The kids who came on loud and boisterous, for example, had big, ostentatious scripts, and the bookworms who kept to themselves had small, precise writing.

I was seeing a psychologist in those young school days, and I related my handwriting experiences to her. She encouraged me and told me that I would need to go to Europe to study graphology because virtually nothing was offered on the subject in this country. She helped me arrange such studies at the Sorbonne in Paris and at the University of Heidelberg in Germany.

When I returned from Europe, I went off to the University of California, Berkeley, where I continued my studies by obtaining permission time and time again to write papers on graphology as related to such subjects as education, criminology, sociology, psychology, biology, and physiology.

After graduating from Berkeley, I undertook eight years of independent research in the field of graphology. I sought out psychiatrists and other medical doctors who were willing to participate in experiments correlating handwriting characteristics with mental and physical conditions.

In pursuing my research, I also received the cooperation of Alcoholics Anonymous, the National Association of Educators, four California penal institutions, and a variety of business groups. In these studies, I explored the relationship between handwriting and such traits as alcohol and drug use, intelligence, aptitudes, criminal tendencies, potential for success and/or failure, likely emotional behavior, drive, reliability, self-confidence, and physical condition.

Because I published the results of my research in the proper manner, I was allowed to design and teach a course in graphology at UCLA. The credibility of being an instructor of graphology on such a campus led to my first clients in the field. The rest, as they say, is history.

For many years now, I have been deeply troubled by the fact that the American public is both uninformed and misinformed about graphology and, therefore, is missing out on a truly wonderful and practical diagnostic tool. The main reason for this is that most people do not believe that our handwriting reveals anything useful about us. I've written this book in hopes of changing all that.

In the book, I have tried to employ the same method I use in my college classes. That method is to let you, the reader, interpret handwriting for yourself, right off the bat, rather than simply telling you what a given trait means. In this way, you can see and be convinced first hand of the logic behind the science.

Most chapters of this book start off with a quiz for you to take. These are designed to show you that the science of graphology is built on common sense and on simple, logical deductions that most people can already make without realizing it. In this way, I hope to demonstrate the validity of the science.

Because I also want to show you how useful graphology is in all segments of life, throughout the book I've included numerous real-life cases on which I was consulted. These cases cover many topics—crime solving, employment predicaments, and psychological problems, to name a few. You'll have a chance to look at handwriting samples like those I examined and to solve each case yourself. Then I'll reveal how the cases actually unfolded in real life.

After reading this book, you can expect to be able to know a great deal about a total stranger after just a few minutes of looking at his or her handwriting. You will be able to discern, for example, whether the writer is sane or insane, honest or dishonest, intelligent or not so intelligent, emotionally stable or unstable, motivated or lazy, in good health or poor health . . . and many other important characteristics. While you'll acquire a great deal of expertise after reading this book, it takes many years to become a thoroughly skilled graphologist, so don't go out and fire all your employees just yet!

I originally got interested in graphology because I was amazed by the idea that it was possible to know all about somebody just from his or her handwriting. You may share the same reason for your interest in the subject. Or perhaps you want to find out the meaning behind a few handwriting traits of your own, or those of someone else. Maybe you just want to see if there's really anything to graphology.

Whatever your reasons for reading this book, you are on your way to learning about one of the most fascinating "people sciences" in existence today. You will learn information that you will use the rest of your life. And, hopefully, you're going to have a lot of fun in the process.

Welcome to the world of graphology!

Andrea McNichol

LAST-CHANCE PAGE

I promise you that after reading this book, you will never feel the same about any handwriting again! You will never again be able to pass by a handwriting sample without wanting to analyze it, whether it be on a postcard, on a bulletin board, or in someone's underwear drawer.

So, before you read a single word about the subject, I know you will want to have one last unbiased sample of your own handwriting to analyze when you finish the book.

After more than fifteen years of teaching graphology, I can tell you that once you read even one chapter of this book, you will find yourself subtly starting to eliminate the "sickie" traits in your writing and adopting the positive ones.

So here's your last chance!

Get a blank, *unlined* sheet of 8½" by 11" paper and a good ballpoint pen, and write at least two paragraphs about anything you want. (In fact, please have several sheets of unlined paper and a scratch pad handy, as you will be using them throughout the book.) Do not copy your two paragraphs from somewhere else; the writing should be spontaneous. Then sign and date it. *Pretend that you are writing this for someone else to read.*

Always place several sheets of blank paper underneath what you're writing to prevent any nooks and crannies in the writing surface from coming through and affecting your writing, perhaps making it look as though you're about to have a heart attack or are on drugs!

The more you write now, the happier you'll be later when you find out what it all means.

Also, somewhere on your page you may want to include a factual lie. By a "factual" lie I mean something that can be proven, such as "My birthday is July 17." You have a birth certificate, which can prove that right or wrong. A "nonfactual" lie would be "I love spaghetti." You probably don't love *all* spaghetti, and anyway, how can we prove it?

Ready? Set? Go!

Handwriting Analysis
Putting It to Work for You

No one can get out of his own skin. We act as our psychological past, i.e., as our cerebral organization dictates. For this reason, we are bound to expose ourselves in the association experiment in exactly the same way as we do in our own handwriting.

—C. G. Jung, 1906

PART I
GETTING YOUR HANDS WET

1
FUN QUIZ

This quiz is designed to get you started in graphology, to give you a feeling of how and why it works. Please answer each of the following questions in five seconds or less, using plain old common sense. Put down your answer, A or B, on your scratch pad. (Answers are on page 8.)

1. Who's moodier, *A* or *B*?

A.

B.

2. Who's more extroverted, *A* or *B*?

A.

B.

3. Who likes to be in the middle of everything, *A* or *B*?

A.

B.

4. Who's feeling more aggressive, *A* or *B*?

A.

B.

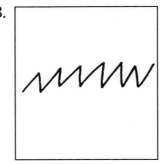

5. Who's feeling more depressed, *A* or *B*?

A.

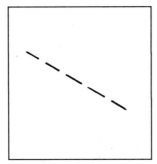

B.

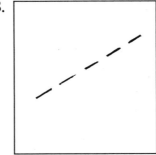

6. Who's feeling more uptight and narrow-minded, *A* or *B*?

A.

B.

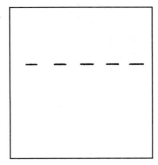

7. Who holds back his feelings, *A* or *B*?

A.

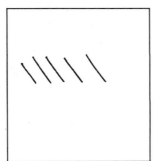

B.

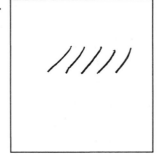

8. Who's feeling more economical, *A* or *B*?

A. 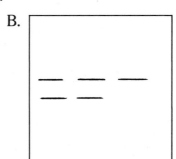   B.

9. Who ventures out more, *A* or *B*?

A. 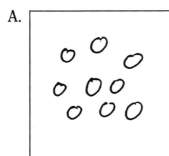   B.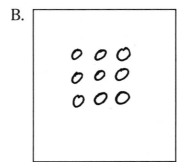

10. Who's feeling more organized, *A* or *B*?

A. 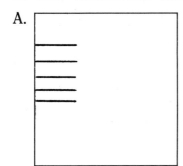   B.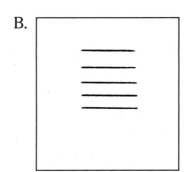

11. Who's writing about the future, *A* or *B*?

A. 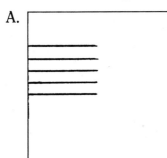   B.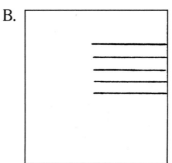

Now let's do some samples using actual words.

12. Who's Japanese, *A* or *B*?

A.

さらに　ご希望に応じ、移民法に
無料で行いたく存じます。　ご多忙に
あるいは　お電話にて　ご回答のほど賜

B.

probably get this way
so I want to say,
is 5 people here taking
sabotage all the people

13. Who is communicating better, *A* or *B*?

A.

Woll, I am really
but I late to see
to the Wrong reason
on. & as) the defense

B.

Wow! I am really
but of late to see
has been very di

14. Who's feeling more active, *A* or *B*?

A.

active

B.

active

15. Who's feeling defensive and has something to hide, *A* or *B*?

A.

hide

B.

hide

16. Who's more reliable and predictable at this time, *A* or *B*?

A.

who's more reliable AND PRE-dictable ?

B.

who's more reliable and predictable ?

17. Who's more dishonest about money, *A* or *B*?

A.

We agreed on:
$ 765,498.⁰⁰

B.

We agreed on:
$ 103,498.⁰⁰

18. Which Mrs. Smith wants a divorce from Mr. Smith, *A* or *B*?

A.

Sincerely,
Sally Smith

B.

Sincerely,
Sally Smith

Extra Credit

19. Jack works for both Mr. *A* and Mr. *B*. Based on the way each wrote the name *Jack*, who is more likely to give him a raise?

Mr. A

Please have Jack come see me

Mr. B

Please have Jack come see me.

20. Which writer is a convicted killer, *A* or *B*?

Sample A

have, Nothing to loose but and a world to win —

Sample B

seek new and better ways, to challenge and to oppose, where necessary, to make our

Answers to Fun Quiz

1. A	7. A	13. B	EXTRA CREDIT
2. B	8. A	14. A	19. Mr. A
3. B	9. B	15. B	20. A
4. B	10. B	16. B	
5. A	11. B	17. A	
6. A	12. A	18. B	

Did you get most or even all of these questions right? Why? Let's take a closer look in the next chapter.

2

EXPLANATION OF ANSWERS

Let's take a closer look at the answers to the Fun Quiz.

1. Who's moodier, *A* or *B*?

A.

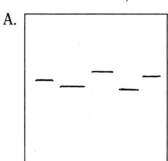

B.

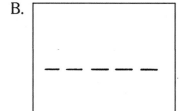

The answer is *A*. Why *A*? Because the lines are uneven. When people are moody, we say that they are "up and down," not on an even keel," that they "don't have both feet planted firmly on the ground." You already realize this connection to handwriting instinctively, but perhaps didn't consciously know it until this moment.

2. Who's more extroverted, *A* or *B*?

A.

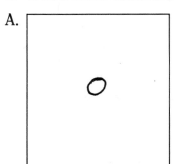

B.

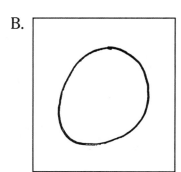

The answer is *B* because the circle is bigger. What do you think of when you think of an extrovert? Don't you think of someone who enjoys getting a lot of attention, who makes expansive gestures and speaks in a way that invites people to listen, who comes on big?

3. Who likes to be in the middle of everything, *A* or *B*?

A.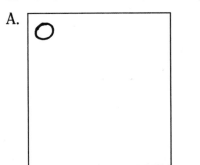

B.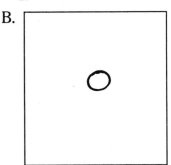

Again, the answer is *B*. In graphology, the blank piece of paper represents life itself, and where you choose to put your words on the paper represents how you choose to interact with your environment and other people.

If I give you a blank sheet of paper and ask you to sign your name on it, and you choose the corner, that's what you do in life. You stay on the edges, the fringes. You don't see yourself in the middle of what's going on.

4. Who's feeling more aggressive?

A.

B.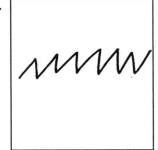

B is more aggressive because his lines are angular, while *A*'s are round.

Aggression by nature causes your muscles to tense. When your muscles tense, you can only make an angle. When do you tense up? When you're angry, nervous, uptight, aggressive, fearful, determined, competitive, hard-working, hard-driving.

Some angularity in your handwriting is desirable. When there is too much of it, though, we know that the writer is too constricted.

Roundness can be created only by relaxing the muscles. All the things that encourage relaxation such as love, peacefulness, flexibility, communication, and agreement are associated with roundness.

5. Who's feeling more depressed?

A. 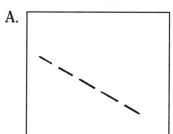   B.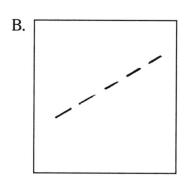

A is feeling more depressed. We know this because the lines are going downhill. We say things like "down in the mouth," "downtrodden," "down-hearted," and feeling "down."

6. Who's feeling more uptight and narrow-minded?

A. 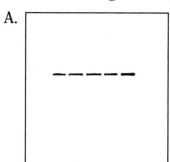   B.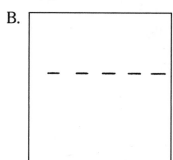

Did you say A? Why is A more uptight and narrow-minded? Please take your pen and scratch paper, and try imitating the handwriting in samples A and B below, and see how it feels. This is the best way I know for you to see for yourself.

A.    B.

Did one way of writing make you feel constricted and the other way make you feel open and more relaxed?

Are you starting to get a feel for how graphology works?

7. Who holds back his feelings?

A.   B.

The answer is *A*. Now, how could you know that *A* holds back his feelings? You see only five lines leaning to the left and five lines leaning to the right. Why is leaning to the left "holding back"? Left is back, and right is forward—where do we get that from? For now, I ask only that you think about this question; we'll look at it in greater depth later.

8. Who's feeling more economical?

A.   B.

The answer is *A*. If you conserve paper, you tend to be the type who, no matter what you do, wants to conserve. You automatically want to leave room in case you have something to add later.

9. Who ventures out more?

A.   B.

The answer here is *B*. Adventurous people tend to go toward the center and do not cling to the side as we see in *A*'s sample. They will venture further out.

10. Who's feeling more organized?

A. 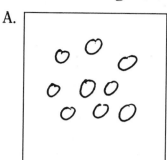   B.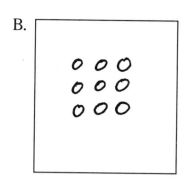

B is feeling more organized. You can tell because the little circles are arranged in order. When you're feeling organized, you do things neatly, even if you're doodling. If you're feeling disorganized, your movements and productivity are haphazard, going in all directions, not forming any shape or pattern, aimless, like *A*'s sample.

11. Who's writing about the future?

A. 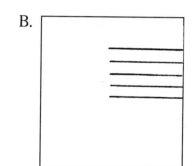   B.

I'll bet you said *B*. Why? It's only five lines on the right side of the page. Why is the right associated with the future and the left with the past?

Which foot do you get started on? Is someone your "left-hand man" or your "right-hand man"? Why do we shake with our right hands . . . ? As we will see later, there are a number of subconscious associations for right and left, such as past and future, that are shared universally and are just as significant in graphology as anywhere else in life.

OK, now let's see how you did when analyzing actual words.

12. Who's Japanese?

A.

さらに　ご希望に応じ、移民法に
無料で 行いたく存じます。 ご多忙に
あるいは お電話にて ご回答のほど賜

B.

*probably get this way
so I want to say,
5 people here taking
sabotage all the people*

Well, I just wanted to make sure you got *one* right!

13. Who is communicating better?

A.

*Wow, I am really
but late to sell
to the wrong illion
in. A a) the defer;*

B.

*Wow! I am really
but of late to sell
has been very di*

OK, I wanted you to get *two* right! I hope this answer is obvious, because the only sample you can read is *B*. If you take a pen in hand to write something meant for someone else to read, and you can't write legibly, like *A*, then you've accomplished absolutely nothing, because the reader has no idea what you've written. You are not communicating well at all.

14. Who's feeling more active?

A.

active

B.

active

A is feeling more active. What is it about *A*'s sample that makes you think the writer is feeling more active? It looks as if it were written *faster*; it's more *energetic*.

These samples remind me of the two pedestrians in the crosswalk when you're driving somewhere in a big hurry, and you have to stop to allow them to cross. One pedestrian (*B*) just saunters across the street, wearing earphones and taking his sweet old time, rocking to the music, and you know he has nowhere to go and nothing to do, and you want to kill him! He writes slowly for sure.

14

The other pedestrian (*A*) races across the street with purpose, and you know he's got a lot to do, places to go, and people to see! He writes quickly.

The same common sense we use in reading body language applies to our understanding of handwriting. But handwriting tells us so much more than body language.

15. Who's feeling defensive and has something to hide?

A.

B.

B feels defensive and has something to hide. If you're afraid someone's going to attack you, are you going to stand there like this?

Or like this?

When you're defensive, you close up, you take cover. The line on the end of *B*'s word is called a "cover stroke," and it means defensiveness. It means, "I have something I don't want you to see."

16. Who's more reliable and predictable at this time?

A.

B.

Predictability means being able to predict what a person is going to do next. Here we wonder about *A*. Is he going to keep the punctuation the same, the style the same, the rhythm, spacing, size the same? The more a person keeps changing his writing in the same sample, the more unreliable and unpredictable that person is at the time. *B*, on the other hand, is consistent in all aspects of his writing and is therefore deemed more reliable at the time.

17. Who's more dishonest about money?

A.

We agreed on:
$ 765,498 <u>00</u>

B.

We agreed on:
$ 103,498. <u>00</u>

A is more dishonest about money because his numbers are indistinct and touched up. *B* is more honest about money because the numbers are easy to read. Who knows *what* numbers *A* is writing?

There are only ten digits (0 through 9), and unlike words, numerals must be completely legible. You can be illegible on a few letters or words and still preserve and communicate the content of your writing. When writing a number, however, you must be 100 percent legible, or the dollar amount, address, telephone number, or whatever may be misread.

Graphologists find that people who feel dishonest about money, represented here by numbers, often make a number look like any other number so later they can say, "No, that was a 4," or, "No, that was a 9."

When you can't write a number clearly, it's either because you've lost neurological control or because you consciously or subconsciously want to be unclear about it. Writing numbers illegibly is the number one handwriting trait shared by convicted embezzlers.

18. Which Mrs. Smith wants a divorce from Mr. Smith?

A.

Sincerely,
Sally Smith

B.

Sincerely,
Sally Smith

I hope this was obvious: *B* is crossing out her husband, "Smith." Not the happiest marriage!

19. Jack works for both Mr. *A* and Mr. *B*. Based on the way each wrote the name *Jack*, who is more likely to give him a raise?

Mr. A

Please have Jack come see me .

Mr. B

Please have Jack come see me .

Mr. *A* is much more likely to give Jack a raise. If you got this extra credit question right, it is because you know that we automatically give stature to something we think is important and reduce the stature of that which we think small.

Mr. *A* subconsciously enlarged the *J* when he wrote "Jack"; he thinks "big" of Jack, Jack looms large in his mind. On the other hand, when Mr. *B* wrote "Jack," he made it the same size, perhaps even smaller. He's not thinking of Jack in the same way at all. He doesn't think very much of Jack.

20. Which writer is a convicted killer, *A* or *B*?

Sample A

have, Nothing to loose b: and a world to win —

Sample B

seek new and better ways, to challenge and to oppose, where necessary, to make our

The convicted killer is *A*. This is the writing of Sirhan Sirhan, who assassinated Robert Kennedy in the late sixties. It's logical that someone like Sirhan, who exhibited highly unstable behavior by assassinating a presidential candidate, would have highly unstable handwriting. In unstable handwriting, the aspects of the writing are not even, as in *A*'s sample.

17

B's writing is that of Mayor Tom Bradley, who was chief of police of Los Angeles for twenty years before becoming mayor. We would hope such a man would exhibit stable traits and that therefore his writing would look more even than that of a convicted killer.

How many did you get right?

If you're like the vast majority of people, you got most, if not all, of these twenty questions right.

Now, how could this be possible if there were no validity to graphology? You have not yet learned a single thing about how to interpret graphologic movement or handwriting. . . .

3
WHAT DOES GETTING THE RIGHT ANSWERS MEAN?

My method for demonstrating that graphology is valid is to ask you to be your own guinea pig and see the logic of graphology for yourself, as I hope you've begun to do.

Here's the idea: If I asked you a question on a subject you knew nothing about, gave you five seconds or less to give me the right answer from two choices, and without any help you gave me the right answer, what would this mean?

For example, look at samples *A* and *B* below. One of them was written by a flamboyant salesman, and one was written by a shy, introverted accountant. Which one was written by the flamboyant salesman, *A* or *B*?

Sample A

Sample B

I'll bet you correctly said that sample *B* was written by the salesman. Now, could the fact you gave the right answer have happened just by chance?

Well, what if I asked you twenty questions and gave you five seconds or less to give me the right answer to each, and it turned out that you got all twenty answers correct? Could that happen by chance?

What if I asked *ten thousand* people a *hundred* questions, and it turned out that every one of those ten thousand people, in less than five seconds, gave me the right answers to each of the hundred questions? Could *that* happen just by chance? Of course not!

19

Well, that is exactly how I hope to show that graphology works:

1. Before giving any explanations, I'm going to ask you a series of questions calling for you to interpret graphic movement.
2. I'm going to give you five seconds to answer each question, and I'm certain that you will get *nearly every answer right*.
3. When that happens, I hope you will agree there must be some logical reasons why you—and everybody else who answers these questions—get the right answers. At that point, I hope you will also agree that there must be some logic to the science of interpreting graphic movement. After all, everybody couldn't get all the answers right just by chance, could they?

No. They could not.

PART II
THE SCIENCE OF GRAPHOLOGY

4

HANDWRITING AS "BRAIN PRINTS"

What Is Graphology?

Graphology is the study of all graphic movement; it is not simply "handwriting analysis." In addition to handwriting, the graphologist studies doodles, drawings, sculptures, and paintings in order to gain insight into the physical, mental, and emotional states of the writer or artist.

Communicating through written symbols is a uniquely human endeavor. Of the millions of species of life on earth, only *Homo sapiens* has the ability to paint the ceiling of the Sistine Chapel, design the graceful span of the Golden Gate Bridge, or scrawl "For a good time call . . ." on a bathroom wall. We are also the only species that can use graphic symbols to communicate long after we are dead, through art, books, wills, music, and so on.

Although all graphic movement can be analyzed, this book concentrates on handwriting because we teach the subject in our schools and most people can write.

"Handwriting" Without a Hand

Can you produce "handwriting" without a hand?

Well, let's try a little experiment. Please hold your pen in your mouth, between your teeth. On your scratch paper, sign your name.

Did you try to do it? If not, please try it before you go on.

Now, whose handwriting were you trying to imitate? Mine? Richard Nixon's? Of course not. You were trying to imitate your *own* handwriting. And if you were really forced to learn to write this way, after enough practice you would eventually produce the same "handwriting" with your mouth that you currently produce with your hand.

Studies of thousands of people who have lost the use of their hands and have had to learn to write with the pen in their mouths or between their toes show that they eventually produce their own unique "handwriting," the same handwriting they had when they could use their hands.

23

The point is it's not the hand or mouth or toes that decide which way we'll slant our writing or how big we'll write. Those decisions actually come from our brains.

So when we produce any graphic movement, such as handwriting, we are actually "brainwriting" and leaving our "brain prints" behind on the paper.

What Do Our "Brain Prints" Reveal?

Our brain prints reveal who we are and how we think, feel, and behave. They are an x-ray of our mind. And, like our fingerprints, they remain uniquely our own forever. No two people ever have the exact same brain prints.

Brain Prints: Conscious vs. Unconscious

Once we have learned a system of writing, whenever we take pen in hand much of what we're doing comes automatically. These aspects of writing are rote, like speaking. They are the part of our handwriting we do *unconsciously.*

For example, when asked if they lean their writing to the left or the right, many people will say, "Gee, I don't know. I'll have to look. I've never thought about it."

Most aspects of handwriting are unconscious. We write along in our own style without really thinking about it.

Sometimes, though, we'll stop and think, "Hey, I want to make this a fancy letter!" This would be an example of a *conscious* part of handwriting. Have you ever practiced writing your signature in many different styles, to find one you like? Do you jazz up certain letters in your writing? Do you stylize your *e*'s, or have funny *f*'s or strange capital *M*'s? That's all conscious stylizing.

So your writing is both conscious and unconscious, and both can be analyzed. Analyzing the former tells us about your conscious self; analyzing the latter tells us about your unconscious self.

Fixed vs. Unfixed Traits

What qualities of ourselves, and therefore what qualities of our writing, are fixed? And what parts of us are unfixed, or temporary aspects that can change?

FIXED TRAITS	UNFIXED TRAITS
IQ	Ability
Aptitudes	Attitudes
Temperament	Moods
Identity	Beliefs
	Motivation level
	Physical condition

Fixed Traits

Many scientists believe that we are born with a given intelligence level and that, while it can be enhanced or diminished by environment, we are basically born with that innate, fixed IQ. Many people believe we are also born with innate aptitudes and with an innate temperament.

In addition, our identity is also fixed, which is why we can recognize our own handwriting from any other. For example, if I hid your writing in a hundred samples of other people's writing and asked you to find the one you wrote, no matter when you wrote the sample, no matter what the slant, size, or look of your particular sample, you could pick it out from the pile. That's because, although your moods may change, part of your writing always stays the same, just as part of *you* always remains the same.

Unfixed Traits

What can change? For one thing, our health or physical state of being can change. We can be sick Tuesday but healthy Wednesday. We can have drugs in our system on Friday and be drug-free the next week.

The ways we think, feel, and behave are also temporary states for many of us. We may be in a good mood or a bad mood. We can feel uptight and angry one day, mellow the next. Those are the kinds of things that can change.

5
SCIENCE QUIZ

Please take this little quiz before reading further. (We're making a practice in this book of helping you see how much you already know.) (Answers are on page 31.)

1. Why do we have to sign checks, wills, and other legal documents? Why can't we just type our names on them?

2. Which questioned signature of Andrea McNichol is a forgery, *A* or *B*?

Authentic signature:

Questioned signatures:

A.   B.

3. Which one of the following signatures is easier to forge, *A* or *B*? If you don't know, try it for yourself!

A.   B.

4. Who's drunk, *A* or *B*?

Sample A

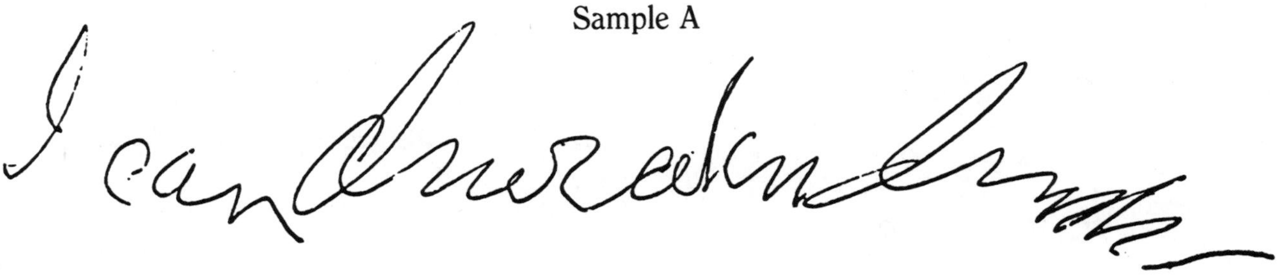

I can Inredknrnka (handwritten)

Sample B

I can drive when I drink. (handwritten)

5. Who has a higher IQ, *A* or *B*?

A.

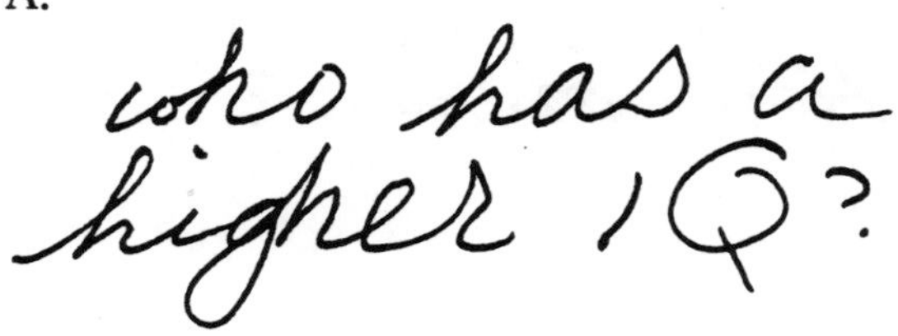

who has a higher IQ? (handwritten)

B.

who has a higher I.Q.? (handwritten)

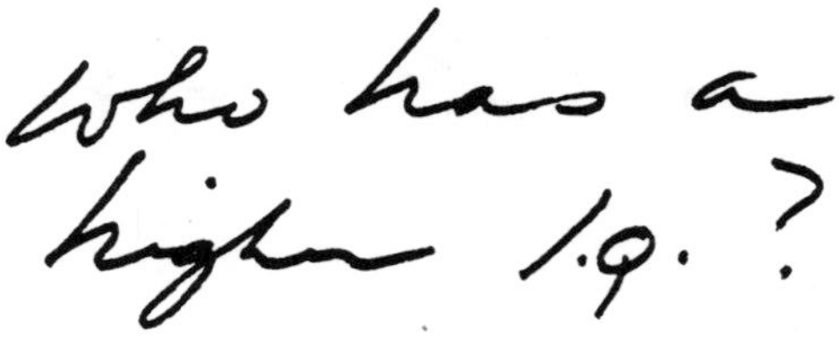

6. Which famous actress always fought with her directors?

A.

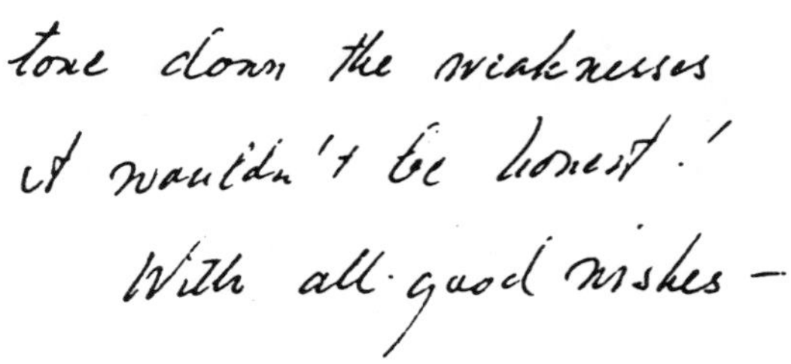

tone down the weaknesses it wouldn't be honest! With all good wishes — (handwritten)

B.

How kind of you! appreciate the spirit which prompted you to write me, & may hope my performances may continue to please! (handwritten)

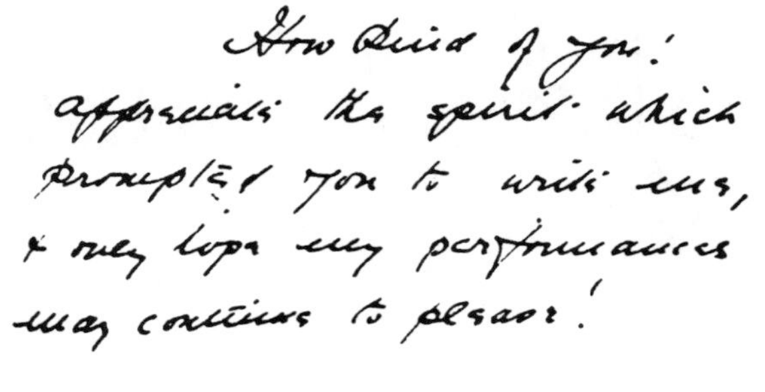

7. Which person would make the better salesperson, *A* or *B*?

A.

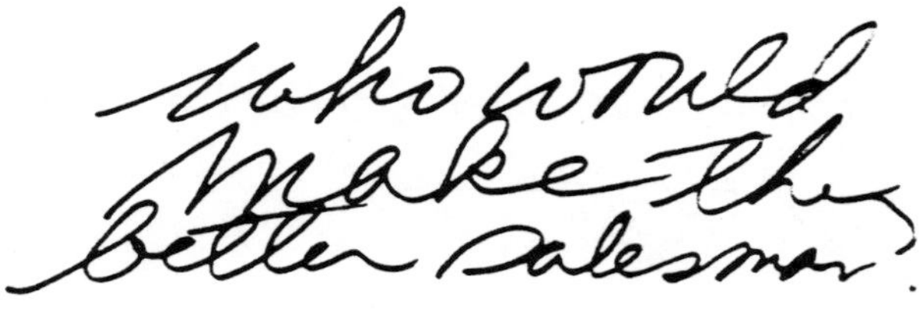

who would make the better salesman! (handwritten)

B.

I would like to go into sales. I think I could be very good. (handwritten)

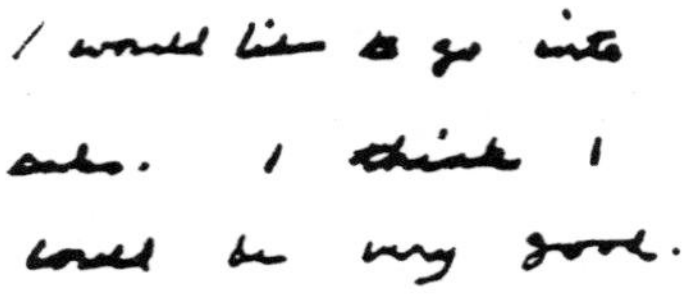

8. Who is more suited to a conventional job, *A* or *B*?

A.

I Think I AM Suited 2 A ConVEntionaL Job!

B.

I think I am suited to a conventional job.

9. Who is better at working with small details, *A* or *B*?

A.

Now tell whos better at working with details? or me.

B.

Now tell me. Who's better at working with details? Him or me?

10. Who has more pride, *A* or *B*?

A.

John Thomas

B.

John Thomas.

11. Who has more vitality, *A* or *B*?

A.

who has more vitality?

B.

who has more vitality?

12. Who is more generous with his personal time and energy, *A* or *B*?

A.

have

B.

have

13. One of the writings below is that of Marilyn Monroe, and the other is of Abraham Lincoln. Which one is Marilyn's?

A.

You will be Seeing more of me Soon in —

B.

Your very agreeable letter of the 15th is received — I regret the necessity of saying I have no daughter. I have three sons — one seventeen; one nine, and one seven, years of age — They, and their mother, constitute my whole family.

14. Who's physically sick, *A* or *B*?

A.

take a long time — you for the letters

B.

youre in the hospital. But god youre doing so well. You deserve the best! Take care.

15. Which writer is barely literate, *A* or *B*?

A.

and Marvin for other night. It in Catching up on I. From time to ti

B.

Work mother to me looking for the

29

16. Who's feeling neater, *A* or *B*?

A.

By August 6th, it weighs 9 am ~ 193# on th (handwritten)

B.

to hear about the household from Marg Patty, and Lynn. We get together again soo (handwritten)

17. Who doesn't like his first name, *A* or *B*?

A.

Shelton (handwritten signature with illegible first name)

B.

Leslie Shelton (handwritten)

Extra Credit

18. Which man's doctor actually told him he was *not* in great shape, *A* or *B*?

Sample A

the doctor said I was in great shape! (handwritten)

Sample B

the doctor said I was in GREAT shape! (handwritten)

19. Who's lying, *A* or *B*?

A.

I am 36 years old. (handwritten)

B.

I am 36 years old. (handwritten)

20. The two samples below represent margins on a page of writing. Who's the lawbreaker, *A* or *B*?

A.

B.

21. Who's the liar, *A* or *B*? (*Hint:* Which writer "speaks with forked tongue"?)

A.

Do you want cake?

B.

Do you want cake?

Answers to Science Quiz

1. To make them legal.	7. A	13. A	EXTRA CREDIT
2. B	8. B	14. B	18. B
3. A	9. B	15. B	19. B
4. A	10. A	16. B	20. A
5. B	11. B	17. A	21. A
6. B	12. A		

The next chapters explain the answers to these questions.

6

GRAPHOLOGY AND THE THREE FACETS OF MAN

Over two thousand years ago, Aristotle spoke of dividing man into three separate aspects: the body, the mind, and the spirit. A more modern way of referring to the same things might be the physical, the mental, and the emotional.

When you pick up a pen to write something, you are using all three of these aspects. You must hold a pen with part of your body. You have to have intelligence to communicate in written symbols. And your emotions are guiding everything you do.

Because each of these aspects comes into play when you handwrite, graphology contends that your writing will reveal a great deal about your individual characteristics in each area:

1. Physical
2. Mental
3. Emotional

Let's take a closer look at each of these three areas and see how this is true.

What Handwriting Reveals About Our Physical Aspects

Handwriting reveals the following physical aspects about us: our identities, the state of our physical health, and the presence of drugs, alcohol, or other foreign substances in our bodies.

Identity

Part of the science of graphology is known as examination of questioned documents, which involves authenticating handwriting or other graphic renderings.

1. Why do we have to sign checks, wills, and other legal documents? Why can't we just type our names on them?

   The fact that people can be identified from their handwriting is the reason we require people to sign checks, wills, deeds, and contracts. A typed name doesn't prove a person's identity. Thus, when a signature is required it means that we want *proof* of who the person is that signed the document.

2. Which questioned signature of Andrea McNichol is a forgery, *A* or *B*?

Authentic signature:

Questioned signatures:

A.

B.

The answer is *B*. Here the forger did a very good job. On a superficial look, everything appears the same. But upon closer scrutiny, we realize the giveaways. For one, the pressure is much heavier in *B*. One sign of forging is the concentrated effort, tenseness, and uptightness caused by having to focus on emulating the letter shapes. Frequently this produces greater writing pressure. Also, the length of the writing line frequently is either too long or too short on the forged signature. There are many other giveaways, too, such as the shape of the *r* in *Andrea*.

3. Which one of the following signatures is easier to forge, *A* or *B*?

A.

B.

The answer is *A*. Why? Because you can stop after several of the letters and, hence, take more time to imitate each shape correctly. When you're signing your name, every time you stop, you give the would-be forger a chance to stop, too, and regain composure before going on to emulate the next letter of your name.

Why can't you print your name on a check? Why do you have to use cursive writing to make a valid signature? The reason is that it is in your connecting strokes that you reveal your real personality. It is your connection patterns that identify you uniquely.

For example, do you narrow between an *a* and an *r*? Do you widen between an *l* and an *i*? Do you lighten your pressure on the left side between a *q* and a *u*? These are the things that are unique to each individual. Together they make up what is called a "pressure pattern."

Some people say they want to make sure no one can forge their signature, so they scribble it:

Is this a good idea? No. This is the *easiest* signature to forge! The scribblers are victims all the time. If you're now signing your name in this way, I suggest you change.

The most difficult signatures to forge are those that have the following three elements:

	Good	**Bad**
1. Written as legibly as possible.	*Audrey Grey*	*Audrey Grey*
2. Written as continuously as possible.	*Audrey Grey*	*Audrey Grey*
3. Written as quickly as possible.	*Audrey Grey*	*Audrey Grey*

Can I help you, my dear?

Forgery Tidbits

- It's interesting to note that professional forgers have been known to wait at banks, often dressed as members of the clergy or medical professions, looking for signatures that are easy to forge. Then they're either going to have someone rob you and steal your checkbook, or they're in cahoots with someone at the bank.
- Banks routinely microfiche their documents and throw away the originals with authentic signatures in order to save filing space. This practice is proving costly and sometimes tragic for many people who later deny that their signatures are on a bank document. If a forger did a good job, a document examiner will need the *original* signature in order to determine whether or not that signature is authentic. Unfortunately, the microfiche process removes or distorts many of the nuances an expert must examine; for example, the pressure pattern of the signature is lost and the degree of reduction often blurs the lines.
- I'd like to take banks to task for another reason, too. When banks have you sign a signature card, often they provide only a tiny, microscopic line on which to write your name, forcing you to write in a wholly unnatural manner. This is the specimen they will use later to authenticate your signature. It's often useless! And yet

sometimes it may mean the difference between whether or not you lose your home, or your boat, or your business.

Pop Quiz

A wealthy elderly man handwrites his last will and testament, then drops dead just before signing it. His wife and sons panic and forge his signature on the will. A disinherited son recognizes the signature is forged and cries foul. In court, the wife maintains that since the content of the will is in the authentic handwriting of her deceased husband, the will is valid.

How do you think the judge ruled in this actual case?

The judge ruled that a handwritten will is not valid without a handwritten signature because the deceased may have wanted to add more. He may have intended to add a final paragraph that would have changed the whole intent of the will or, in rereading it before he signed it, may have wanted to change something. Without his signature, there is no way of knowing.

State of Physical Health

Our handwriting is partly physiological, so whatever state of health we're in is reflected in our writing. If you are physically ill, your handwriting will reflect that (see question 14, page 42). The next time you are sick, write a paragraph and compare it to your writing when you were healthy. Note the differences.

Presence of Alcohol or Other Drugs or Foreign Substances

4. Who's drunk, *A* or *B*?

Sample A

Sample B

This answer must seem all too obvious, and well it should. You knew that *A* was drunk because that person's handwriting looks crazy, sloppy, inebriated. Writing is a motor skill produced by a physical mechanism, and anything that interferes with motor functions, equilibrium, circulation, neurological processes, and so on will show up in handwriting.

In addition, it is possible to determine whether a writer has a depressant or stimulant in his system at the time of the writing because each drug affects the body, and thus the handwriting, in different ways.

While numerous studies have identified specific patterns in handwriting brought on by each of these drugs, graphology isn't likely to take the place of the urine test. A skilled graphologist may have little trouble detecting the influence of stimulants or depressants, such as cocaine versus marijuana, but it is more difficult to determine combinations of such drugs in the system as well as dosage and frequency.

Summary

Our identity is a totally fixed trait. It doesn't matter what your writing looks like. No matter how sick you are, how much alcohol you've had, your identity—you—is always reflected in your handwriting. But the state of your health is a temporary condition, as is the presence of drugs or alcohol in your system.

What Handwriting Reveals About Our Mental Aspects

The mental aspects handwriting reveals about us are our intelligence and our aptitudes.

Intelligence

Why is it that humans are the only species that can communicate through written symbols? While we can give an ape a pen and it can leave a symbol, it will not be able to communicate with another ape using that symbol. Why not? The answer is that the ape does not have the intelligence required to do so.

The very fact that we can use written symbols to communicate thoughts, ideas, and feelings distinguishes human intelligence from animal intelligence. And just as there are degrees of intelligence between human and animal, so there are degrees among humans. These degrees of intelligence are revealed through graphology.

But before we can determine how this is done, we must first agree on a definition of intelligence. Actually, let's agree on several.

One type of intelligence is that measured by IQ tests. Although the notion of an "intelligence quotient" has been criticized in many circles, it is in this area that the most research on intelligence has been done. After all, IQ tests measure *something*, even if it's only the ability to do well on standardized tests.

5. Who has a higher IQ?

A.   B.

who has a   *who has a*
higher IQ?   *higher I.q.?*

I've asked this question to literally thousands of people. The only one who ever got it wrong was *A*!

What is it about *B* that you identify with intelligence? It is the fact that the letters got *smaller* as *B* wrote, while *A*'s letters got *bigger* as he wrote. The tendency of letters to grow smaller in words shows that the writer is picking up concentration as he writes.

"Innate" Intelligence vs. "Functioning" Intelligence

"Innate" intelligence refers to the intelligence a person is born with, as opposed to "functioning" intelligence, which is how intelligently the person is behaving. It's interesting to note that some people have genius-level IQs but are sitting in prison because they couldn't control their emotions. These people have high innate intelligence but low functioning intelligence, for they've behaved unintelligently! Some other people score low on IQ tests but end up running enormous corporations because they have street smarts, or people smarts, and behave intelligently. They have high functioning intelligence.

Here's an example of having a high IQ, but low people smarts:

6. Which famous actress always fought with her directors?

A.

tone down the weaknesses
it wouldn't be honest!
With all good wishes —

B.

The answer is *B*. *B*'s writing is overly angular, which means aggressiveness, and it's full of little hooks and tics at the beginning of many strokes. Graphologists call these "temper tics." Temper tics are caused by clutching the pen too tightly, and indicate the writer's intense inner frustration. (By the way, *A* is Ingrid Bergman; *B* is Bette Davis.)

Aptitudes

We usually associate aptitudes with the kind of work for which a person is best suited.

7. Which person would make the better salesperson, *A* or *B*?

A.

who would make the better salesman?

B.

 The answer is *A*, the person with large writing. A salesperson has to be outgoing, to have an expansive use of his environment. Such a person should therefore be an extrovert. Large writing means, "Look at me." It indicates someone who wants to go out into his

37

environment. On the other hand, the small writing of *B* indicates introversion and self-involvement.

When determining aptitudes, we want to know whether the person works best alone or is better suited to working with a lot of people. In terms of the handwriting, is it large or small? If it's average, then the writer could probably go either way. But if it's especially large or especially small, then the person has strong extroverted or strong introverted tendencies.

Thus, knowing the tendency for introversion and extroversion is one way of determining aptitudes. There are, of course, many other personality factors that go into making up one's "aptitudes."

8. Who is more suited to a conventional job?

A.

I Think I AM Suited 2 A ConVEntionaL Job!

B.

I think I am suited to a conventional job.

The answer is *B*. Handwriting that's atypical and has a style all its own usually belongs to someone who works best in atypical or artistic fields—acting, art, and so on. Traditional, conventional writing usually belongs to someone who is more suited to a conventional job, whether it's teaching, law, medicine, or a nine-to-five situation.

9. Who is better at working with small details?

A.

Now tell whos better at working with details? or me.

B.

Now tell me. Who's better at working with details? Him or me?

The answer is *B*. This is another aptitude that is important in placing the right person in the right job: does a person like working with small details or not?

If you want to hire a highly detail-minded decorator, don't choose one who ignores details in his writing! If he doesn't care about details in his writing—missing *i* dots, *t* bars, apostrophes, and so on—then he doesn't have an aptitude for working with small details in general.

What Handwriting Reveals About Our Emotional Aspects

Handwriting also reveals how we think, feel, and behave. Let's see how emotions are revealed through handwriting:

10. Who has more pride?

A.

B.

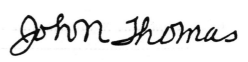

The answer is *A*. How could you get this right if graphic movement didn't reveal anything about people? Just think of the body language of people who have a lot of pride. They tend to walk tall, head above it all, shoulders back and chest forward, thinking tall:

People who put feelings into their body movements put the same feelings into their writing.

11. Who has more vitality?

A.

Who has more vitality?

B.

Who has more vitality?

The answer is *B* because there's more "oomph" to the writing.

The next time you meet someone with a firm handshake who looks you in the eye and greets you heartily, the odds are good that the pressure of that person's writing is like *B*'s. *A*'s handshake, on the other hand, may remind you of an old banana peel. The more intense you're feeling, the more you will bear down when writing.

12. Who is more generous with his personal time and energy, *A* or *B*?

A.   B.

have   *have*

The answer is *A*. What's the difference between the two samples? *A*'s writing has a longer ending stroke on the *e*.

Subconsciously each word becomes a unit, the ego, the writer's self. What the writer does at the end of a word represents his attitude toward the future and other people. *A* reaches out at the end of the word, as if extending a hand out in friendship.

B, however, gets to the end of the word and pulls in, as if to say, "Oh no! You ain't gettin' nothin'!"

People who chop off the ends of cursive words this way, especially words ending with an *e*, are stingy with their personal time and energy. This does not necessarily mean that they are stingy with money, however.

For example, a father may respond to his son's invitation to come play catch by giving the kid twenty bucks and sending him off to the movies. He's generous, maybe, but not with his time and energy.

We've seen how graphic movement can reveal a great deal about a person's physical, intellectual, and emotional states. Now let's take a more detailed look at the methods most used when making graphological deductions.

7

GRAPHOLOGICAL DEDUCTIONS:
THE FIVE WAYS THEY ARE MADE

Let's take a look at this question from the Science Quiz:

One of the writings below is that of Marilyn Monroe, and the other is of Abraham Lincoln. Which one is Marilyn's?

A.

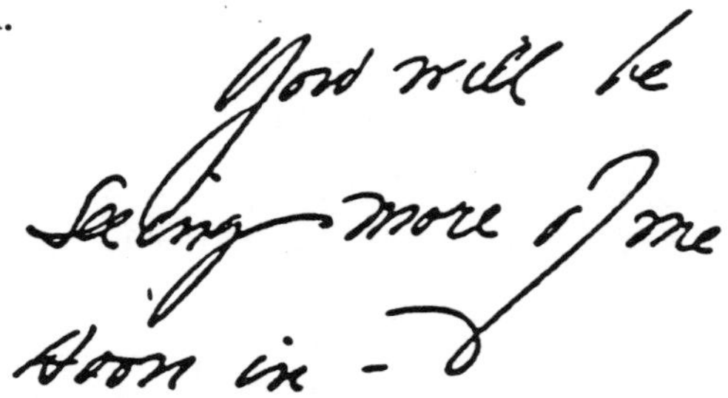

You will be Seeing more of me soon in —

B.

[handwritten text]

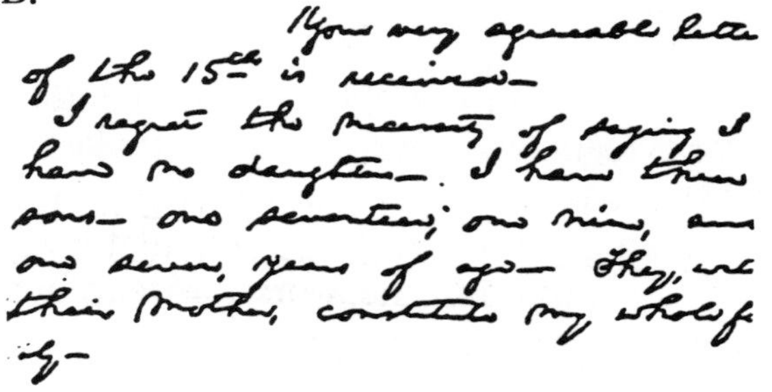

Marilyn's writing is sample *A*. But how did you know that? There are no signatures there. What is it about Marilyn's and Lincoln's writings that made you able to deduce whose was whose?

Most likely, you instinctively used graphological clues to reach that conclusion. In this section we're going to take a look at the five major ways (and combination of these ways) such judgments are made. The techniques are:

1. Physiological deductions
2. Basic common sense
3. Universal concepts
4. Simple psychological interpretations
5. The scientific method

Physiological Deductions

Graphologists use physiological deductions to make determinations about the *physical* state of the writer. As explained in Chapter 6, this includes using handwriting to determine a writer's identity, whether he or she is sick, and whether drugs or alcohol are present in the body.

When we looked at the forgery of my signature on page 33, we saw how one's identity can be determined from such traits as pressure pattern. Then we saw the difference between drunk and sober writing in the same individual. Now, what about spotting illness using handwriting? Let's take another look at this question from the Science Quiz:

Who's physically sick?

A.   B.

B is physically sick. What is it about *B* that makes us think of illness? It is probably the uneven pressure, light spots, bends, and jerks in the sample. We instinctively know that when there is something wrong with our health, we cannot write as well.

This is an example of a physiological deduction. It is based purely on physiological evidence: if a writer's hand shakes, his writing will shake. If you have a disorder of the nervous system, or suffer from tremors as a result of a disease, or if you suffer from an obstruction in your circulatory system, these will all show up in your writing.

Throughout the world, research has been under way for several decades to identify which handwriting traits are shared by the victims of various diseases. These diseases include cancer, heart disease, Alzheimer's and Parkinson's diseases, learning disorders, and stuttering, to name a few.

——————— ———

Tidbit

Do you remember the case of the Howard Hughes will? Howard Hughes had a degenerative nerve disease that was definitely reflected in his handwriting over the latter period of his life. Any writing during this part of his life would have had tremors and other indicators associated with this disease. Yet the writing in the will that surfaced and was disputed was smooth and had no evidence of the physiological shakiness that should have been present. Thus, it was concluded that the will could not possibly have been written by Hughes at the time it was purported to have been written. Because of this and other factors, the will was deemed bogus.

Commonsense Deductions

Sometimes there's just no other way to describe a particular conclusion except to call it "common sense." The answers to these questions on the next page should be obvious.

Which writer is barely literate?

A.

*and Marvin for
other night. It in
catching up on i.
From time to te*

B.

*work
mother
to me looking for the*

Who's feeling neater?

A.

*By August 6th,
it weight 9 om
~ 193# on Th*

B.

*to hear about the
household from Marg
Patty, and Lynn. We
get together again too*

Who doesn't like his first name?

A.

Shelton

B.

Leslie Shelton

Common sense. There's not much more to say about this type of deduction.

Deductions Using Universal Concepts

To help understand how universal concepts work, please take the following quiz:

1. Who's feeling more up? (Up versus Down)

A.

who's more up?

B.

who's more up?

2. Who feels bigger about herself? (Big versus Small)

A.

My name is ann

B.

My name is Ann .

3. Who holds back his feelings? (Left versus Right)

A.

who holds back

B.

who holds back

4. Who is more heavy-handed? (Light versus Heavy)

A.

who's more

B.

who's more

5. Who's feeling more organized? (Neat versus Sloppy)

A.

who's feeling more organized? Neat versus Sloppy?

B.

who's feeling more organized? neat versus sloppy?

6. Who's more traditional and conventional? (Traditional versus Nontraditional)

A.

who is feeling more

B.

Who is feeling more traditional?

7. Who walks taller? (Tall versus Short)

A.

WHO WALKS TALLER DO YOU THINK?

B.

who Walks taller, do you think?

8. Who's more narrow-minded? (Wide versus Narrow)

A.

narrow

B.

narrow

9. Who's more social and friendly? (Round versus Angular)

A.

who's more sociable And friendly?

B.

Who's more sociable and friendly?

10. Who's more consistent and stable? (Consistent versus Inconsistent)

A.

Who's more Consistent And stable?

B.

who more consistent and stable?

11. Who's faster? (Fast versus Slow)

A.

who is 'faster'

B.

who is faster?

12. Who's more pretentious? (Simple versus Ornate)

A.

Who's more PRETENTIOUS?

B.

Who's more pretentious?

13. Who's more closed up? (Open versus Closed)

A.

who's more closed up?

B.

who's more closed up?

14. Who's feeling more intense and sensual? (Shaded versus Nonshaded)

A.

who's feeling more intense +

B.

who's feeling more intense ↓

15. Who's functioning more smoothly? (Smooth versus Rough)

A.

who's functioning smoother - Him or me?

B.

who's functioning smoother - Him or me?

Answers to Universal Concepts Quiz

1. A	5. B	9. A	13. B
2. B	6. B	10. B	14. A
3. B	7. B	11. A	15. A
4. A	8. A	12. B	

You knew the correct answers to all of these questions by applying "universal concepts."

Where Do Universal Concepts Come From?

In researching his book *Manwatching*, anthropologist Desmond Morris went around the world to find out which body language traits are universal to all cultures, and which are not. He found, for example, that if someone was scowling and pounding furiously on a table, any observer, regardless of culture, would interpret it as the expression of anger or frustration.

Morris also found there are other body language behaviors that are unique to a particular culture, and someone of another culture would not readily understand them. For example, in America, if you stick your hand out your car window with your middle finger thrust out, this would mean something obscene. In another culture, however, this might mean nothing at all, or perhaps something quite different from what it means in America, perhaps something like, "Come over for dinner."

In essence, Morris concluded, the traits with which all babies are born constitute universal body language concepts. For example, all babies express happiness and sadness, pain and pleasure, and anger and affection in ways that are immediately and universally recognizable.

The most vivid proof of identifiable body language behavior comes from athletes. The next time you view a sporting event, watch the players as they succeed and fail. They show you all the emotions with their bodies.

Handwriting is a trace of your body movements that you leave on the page. It is body language on paper, and all the same subconscious associations apply.

To understand this better, let's take a deeper look at the universal concepts illustrated in the first two questions of the Universal Concepts Quiz:

Who's feeling more up?

A.

who's more up?

B.

who's more up?

A is feeling more up. As with all universal concepts, people all over the world would answer this question the same way. The meanings we associate with "up" and "down" come from body language, because when we are feeling positive emotions, our bodies go up, and when we're feeling negative emotions, our bodies go down.

Just look at some of the meanings we give to these concepts in the English language:

UP (*associated with hopefulness, aspirations, happiness*)	DOWN (*associated with depression, negativity, failure*)
Are you *up* for the game? *Up* and at 'em! Do you feel *up* to it? Are you in *high* spirits? It's *up* to you. On *cloud* nine. On the *up* and *up*. Get the *upper* hand.	He was *down* in the dumps. *Down* for the count. *Down* in the mouth. *Down*trodden. *Down*hearted. On a *downer*. *Down* and out. And worst of all: Can't get it *up*!

This is an example of a universal concept that comes from body language. But universal concepts come from many sources. Let's look at another:

Who feels bigger about herself?

A.

My name is Ann

B.

My name is Ann.

The answer is *B*, because the name *Ann* is bigger in relation to the rest of the writing. Like "up versus down," "big versus small" is another universal concept.

In a study conducted at the University of California, Berkeley, a man gave a speech to two different groups of people. The man wore the same suit, stood in the same spot, and gave the same speech to both groups of average people. Everything was identical in both situations—except that to the first group, the man was introduced as the president of one of the largest, best-known corporations in the world, and to the second group, he was introduced as a typical man off the street who wanted to give his opinion.

At the end of the speech, the audience was given a series of questions to answer about the man. One question was "How tall was this speaker?" The group that thought the speaker had been the president of a major corporation estimated him to be approximately three inches taller, on the average, than the group who thought he was an ordinary man off the street.

What this study showed is that we subconsciously give stature and size to what we consider to be better or more important. "Bigger is better," we find, is another universal concept. And we reduce the stature of that which we consider "small."

Again, we have only to examine some of the meanings we attach to these concepts in language:

BIG	SMALL
Big time.	*Small* time.
Comes on *big*.	*Small*-minded.
Made a *big* impression.	*Short*sighted.
That was *big* of you.	On a *small* scale.
Think *big*!	*Limited* mentality.
Big shot.	*Short*comings.
*Big*wig.	*Small* potatoes.
Onto *bigger* and better things.	
Made *enormous* strides.	
In the *big* leagues.	

Simple Psychological Interpretations

A great deal of graphological analysis is based on simple psychological interpretations. Remember this question from the Fun Quiz?

Jack works for both Mr. *A* and Mr. *B*. Based on the way each wrote the name Jack, who is more likely to give him a raise?

Mr. A

Please have Jack come see me .

Mr. B

Please have Jack come see me .

As you learned earlier, Mr. *A* was more likely to give Jack a raise. This is an example of a simple psychological interpretation, because the conclusion is based on the fact that Mr. *A* enlarged the name Jack, thus revealing that he gave Jack stature and importance.

49

Here's another example, this time from the Science Quiz:

Which man's doctor actually told him he was *not* in great shape?

Sample A

The doctor said I was in great shape!

Sample B

The doctor said I was in GREAT shape!

Now, the answer is based on an even more sophisticated psychological deduction. The answer is *B*. The difference between these samples is that when *B* wrote the word *great*, he overdid it to the point where it had to be a conscious act. He overdid it because he knew it wasn't true.

Note the difference between this question and the one about Jack's raise. Jack's name was enlarged only mildly, indicating that it was an unconscious act. Because it was unconscious, we know that this was the way Mr. *A* was really feeling—that Jack looms large in his mind.

But when something is *over*done, as in *B*'s sample, "I am in GREAT shape!," it actually means the opposite. When people need to exaggerate, it's to compensate for an inner feeling of just the opposite. So if I tell you that I'm feeling GREAT, and I overemphasize the word *great*, it's to compensate for a lack of conviction. As Shakespeare said, "The lady doth protest too much, methinks."

To make accurate psychological interpretations, one has to be aware of basic psychological principles. As we will see again and again, whenever someone overdoes something, it is to compensate for that which he feels he lacks in the area that he is overdoing.

Freud broadly applied this basic psychological principle. For example, if you're always bragging about your sexual conquests, you doubt your sexuality; if you go on and on about how smart you are, you doubt your intelligence. (So what do you think it means if someone is so obsessively clean he runs after you wiping up behind you? Answer: He has a dirty mind!)

Let's look at another example of a psychological interpretation from the Science Quiz:

Who's lying, *A* or *B*?

A.   B.

I am 36 years old.   *I am   36 years old.*

The answer is *B*. What is it about *B*'s writing that looks odd? The large space before 36, right? What psychological principle were you using?

50

As *B* was filling out her application, she wrote, "I am . . . ," but then for some reason she stopped. Maybe she was thinking, "I don't want to tell them my age!" So as she paused to think of what she was going to say, she lost spontaneity, but she subconsciously kept moving her hand to the right.

Thus, whenever you see an abnormally wide space between two words, you know the writer lost spontaneity. Maybe he or she didn't know how to spell the next word or was groping for the right adjective. You have to use common sense. But if what follows the gap is something like a person's age, you have to ask yourself, "Now why would someone have to stop before writing her age?" Usually it's because she's lying about it!

When we see such things as a sudden change in the size of a word or a sudden enlargement in the space between two words, we know that something interrupted the natural flow of the writer's thoughts.

Also, what we *don't* see is subject to psychological deductions. For example, if we don't see periods, commas, and quotation marks, we might deduce that the writer is not schooled. Or if there is no capital letter on a word that calls for one, or we don't see any *i* dots, or only some *i* dots, or there's no date written on a letter—all of these omissions mean something as well.

The Scientific Method

The science of graphology is also based on empirical research.

The two samples below represent margins on a page of writing. Who's the lawbreaker, *A* or *B*?

A.    B.

The answer is *A*. You probably got this answer right by using common sense or by using a simple psychological deduction. The psychological concept would have to do with the fact that *B*'s writing is lined up and *A*'s isn't. We know that the criminal is more likely to get "out of line," not to order himself, while *B* looks more law-abiding because there is a straight left margin.

This trait, like all traits in graphology, was validated using the scientific method, through empirical study. To determine which handwriting traits correspond to a particular human characteristic, graphologists study large numbers of handwriting samples from people who have been identified as having that characteristic. In studying these samples, we look for handwriting traits that occur more frequently in these people's writing than in that of the general population.

51

The preceding example comes from a prison population study that sought to corroborate European studies identifying specific handwriting traits associated with antisocial and criminal behavior. This study found, among other things, that when convicted felons are asked to write on a blank page, a statistically significant number of them do not line up their left margins, while in the general population 99 percent have a straight left margin. Criminals, obviously, do not toe "the line of society."

Graphologists have identified twenty-five different handwriting traits that are significantly more common among convicted felons than in the general population. (It is interesting to note that none of these traits is related to IQ. Actually, the average IQ of the prison population is exactly the same as the average IQ in the outside world.)

Different traits are associated with different types of criminal behavior. Some handwriting traits are associated with those capable of out-and-out dishonesty—"I will lie, cheat, and steal from you." Other traits are associated with those who are capable of committing bodily harm. Graphology has become sophisticated enough to distinguish the traits associated with white-collar crime from those associated with violent crime, for example. Obviously, an embezzler is a totally different type of criminal than a rapist (unless, of course, the rapist is also an embezzler!).

Who's the liar, *A* or *B*? (*Hint:* Which writer "speaks with forked tongue"?)

A.   B.

Do you want cake?   *Do you want cake?*

The answer is *A* because there are little lines inside the ovals. Studies of people found to be "chronic liars" show that an overwhelming percentage of them have these stabbed ovals throughout their writing. Similarly, an overwhelming percentage of people who continuously stab ovals are found to be liars. This is another example of using the scientific method to come to conclusions based on empirical evidence.

Graphological data are gathered and interpreted in the same way as psychological data. For example, on the Rorschach ink-blot test, a psychology test used widely, there are certain cards on which most people see a butterfly. Ninety-nine percent of people who take the test do see a butterfly, and 1 percent do not, so the 1 percent that do not are therefore automatically labeled "abnormal." When we later study those "abnormal" people, lo and behold, we find that many don't fit in with society. They may be creative geniuses or social misfits, but either way they're abnormal.

The same type of analysis works with handwriting. For example, we can gather all kinds of data on violent schizophrenics and find that 95 percent of them do certain things in their writing that the average population does not do. At this point, we can safely conclude that individuals who exhibit these handwriting traits have the potential to be violent schizophrenics.

A good way to remember the trait of stabbed ovals is to think of ovals as little mouths. The writer who stabs his ovals can be thought of as "one who speaks with forked tongue."

Oval shapes appear in the letters *a*, *o*, *d*, and *g*.

a o d g

You can open your ovals—or "open your mouth"—and the words just come tumbling out.

a o d g

Or you can be secretive, and put a loop in your oval.

a o d g

Or you can be *very* secretive and put a double or triple loop in your oval.

a o d g

Or you can "stab" your oval.

a o d g

LIAR

53

8

SUMMARY:

GRAPHOLOGY AS A SCIENCE

You've just seen how our physical, intellectual, and emotional states combine to produce our style of handwriting. You've also begun to see how individual characteristics in each of these areas are revealed and logically interpreted through graphology.

Does this mean graphology is truly a "science"? Consider what the dictionary has to say. According to *Webster's New Twentieth Century Unabridged Dictionary,* graphology is "the study of handwriting, especially as it is supposed to indicate the writer's character, aptitude, etc." So Webster's does not consider graphology a "science" as it does, for example, psychology, "the science dealing with the mind and mental processes." What, then, is Webster's definition of a "science"? It is as follows:

1. originally, state or fact of knowing; knowledge, often as opposed to *intuition, belief.* 2. systematized knowledge derived from observation, study, and experimentation carried on in order to determine the nature or principles of what is being studied. 3. a branch of knowledge or study, especially one concerned with establishing and systematizing facts, principles, and methods as by experiments and hypotheses. . . . (Italics added.)

Does graphology fit this definition? As you've just seen, graphological data are, in fact, derived from observation, study, and experimentation. And graphology uses hypothesis and experiments to establish a body of facts.

Graphology: Research

Let's look at how this works. Suppose we set out to prove the following hypothesis: "Alcoholism is discernible in handwriting." Another way of stating our hypothesis might be: "Alcoholics all share certain, identifiable handwriting traits common only to them."

To see if this hypothesis is true, we must first agree on a definition for an "alcoholic." If we accept the premise that people who are members of Alcoholics Anonymous are alcoholics, then we can find test subjects through the Alcoholics Anonymous organization.

We take writing samples from one thousand confirmed alcoholics, and we take writing samples from one thousand people who are not alcoholics and who do not have drinking problems of any kind (a control group of "nonalcoholics"). We then compare the two sample groups to determine what handwriting characteristics, if any, the alcoholics share that are not found in a statistically significant number of the nonalcoholic population.

54

What emerges from studies such as this is that there are several major combinations of handwriting traits found in the writing of alcoholics that are not found in the writing of nonalcoholics. These combinations of traits, then, are said to be associated with alcoholism.

To test whether or not our hypothesis works, we try to use it. An outside party independently collects and submits to us a minimum of one thousand handwriting samples. Among these samples are alcoholics and nonalcoholics, the identity and number of which are known solely to the outside party. Only if we are able to accurately determine which writings belong to the alcoholics and which belong to the nonalcoholics can we then say our hypothesis works.

When experiments such as this one are repeated by other competent researchers using different alcoholic and control groups, the findings are the same. Thus, it is not intuition but systematized knowledge that is being applied.

Graphology uses this approach—the empirical method—to prove its hypotheses. That is the same standard required when establishing the principles of chemistry, biology, or any other science.

Because we have hospitals, prisons, and psychology professionals, it is possible to prove or disprove many of graphology's hypotheses—such as: "Heart disease is discernible in the handwriting"; "Dishonesty is discernible in the handwriting"; and "Mental instability is discernible in the handwriting."

A problem some people have regarding graphology as a science is that it often makes interpretations in areas that, unlike those just mentioned, are exceptionally subjective. This class of skeptics asks, "How do we judge traits such as stubbornness, kindness, extroversion, or anger?" The answer is to find individuals who are considered by many people who know them to possess the quality under scrutiny, and to determine which handwriting traits these people share in common.

These skeptics, though, consider these areas too elusive in the first place and, therefore, not really measurable.

Psychology—which, as noted earlier, *is* considered a "science"—is in exactly the same boat. For example, a psychologist might say a person fears his mother. Well, maybe the person does or doesn't, or maybe he fears his mother only at family gatherings, or only when she's angry, and so on. In any event, there's no real way to prove it.

Similarly, if a graphologist says a person is sweet and kind, there are the same gray areas. Maybe the person is not always sweet and kind, or maybe she's only sweet and kind to people she likes and knows, and so on.

When describing anything except numbers, there's always going to be a subjective element involved. If a person says he is twenty-seven years old today, he can prove it. But if he says he's feeling older today, or sad or angry or some other emotion, there's no way to really prove these things. But wouldn't you agree that these subjective feelings and thoughts really do exist?

Summary Graph

THE SCIENCE OF GRAPHOLOGY

People Produce

HANDWRITING

This handwriting is a result of aspects of people that are

UNCONSCIOUS	and	CONSCIOUS

Through analysis of handwriting, we see traits that are both

FIXED	and	UNFIXED

Graphology gives insight into the three facets of people:

PHYSICAL (the body)	MENTAL (the mind)	PSYCHOLOGICAL (the spirit)
Identity (fixed)	IQ (fixed)	How we think, feel, and behave (unfixed)
Physical health (unfixed)	Aptitudes (fixed)	
Presence of drugs/alcohol (unfixed)		

Graphological interpretations are made in five ways:

1. Physiological deductions
2. Basic common sense
3. Universal concepts
4. Simple psychological interpretations
5. The scientific method

PART III
AN IN-DEPTH LOOK
AT SOME SPECIFIC
HANDWRITING TRAITS

9

A FEW THINGS TO KNOW
BEFORE GETTING STARTED

Two Approaches to Analyzing Handwriting

We can take individual *handwriting traits* one at a time, and determine what each one tells us about the writer. For example, we might start with the slant of the writing and see what that reveals about the writer. Then we might look at the size of the writing to determine what that means, and so on. This is the approach described in this section.

The other approach is to start with a *personality characteristic*, and then see whether or not the writer has the traits associated with that particular characteristic. An example of this approach would be to start with, say, the personality characteristic of dishonesty, and ask, "Does this writing contain any signs associated with dishonesty?" If we know the handwriting traits associated with dishonesty, we can then use graphology to answer that specific question. This is the approach examined in Part IV.

Applying Universal Concepts to Handwriting

Graphology is based on the Gestalt of the handwriting; it takes into account the writing as a whole. Is it big or small? Is it neat or sloppy? Is it round or angular? Is it left or right? Is it up or down?

Before a skilled graphologist comes to any strong conclusions, a handwriting generally must exhibit *several* traits that mean the same thing. So bear in mind as you read on that, while graphology must be learned one trait at a time, it works only when applied as a whole.

When analyzing a handwriting, we begin by applying universal concepts (such as Up versus Down, Heavy versus Light, Big versus Small). From there we can begin to look at specific deviations in the handwriting, such as, "What does it mean if you are taught to make an *m* overhanded but you make it underhanded?" To make these kinds of analyses, we must first know what writing system a person was taught, in order to know what he is deviating *from*. For that reason, a few of the specific

59

interpretations in this book will only apply to people who were taught the Palmer method or a variation of it.

The Palmer method, in case you don't remember it from elementary school, looks like this:

The quick brown fox jumps over the lazy dog.

It's important to mention, however, that all graphological principles drawn from universal concepts can be applied to any writing, in any language, except the concept of Left versus Right. Those cultures that write from right to left would derive opposite interpretations from those directional movements.

Little Guys

Bad News!   *Good News!*

In the coming chapters, whenever you see the little guy on the left with his thumb pointing down, it means a very negative trait. If you see this trait in someone's handwriting, sirens should go off!

When you see the little guy on the right with his thumb pointing up, it signifies an especially favorable trait.

How Many Handwriting Samples Do We Need in Order to Analyze Someone?

When analyzing an individual, it is ideal to have several samples written over a week's time (while at work, at play, at rest, and so forth). Most people manifest all phases of their personalities in such a time span. If you work with only one sample, you run the risk, albeit a small one, that the sample you get represents the *one* time that writer had just guzzled down two bottles of vodka, or had just had a major car accident, or had just been fired. This might mean that the sample would not represent that writer's usual nature. Of course, the more writing you have, the more evidence you have with which to work. Nevertheless, we often have only one sample to work with, so we make do.

What Type of Handwriting Samples Should We Analyze?

Graphologists should analyze only handwriting that was meant to be read by another person. Some of us write to ourselves in our own hieroglyphics, which we might be able to read but which no one else can. If we were judged by the garbled notes we often write to ourselves, we would all be locked up!

Also, whenever possible, analyze handwriting that was written under normal writing conditions. Obviously, if someone has written while crouched on one knee or while riding on an airplane, train, or boat, the writing could be distorted.

What Does It Take to Be a Skilled Graphologist?

To be a skilled graphologist, a person needs technical skill and interpretive skill.

Having technical skill means being able to correctly assess what you're looking at. Are you correctly assessing a writing as "big" or "small," "heavy" or "light," "consistent" or "inconsistent"? Are you looking correctly at the spacing, the margins, the slant? You have to be technically correct about all of this from the outset, or none of the interpretations will matter.

Interpretive skills require that you know what the various traits in the handwriting mean and what various combinations of traits reveal.

Whom Should We Analyze?

This book applies to people who know how to write well. Children are still in the developmental stages, so we must analyze many aspects of their graphic movement differently than we do adults' writing. And children display many traits in their writing that are quite normal for children but would be horrifying if we saw them in an adult's writing. Therefore, apply what you learn in this book to adults only.

Oh, no! My child has that trait in her writing!

A Final Point

Many graphology students, soon after learning about a horrible trait, suddenly find themselves making it in their own handwriting. They've never written that way before and—whammo—there it is! Out of sheer terror of writing this dreadful way, they can't help but do it.

This is perfectly normal, so please don't worry about it! It only means you're a sensitive and impressionable person. Soon your writing will return to normal . . . that is, if it ever *was* normal!

Oh, my God! I'm starting to write that way!

In the following eleven chapters, we examine ten traits in some depth. Keep in mind, though, that there are scores of different traits to study, and then countless combinations of traits to learn as well. The purpose here is to begin to explain some of the basic handwriting traits of graphology, so that you can get your feet wet.

10

SLANT

Who Burglarized Grandma Bessie's Home?

After the death of her husband, Bessie Ostler, 78, was living alone for the first time in almost fifty years. Because she had poor hearing and was aware of rising crime, Bessie decided that, even though it was expensive, she would feel more secure having an alarm system installed in her home and a security company keeping an eye on her.

She soon signed up with High-Tech Armed Patrol Security Company. They had an alarm system installed and then added her home onto one of their patrol routes, Route 13 of the Greenfield area.

Bessie immediately felt much safer.

Some months later, Bessie became a grandmother for the eighth time and decided to go visit her newest relative the following weekend. She alerted High-Tech Security that she would be away.

When Bessie returned from her trip, she was horrified to discover that she had been burglarized while she was gone. Not only were such things as her television, microwave oven, stereo, and all her jewelry stolen, but all her dead husband's pictures, mounted in silver frames, were gone as well!

You, Supergraphologist, are contacted by Mr. Watson, the head of investigations for High-Tech. "We've heard that you can look at someone's handwriting and tell if they're very dishonest or if they're lying in their statements," Watson tells you. "If that's true, we need your help."

Watson goes on to describe the theft at Bessie's house, explaining that this was the third home guarded by the High-Tech to have been burglarized in the past six months.

"The burglar always knows how and where to de-alarm the system and only strikes while the owners are away. So we're pretty darned sure this is an inside job. Nineteen people in the company have access to this information, and we wondered if you could look at their handwriting and maybe help us narrow the field of suspects. Can you really do that?"

You tell Mr. Watson you'd be glad to give it a try. You then instruct him to have the nineteen suspect employees take ballpoint pens and unlined paper and write down everything they were doing on the weekend that Bessie's house was burglarized. They should end their statements with a sentence such as, "I did not burglarize Ms. Ostler's house, and I have no knowledge about it." You'll then screen the statements and get back to Watson.

Following are portions of three of the suspects' statements. Can you tell which suspect is the guilty party?

Davis

ON ROUTE 7 AND 8 UNTIL MIDNIGHT I SPOKE TO JIMMY TUCKER BEFORE I PUNCHED OUT FOR ABOUT 10 MINUTES. THEN I LEFT AND WENT HOME. I DID NOT COMMIT THE BURGLARY AT THE OSTLER HOUSE.

Nicholas

AND THEN I WENT HOME FOR THE NIGHT. I WAS NOT ANYWHERE NEAR THE GREENFIELD AREA THAT NIGHT. I AM NOT FAMILIAR WITH THE PLACEMENT OF ANY ALARMS ON ROUTE 13.

Carter

AND I ONLY DRIVE ROUTES 4, 5, 9, + 13 ON THE WEEKENDS I DON'T KNOW ANYTHING ABOUT WHAT HAPPEENED AT THE OSTLER HOUSE OR GREENFIELD AREA. I DIDN'T COMMIT THE BURGLARY

After you read this chapter, you will have learned some key clues that will allow you to solve this crime. At the end of the chapter, you will find the solution and then learn how the culprit was actually caught by the authorities.

Slant Quiz

Please take this quiz to see how much you already know about slant and the symbolism of Left versus Right.

1. Who holds back his feelings?

A. *who holds back?*

B. *who holds back ?*

2. Who gets carried away by his feelings?

A. *who gets carried away*

B. *who gets carried away ?*

3. Which teenager would you hire as your baby-sitter?

A. *who would you hire as your*

B. *who would YOU hire as your*

4. Who's lying?

A. *We were so very very happy to see*

B. *We were so very very happy to see*

5. Why are we taught to lean our writing to the right?

6. Why do we write from left to right?

7. Do most left-handers lean their writing to the left?

Answers

1. A	5. Because we write from left to right.
2. B	6. So the vast majority of people, who are right-handed, will not get ink on their hands.
3. A	7. No.
4. B	

Defining Slant

Graphologists use the term *slant* to describe which way a handwriting leans. A handwriting can lean to the right or to the left, be straight up and down, or go in all different directions.

We also have other terms for these four types of slants:

this is backhanded

① Backhanded
or
Reclined

this is straight

② Straight Up
and Down

this is inclined

③ Forward
or
Inclined

this is going in all directions

④ Going in
All
Directions

Where Does Slant Come From?

In all countries except those in the Middle East and parts of Asia, one is taught to write from left to right across the page. Do you know why?

We didn't always write that way. In fact, the earliest cultures started out writing from right to left. The first writing was known as hieroglyphics, and the way people communicated thoughts and feelings with writing was to chisel little shapes and figures in stone. It has been theorized that because the vast majority of people throughout time have been right-handed, hieroglyphics were written from right to left because a right-hander has more force pounding with a hammer when going across his body from right to left.

With the development of the ink pen, however, most cultures switched to the current practice of writing from left to right for one very practical reason: if you're using your right hand and writing from right to left, it's difficult to avoid smearing what you've just written. And, because roughly 85 percent of the world is right-handed, the majority gets its way. So the majority of right-handers switched to writing from left to right so they wouldn't get inky palms.

Why are we taught to slant to the right?

If we are moving from left to right, it only makes sense to lean in the direction we're moving.

Leaning to the left as we write to the right is akin to going up a down escalator. It's not natural. Of course, that doesn't stop some people from doing it.

Do more left-handers slant their writing to the left?

No. It is a common fallacy to think that more left-handers than right-handers lean their writing to the left. The same percentage of left-handed people as right-handed people lean to the left and lean to the right. It's just that there are far fewer left-handers in the world.

In fact, everything in graphology applies equally to left-handers and right-handers. There is almost no difference between the writing of left-handed and right-handed people. The only difference is the way some lefties cross their *T* bars. Fifty percent of left-handers cross their *T*s from right to left when using a separate stroke to cross the *T*. The other 50 percent cross from left to right, as do nearly 100 percent of right-handers.

This is what is meant by a separate stroke: *This is not a separate stroke:*

Although we're all taught to slant to the right, how come approximately 25 percent to 30 percent do not?

I don't know of anything physiological or intellectual that would cause someone to change his slant from the rightward direction he was taught. Therefore, the direction a person chooses to lean his or her letters is caused by *psychological* factors—the emotions.

You might say, "But I'm only copying my Uncle Charlie's slant, that's all . . ."

Why did you choose to copy your Uncle Charlie's writing and not your Aunt Mary's? You did so because there is something about how Uncle Charlie acts or behaves that makes you feel good, that you identify with. And his writing feels more natural to you. That's why you *didn't* copy Aunt Mary's writing. You picked the writing that felt right to you based on your psychological condition.

If you say your writing looks just like your mother's, then you are probably a lot like your mother!

What the Slant of Your Writing Means

Slant reveals the degree to which you express your real emotional feelings to others. It doesn't say to what degree you *have* feelings, but to what degree you will *express* your real emotions to other people.

Rightward

Slanting to the right is to *express* your real emotional feelings, to be demonstrative, affectionate, passionate. It also means oriented toward the future. The words that best describe this slant are *future, compliance, vision, expressiveness, others*. Approximately 70 percent of American adults retain a rightward slant their entire lives.

Vertical

Writing vertically is to *suppress* your real emotional feelings. It's the slant associated with diplomacy in that you neither express nor repress your feelings; you stay on top of things. It means "head over heart," or thinking rather than feeling. It also means oriented toward the present. The words that best describe the vertical slant are *present, self, indifference, suppression, diplomacy.*

Leftward

Slanting to the left is to *repress* your real emotional feelings, to think one thing but say another, to lean over backward to avoid emotional situations. Such a slant is associated with those who do first and last what's best for themselves alone, who are overly materialistic and overly concerned with outward appearances. It also means oriented toward the past. The words that best describe slanting to the left are *negative, past, fear, resistance, doubt, repression, self.*

NOTE: If you no longer want to read one more word of this book because you slant your writing to the left and therefore are negative, past-oriented, fearful, and resistant—don't worry about it! So you're repressed! So what? Sooner or later we "get" everybody in this book! You may strike out here, but I'm sure you'll have something to be proud of in the next chapter! And someone else who's gloating right now will wish he were dead later on!

Do you remember this question?
Which teenager would you hire as your baby-sitter?

A.

who would you hire as your

B.

who would you hire as your

You said you'd hire *A* as your baby-sitter, right? You wouldn't want to entrust your child and house to someone as unstable-looking as *B*!

Please try to copy *B*'s slant just as it looks, on your scratch paper. Remember that really trying these samples helps you understand graphology.

How did it feel to write with an unstable slant? It should feel off kilter, like you're being pulled in all directions. We find that between 70 and 80 percent of convicted felons exhibit an unstable slant. That's remarkable, because only about 10 percent of the general population have a slant wobble.

this is unstable writing

The unstable slant is a slant constantly changing directions and means to lack control over the expression of your emotions, to be emotionally unstable. One minute you're warm, friendly, expressive (rightward); the next you're cold and aloof (leftward). You're impossible to fathom or get along with.

Some people have only a mild slant wobble in their writing, so they're only mildly emotionally unstable at the time. Other people wobble a great deal, which is much more serious. The more severe the slant wobble, the more unstable the writer and the less you want to have to do with this person!

Measuring Slant

In one of the first quizzes, you were introduced to the concept of zones. There are three zones:

Upper Zone ——————
Middle Zone ———— *Harry* ————
Lower Zone ——————

We'll take a more in-depth look at zones later, but it's important to note that graphologists measure only the slant of the *upper*-zone letters, such as *h*'s, *l*'s, *d*'s, and *k*'s. Here's why. Let's start with the lower zone. We see that the extension down of the letter *y* in "Harry" above is leaning to the left, yet the slant of the rest of the writing is rightward. The lower zone, as you'll see later in the discussion of zones, represents the libidinal part of the writer. Often, as in the sample above, it is out of whack with the rest of the person.

We can measure the middle zone, but as you can probably see, it's not as easy as measuring the upper zone.

Now let's look at the meanings of slant in greater detail.

The Slant Chart

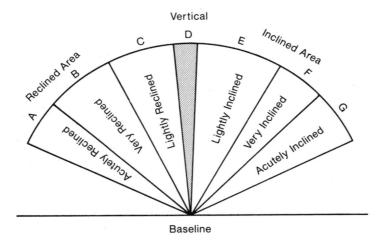

To try out measuring slant, select several upper-zone letters throughout a page of handwriting. Place the line of writing that contains the letter or letters to be measured parallel to the baseline on the slant chart. Center the upper letter and follow its extension upward to determine its slant. Measure several upper-zone letters to find an average. Finally, use the following definitions to interpret what you have measured:

Definitions

A. *Acutely reclined*—Emotionally ill. Totally emotionally repressed and locked up in his or her own world. Cannot be reached. Leans over backward to avoid emotional situations. Past- and self-oriented.

B. *Very reclined*—Represses real emotional feelings. Appears cold, evasive, and self-absorbed. Independent, hard to fathom, and difficult to get along with.

C. *Lightly reclined*—Represses real emotional feelings. Cool exterior masks inhibited reactions. Diplomatic, reserved, not straightforward.

D. *Vertical*—Suppresses emotional responses. Head over heart. Complete emotional self-control. Undemonstrative, independent, detached, cautious, diplomatic attitude.

E. *Lightly inclined*—Moderate expression of feelings. Healthy emotional responses.

F. *Very inclined*—Dominated by emotions. Heart over head. Intensely ardent, affectionate, friendly, sensitive, jealous. Emotional brushfire.

G. *Acutely inclined*—Carried away by emotionalism. A reactionary. Heart rules the head. Excessively fervent, ardent, romantic, touchy, oversensitive, demonstrative, nervous, high-strung, capable of hysterical outbursts. Difficult to get along with. Volatile.

• *Unstable slant*—Unstable person. Unpredictable, nervous, erratic, undisciplined, excitable, fickle, capricious, lacking in good judgment and common sense. Pulled in all directions.

Thus, you can see from these more in-depth descriptions of slant that the *further to the left* you write, the more repressed you are, the more emotionally cold, preferring to talk about "things" or the weather rather than emotional feelings.

Conversely, the *further to the right* you slant, the more emotional you are. A writer with a slant of G—all the way to the right—is an emotional wreck, someone who is *totally* swept off his feet with emotion.

The most difficult slant with which to write is a vertical one, because the hand, arm, and body must remain in a straight up-and-down, rigid posture. The vertical writer cannot lean or relax to either side and must concentrate to keep his slant uniformly straight up and down. This makes the meaning easy to remember: maintaining a hold over oneself, keeping emotional control, suppressing one's emotions.

Let's Practice Measuring Slant

At this point, you don't need to become an expert in slant measurement, but just get a general idea. Look at the sample below. Would you say that the writing on average is rightward, vertical, or leftward?

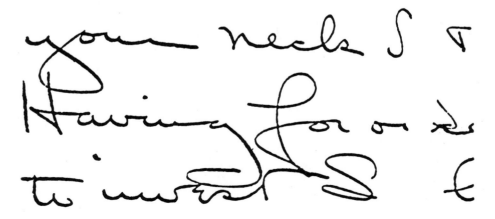

It's rightward. Is it way to the right, slightly to the right, or midway to the right? If you were to measure this on the graph, it would come up very rightward, or F according to the slant chart. The definition for F, "very inclined," is "Dominated by emotions. Heart over head. Intensely ardent, affectionate, friendly, sensitive, jealous. Emotional brushfire."

Remember, the more rightward the slant, the more emotional the writer. The person in this example has an emotional reaction to everything. He feels first, then thinks.

Let's do another. Is the following slant leftward, vertical, or rightward?

It's a little of everything, isn't it? The *k* in *neck* is vertical. The *H* in *Having* is slightly leftward. The *f* in the word *for* is rightward. So already, within just a couple of words, the slant has gone from left to right. And when you take an average, what do you come up with: left, vertical, or rightward?

The sample averages out to around the vertical. What do we call this kind of slant? Unstable. Is it very unstable or slightly unstable? It's slightly unstable. It's not as bad as if it were *really* going left, right, left, right.

Remember that writing with a vertical slant is difficult because it takes the most physical, emotional, and mental control. Thus, we allow a little bit more slant wobble for vertical writers than we do for a leftward or rightward slanter.

Let's do one more. What slant are we looking at here?

While I am not a sceptic, by any means, still, in this particular instance

This sample is slightly rightward, category E, "lightly inclined," without too much wobble. The "perfect" slant is considered to be anywhere between D, "vertical," and F, "very inclined." These are considered ideal slants because the writer is expressive but doesn't get carried away by emotions.

With practice, you should come to the point where you can look at a writing and be able to determine accurately, without the help of a slant chart, what slant you're looking at.

How to Remember the Meaning of Slant

An easy way to remember the meaning of slant is to picture a person walking. The repressed walker leans over backward to avoid getting emotionally into the situation:

So what? That doesn't bother me at all!

The vertical walker is cool, collected, has his head above it all, is in total control of the outward expressions of his emotional feelings.

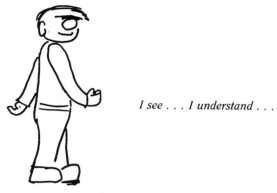

I see . . . I understand . . .

The rightward walker leans into the feeling; he expresses. And if he *totally* leans into the feeling, he is *totally* carried away by emotional feelings.

Oh, my God!

"Left vs. Right" as a Universal Concept

The interpretations of handwriting slants are based on the universal concept of Left versus Right.

Past, Present, and Future

Why is "left" holding back and "right" moving forward?
Remember this question from the Fun Quiz?

Who's writing about the future?

A.

B.

You guessed correctly that *B* is writing about the future, because the writing shifts to the right side of the paper. Now how did you know this?

Universally we associate the right with the future and the left with the past. In fact, numerous studies in graphology, anthropology, psychology, and sociology over many years have shown subconscious links between rightwardness and thoughts of the future, and between leftwardness and thoughts of the past.

In one study, subjects were given three separate blank sheets of paper. On the first they were asked to write about their childhood; on the second, their present life; and on the third, their future plans.

On the page where the subjects wrote about their childhood, nearly everyone exhibited one or more of the following tendencies: the margins shifted to the left, the number of leftward-ending strokes increased, and the length or number of lead-in strokes (the beginning strokes that start the word) increased, as shown below:

When subjects wrote about the future, their margins shifted to the right, and the writing had more rightward-ending and horizontal strokes:

And when writing about the present, most people were between the left and right.

There's ample evidence of this association of left/past and right/future all around us. Think about the days of the week on a calendar, the times on a train or bus schedule, the way *TV Guide* is laid out, or the time line over the blackboard in your sixth-grade classroom. In each case, the left is past and the right is future.

Positive, Negative, and Neutral

"Right" is positive, "left" is negative, and "vertical" is neutral.

We find these associations in virtually every culture that writes from left to right. Why? My guess is that it is because, since the beginning of mankind, over 80 percent of people have been right-handed and right-sided. Therefore, they feel their strength and positiveness coming from that side; right is good and left is bad.

Other Associations

Here are other universal associations we make for right, vertical, and left, found in our everyday language.

LEFT (associated with past and negativity)	VERTICAL (associated with control and formality)	RIGHT (associated with future and positiveness)
It was a *leftover*. A *left*-handed compliment. People with two *left* feet. He's way out in *left* field. Gauche from the French for *left*. Sinister, from the Latin for *left*.	People can be *straight*laced. People stick to the *straight* and narrow. She walks a *straight* line. He gives a *straight* answer. She was told to *straighten* up.	You got the *right* answer. You did the *right* thing. *Right* on. A *right* angle. Sticking up for your *rights*. The *Right* Reverend. *Right*eousness. *Right* a capsized boat. Got started on the *right* foot.

Changes in Slant of Certain Words and Phrases

Take a moment to look at the following four sentences. What additional meaning can you derive from them, based on slant changes?

1. *And then I told her about my*

2. *I love You and I need you right now!*

3. *I was so happy to see you!*

4. *My wife will be home soon!*

Answers

1. *And then I told her about my*

In the above sentence, something isn't slanting to the right. What is it?

The *I*. There is a strange phenomenon in the U.S. culture: about 35 percent of American adults slant just their personal pronoun *I* to the left or make it vertical while they otherwise use a rightward slant. Now what does leftwardness mean? Repression. So this person is going left—repressing—just on his *I*, which represents himself.

People like this cannot communicate their real emotional feelings about *themselves*; they repress those feelings. The rest of the writing may be rightward, which means they can express their real emotional feelings in general: "Oh, I could've just *died* for Tilly when she had her hysterectomy. She was so depressed, I was so upset for her!"

But when it comes to their own hysterectomies, they tighten up. So the leftward personal pronoun means the writer cannot tell you personal feelings about himself. But this is not considered "abnormal" because such a high percentage of Americans do it. This behavior is akin to the expression, "Don't wash your dirty linen in public."

2. *I love You and I need you right now!*

What happened to the slant here? It got very rightward on the words *right now*, which means the writer was experiencing a total loss of emotional control. Whenever the slant in a phrase or sentence goes acutely rightward, you can think of that person falling on his face with emotion; he is totally emotionally involved in it, carried away by emotional feeling.

The writer in this example really wants you "*RIGHT NOW*!!!" If you're the object of this person's affection and you don't want *him* right now, you're in big trouble! Graphologists see these bursts of increasingly rightward slant time and again in people with murderous rages and/or uncontrollable impulses.

3. *I was so happy to see you!*

OK, now what's going on here? Just how "happy" was this person to see you? Ha! Not very, right? Believe me, when you start to look at those old love letters and birthday cards, you're going to wish you had never read this book! It's very depressing!

So what happened on the word *happy*? It got vertical, right? Now why would this happen? You have to be aware of the basic psychological principle that the subconscious always knows the truth, and that it is the conscious mind that lies. When the conscious mind decides to lie, the subconscious is aware of the lie. It's saying, "I really wasn't happy to see you!" and there's a tug of war going on between the conscious and the subconscious:

SUBCONSCIOUS: You weren't happy!
CONSCIOUS: Yes, but *say* you were happy!
SUBCONSCIOUS: No, I shouldn't!
CONSCIOUS: Come on! Come on! Why not?!

Very often, as a result of this subconscious battle, a word will rear up. Sometimes it will become vertical, and sometimes it will actually go leftward, which equals

76

pulling away or back from the feeling. So watch for a sudden variation in the slant. Whenever there's a sudden verticalness or a pulling leftward, take note, because you know that the person is *pulling out the feeling* from what he is writing.

Now we have the classic:

4. *My wife will be home soon!*

OK, now what can you say about this husband and his feelings? Divorce city any day now, right? Heh-heh . . . just kidding! But this man's subconscious is totally withdrawing, going leftward, on the thought of his wife.

You've seen how a change in a slant on a word or phrase gives tremendous insight into the credibility of the statements made and the true feelings behind them. This is only the tip of the iceberg, though!

Graphology and the polygraph both use the same principles to detect when people are lying. Both processes rely on the fact that the subconscious always knows the truth and that the act of lying produces measurable psychological and physiological reactions.

The polygraph measures four phenomena: (1) heart rate, (2) blood pressure, (3) galvanic skin responses (sweating), and (4) respiration (breathing). The use of the lie detector has been greatly restricted for a variety of reasons, among which was the fact that some people learned how to fool the polygraph using a variety of devices. And some polygraphers were so inept or intimidating that just the act of being strapped in to take the polygraph test was enough to make some people feel guilty about everything.

It's impossible to fool an expert graphologist, however. When you're writing a statement—what you know about a crime, for example—you are responding *actively*. You're not just orally giving "yes" or "no" answers as on a polygraph. You have to write coherent sentences; you have to think about spelling and grammar. You have to keep other things constant, such as your slant, sizing, baseline, whether you're connecting or disconnecting, and so forth. Changes in any of the literally *hundreds* of aspects of your writing can provide clues to the skilled graphologist. It's impossible to control all of them at once. And whenever you attempt to deliberately change your writing, you slow way down and, as a trained graphologist knows:

He who writes too slow
Has something he doesn't want you to know!

I know from experience that if you write, "I didn't steal the jewels" and you *did* steal the jewels, some aspect of your writing will go bananas, and I'll know you're the bad guy.

Take a look at a simple thank-you note on the next page. Study it a moment. Is there anything you should doubt? Does the writing suddenly start to get suspicious? If so, where?

77

Dear Jill & Scot —

Thank you for inviting us to your wonderful party. We had such a nice time. The food was simply delicious & spectacular. As hosts you top them all.

Bill & I are going to be living in Europe with longtime friends for a brief period en route to Israel. We probably won't be able to see you before we leave — So until we return we shall miss you terribly. Much love, and many thanks —

Ann

In the first sentence, the letter says:

thank you for inviting us to your wonderful party. We had

What happens suddenly after the word *your*? There's an enormous space, and then the word *wonderful*. As you are calculating what you're saying, your hand keeps moving to the right. When you lose spontaneity, bigger spaces are going to occur where you paused to think. Remember "I am . . . 36 years old" from earlier?

Then look at the word *wonderful*. It starts to fall apart. The writing up until then was very connected, flowing. Then the writer must have stopped and started four times between the letters, after the *w*, after the *n*, after the *d*, and after the *r*.

such a nice time. The food was simply delicious & Spectacular. As hosts you top

Here's an example where the writing actually went to the left—"a *nice* time."

What happened on the word *Spectacular*? It's capitalized. Using common sense, do you think that the author of this letter, "Ann," knows the rules of capitalization, based on the rest of her writing? Is she a literate person?

Yes, she is. Everything else is correctly punctuated and spelled. So we have to wonder whether Ann, in an effort to compensate for her own doubts, is trying especially hard to convince the reader of the strength of her statements.

The same is true for something that is underlined too much. Once again, "the lady doth protest too much, methinks."

Let's continue down this wonderful thank-you letter. Look at the last sentence of the letter:

return we Shall miss you terribly. Much love,

Again, there are huge spaces; the slant changes. What is Ann really thinking? Probably, "We hated the food. It was disgusting, and I hope we don't see you again for a long, long time!"

79

This example shows that not only can we learn a great deal about the writer by analyzing the slant in general (is it left, right, or vertical?), but we can then get so much more information by looking at where the slant changes within the writing itself. So, if a whole page of writing slants evenly to the right, then all of a sudden one word gets vertical or leftward, we have a tremendous amount of added information.

Try Your Hand at Analyzing Slant

Now look at some more writing samples to hone your ability to analyze slant.

Jackie Kennedy (Onassis)

Written shortly after President John F. Kennedy's assassination in 1963

I should have known that it was asking too much to dream that I might have grown old with him.

Jacqueline Kennedy

What slant does Jackie have? Her slant measures B, "very reclined," on the slant chart (page 70), which suggests what? Cold, reserved, indecisive, not straightforward, masks feelings, hard to fathom, difficult to get along with. Leftward slanters tend not to reveal their real emotions.

Remember when President Kennedy was assassinated—people remarked how Jackie showed no emotion whatsoever. You wanted her to cry, to do something, but . . . nothing. That would be typical of a leftward slanter.

While it really doesn't belong in a chapter on slant, there's one feature of Jackie's writing that's noteworthy. It's called "clubbed stroking" and usually indicates the potential for cruelty. Do you see the top crossbar on the first personal pronoun *I*, the first word in the note? Each end of that crossbar has a clublike quality. The only way you can make these clubs is to bear down on the pen at the beginning or end of the stroke. Please get your scratch paper and try to make a clubbed shape on a *g*, as Jackie did on the word *asking*.

Did you do it? Doing this should make you feel tense and angry.

Pop Quiz
Which writer liked what he wrote better, and wants to be associated with it?

A. 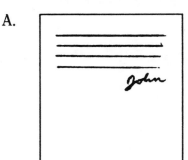   B.

The answer is *A*. *A* put his signature right near what he wrote, and *B* didn't. *A* obviously wants to put himself closer to the words he just wrote, and therefore is probably proud of them. *B* does not like what he just wrote and therefore put his signature far away, revealing a subconscious disassociation from what he said.

What did Jackie Kennedy do with her signature in relation to what she wrote? She put it far away. Thus, we might conclude that she disassociated herself from the words she has just written; she separated herself from them.

Madame Marie Curie

How would you classify Marie Curie's slant? Is it stable?
Yes, it is a stable far-rightward slant. Therefore, she's extremely emotional, passionate, ardent, sensitive, demonstrative, and readily expresses her real emotional feelings. Since she's stable, we don't have to worry about such a passionate nature getting out of control.

[handwritten note:] slant ... matter to give you a basis for analysis. If so I will write again. Sincerely, Eugene Mc Carthy

How would you classify Eugene McCarthy's slant? It's a little wobbly, isn't it? It looks somewhat vertical, C, D, or E on the slant chart (page 70). Did you notice anything about the slant in line three? McCarthy has the reclined personal pronoun *I*. Remember that 35 percent of Americans have this trait. Do you remember what it means?

It means that the writer represses his true emotional feelings about himself. These people can't say what's really bothering them or how they really feel about themselves.

Note the lower zone in McCarthy's signature, and you'll see one of the reasons why graphologists don't measure the lower zone. See how rightward he writes the *g* in "Eugene" and how it is at another angle than the rest of the writing?

Also in the third line, did you notice how rightward the word *write* became in relation to the rest of the note? McCarthy gets very emotional about the word *write*.

Tidbits on Slant

Tidbit #1

About 70 percent of American adults write with a rightward slant, 5 percent write vertically, 15 percent write with a leftward slant, and 10 percent write with an unstable slant.

Tidbit #2

I'm often asked what combinations of slant get along best. If I'm a rightward slanter, should I marry another rightward slanter?

Well, we have found in affairs of the heart—romantic love—that people do not always use rhyme or reason. There is no set pattern of what is preferable. However, it is interesting to note that when a far-rightward slanter marries a far-leftward slanter, after a time the rightward slanter becomes more leftward. In other words, the more expressive person becomes more repressed. Why? I suppose it's easier to shut down than to open up.

Tidbit #3

Often an insecure person will shrivel around a vertical writer. The control displayed by the seemingly confident and self-contained vertical writer makes an insecure soul feel all the shakier.

Tidbit #4

A high percentage of teenagers, especially girls, experiment with a backhanded slant. At the time of this experimentation, the teenager may be experiencing unhappy or rebellious feelings.

Tidbit #5

A study of one hundred gourmet cooks found a preponderance of what slant? The answer is a rightward slant. They got very emotional about their soufflés and sauces!

Tidbit #6

Occasionally you'll see a writing where a few or several of the upper letters will unexpectedly slant far to the right:

We wanted to go, but Brad didn't

The letter *d* is more likely to lean drastically to the right than any other letter in many of these types of writings. That is probably because in English the past tense ends in *ed*, and thus so many more words end in *d*. (The *d* is one of only a few letters that lend themselves to a variety of distortions, but that's another book.)

The trait of suddenly going rightward on a given letter, usually the *d*, here is called the "Maniac *d*" and means maniacal behavior. What it actually indicates is a loss of control over hand movement to the right, indicative of loss of mental and emotional control. (Remember that an overly far-rightward slant is loss of emotional control.)

The Maniac *d* maker is someone who is suddenly pulled off balance and out of emotional control, prone to explosive behavior. The further rightward these *d*'s or other letters lean, the more the writer is at the mercy of his emotional outbursts. And the more frequently these Maniac *d*'s appear, the more often the writer goes off the emotional deep end.

This trait is evident in many of the most notorious murderers of our time. Here is the writing of Steve Grogan, a member of the infamous Charles Manson family. Notice how unstable the slant is.

*Steve Grogan is great.
and the best guitar
player in the world
fascinating and lovely*

Here is the writing of Lee Harvey Oswald. Notice how large and rightward the ending *d*'s are, especially in his signature. Also, note the reclined personal pronoun *I*'s.

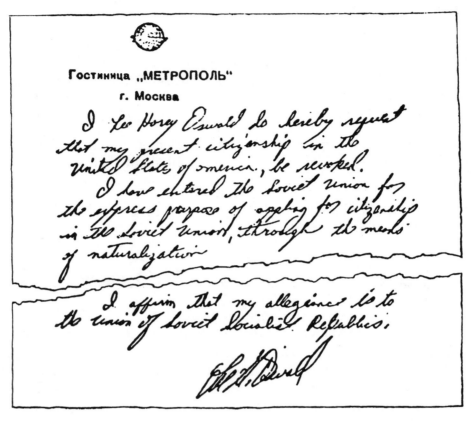

Pop Quiz

1. Which man holds his feelings back, *A* or *B*?

A.   B.

¿Cómo estás, hombre?   ¿Cómo está, hombre?

¿De qué color es tu   ¿De qué color es tu

The answer is *A*, the leftward slanter. Remember, graphological interpretation holds up in any language that writes from left to right.

2. Suppose Mary falls hopelessly in love. She cannot eat or sleep and thinks everyone she sees is her lover, even people who look nothing like him. Her heart starts pounding whenever her phone rings. Which way does Mary's writing probably slant?

Mary's writing probably slants far to the right. Her inability to function smoothly while in love is a result of her heart-over-head emotional nature. She cannot "stop the feeling." Her body and mind are at the mercy of her emotions.

3. Tom falls in love but never shows much excitement about it. He becomes a loyal and devoted husband but seldom brings his wife flowers or gifts. Tom never shows much emotion about anything. Which way does Tom's writing probably slant?

Tom is probably a vertical writer. Typically, a straight up-and-down writer is undemonstrative of strong emotional feelings but usually manages to display moderate sentiments and to make his loyalty and devotion known.

4. Do you normally write your shopping lists more rightward, more vertically, or more leftward than your normal handwriting?

You usually write them more vertically. (Most people don't get too hysterical about cabbage and sprouts. . . .)

5. Who's more dangerous to society, A or B?

A.   B.

B is far more dangerous. While both samples are acutely slanted to the right, A is stable, and B is unstable in every way! Both writers are capable of being overly emotional, but the unstable writer is far less likely to exhibit *self-control*, so this is a red flag.

After collecting and studying the writing of hundreds of murderers, graphologists have found that most of them have very far-rightward slants. They lack emotional control. We may all have murderous feelings, but we don't act upon them. It is this overly rightward slant in combination with unstable qualities that so often accompanies "aberrant behavior."

6. If you have sworn you wouldn't say something when you saw a certain person, and the first thing you did when you saw that person was to find yourself blurting out the very thing you swore you wouldn't say, then you are probably what type of slanter?

You are probably a very far-rightward slanter. As you recall, that's the slant that indicates extreme emotional impulsiveness; your emotions dominate, and you are controlled by them.

7. Some time ago your friend Sarah moved away, and the two of you have been corresponding ever since. Suddenly one day you notice her handwriting slant is completely different; it used to slant far to the right, but now it's becoming more and more vertical. What do you make of this sudden change in her slant?

There is no single answer to this question. Since Sarah has always been a rightward slanter, something has occurred in her life that is causing her to withhold the expression of her real feelings and to become less emotional, more reserved. Perhaps she has become dedicated to her work and cannot afford to be guided by her feelings. You would have to examine all of her writing to see if there are other changes in it that would shed some conclusive light here.

When a rightward slanter starts becoming a vertical or reclined slanter over an extended period of time, however, it is usually an indication of unhappiness. The person stops himself from feeling and instead holds himself upright or leftward, attempting to ward off painful feelings. Many people who experience trauma in their lives defensively try to become immune to their feelings; they repress them and become vertical or leftward, thereby "stopping the feeling."

I came to this conclusion after studying hundreds of cases in which rightward slanters became vertical or backhanded. I noticed repeatedly that signs of depression, fatigue, ill health, disillusionment, disappointment, resignation, or pessimism seemed always to accompany the change in the slant. My findings were substantiated by the writers themselves in my interviews with them.

8. Which writer is more likely to be dangerously compulsive, one step away from cracking up?

A.

this has been a very trying day for me .

B.

this has been a very trying day for me.

The answer is *B*, because the writing is too perfect. When graphologists see a totally unstable handwriting, they know immediately that the writer is totally unstable. But when a writing is too pretty, too perfect, too tight, everything alike as though it were produced by a typewriter (as in the writing by *B*), it means the writer is compensating for an inner feeling of loss of control. These people are one step away from cracking up.

So, although *A* and *B* both have nice, moderately rightward slants, sample B is *too* perfect, too overly controlled, and, thus, unhealthy. These are the types of people who often put rulers under their writing, who write too mechanically. They go along in life seemingly handling everything until, boom! They lose control and go berserk.

9. Here we have two very disturbing handwritings. Which writer should we be more scared of?

A.

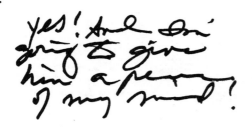

B.

plans too much. Unless I drop dead I will leave here "Friday" morning and be there as soon as

In actuality, *B*, the overly controlled person, is a lot scarier than the person who's showing how unstable he is. Person *A* acts exactly like his handwriting; it's out of control, and when you meet person *A* you know that something's wrong with him. He acts unstable, just like his handwriting.

But person *B*, who also acts just like his handwriting, is perfect, too controlled. So what you see is a person who seems to have it all together to a very strong degree, when in fact his handwriting reveals that this overcontrolled outward behavior is masking a person who is one step away from cracking up.

Thus *B*'s handwriting is, in effect, much scarier because you don't know from his outward behavior just how dangerous he might be. What you see is not what you get. The next time you hear or read of a seemingly normal person who suddenly goes crazy and guns people down at work or at home, note whether his or her handwriting is published by the media. Then note how frequently the style is overly controlled.

10. Both of these people had the same size paper to work with. Who's more extroverted, *A* or *B*?

A.

I don't have my script anymore be by writing it

B.

I put in seven hours on the project non stop! I should at least get paid for that time.

A is more extroverted. Slant has nothing to do with whether you're an introvert or extrovert. You will see later that it is the size of the writing that determines this trait. But even a leftward slanter who is feeling very extroverted and sociable, like *A*, is innately self-oriented, represses his or her true emotions, and remains, in fact, a very private person. Incidentally, *A* is actress Jane Fonda.

11. Would Marie Curie and Jackie Kennedy Onassis work well together? Would they get along?

Jackie Kennedy (Onassis)   *Madame Marie Curie*

Oh, no, no, no, no! Most likely these two women would be tearing each other apart if they had to work together.

In the workplace there is a definite tendency for people of the same slants to get along best. The worst, most disastrous combination would be the one depicted above, a far-leftward slanter working side by side with a far-rightward slanter. The rightward person is so expressive: "This is fantastic! You're a genius! I *love* it! And I'm proud of you! But you know what? I'm really *worried* about whether he's going to like it! I really *hope* he does!" The rightward slanter gives compliments and wants to be stroked; everything is emotional. But the leftward person doesn't want anything to do with emotion, clams up, leans over backward to avoid emotional situations.

So the rightward person thinks of the leftward person, "What a cold fish! Just like a stone wall! You can't get through to that person! What's wrong with her? She's so detached, so cold, so aloof!" The leftward slanter is thinking about the rightward slanter, "What an emotional wreck! That person's just loony-tunes! You say hello, and she falls apart!" By the way, this opposite-slant combination can be disastrous in the work force but not necessarily in affairs of the heart.

Generally a vertical slanter can get along with a leftward or rightward slanter in the workplace. Of course, additional factors are used to determine compatibility, but we're considering only slant at the moment.

12. Which note was written by the Zodiac killer? Which note is a fake?

This is the Zodiac speaking
By the way have you cracked
the last cipher I sent you?
My name is ——

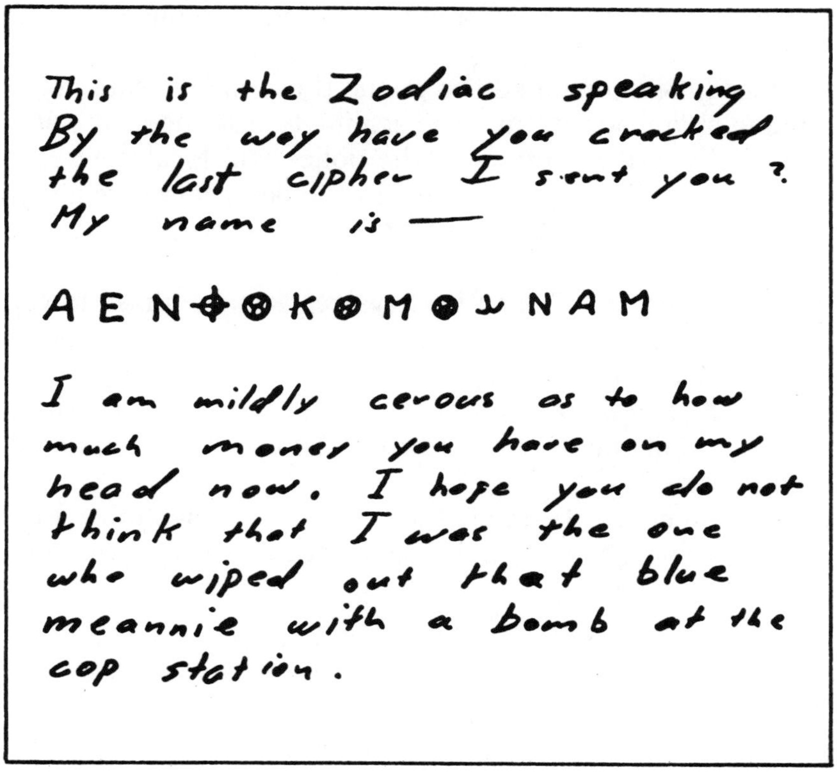

A E N ⊕ ⊗ K ⊙ M ⊙ ↲ N A M

I am mildly cerous as to how
much money you have on my
head now. I hope you do not
think that I was the one
who wiped out that blue
meannie with a bomb at the
cop station.

Sample B

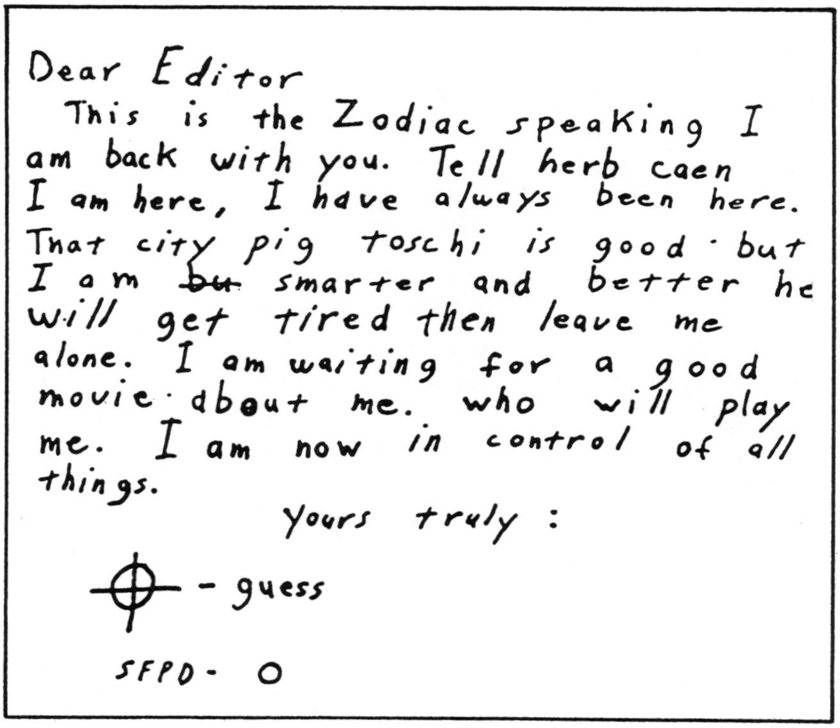

Dear Editor
   This is the Zodiac speaking I
am back with you. Tell herb caen
I am here, I have always been here.
That city pig toschi is good but
I am ~~but~~ smarter and better he
will get tired then leave me
alone. I am waiting for a good
movie about me. who will play
me. I am now in control of all
things.
              Yours truly :

⊕ — guess

SFPD - O

The Zodiac killer, you may recall, is suspected of murdering more than sixty people in the San Francisco Bay area during the late 1960s and the 1970s.

He is also suspected of killing two students at the University of California, Riverside, where his handwriting was found etched in one of the victims' classroom desks.

The Zodiac killer tormented the public those many years not only by cleverly eluding apprehension time and again—to date, he is still at large—but by continually writing letters to the police and local newspapers. In these letters, he would frequently go so far as to describe where and how his next victim would be killed. Often, he included bloodstained clothing belonging to his recent victims.

Everyone was frantic. The entire Bay Area was mobilized to catch the Zodiac. A rash of copycat letters was received by the authorities and newspapers, and each one had to be examined for authenticity.

Even though you do not know what the real Zodiac's handwriting looks like, it contains a trait you have just learned about that is often found in the writing of murderers.

One of the preceding two notes was written by the Zodiac killer, and one is a fake. Your job, should you decide to accept it, is to determine which is which.

Sample *A* is the handwriting of the Zodiac killer. Sample *B* is the fake.

The clue I hope you spotted is the "Maniac *d*" in sample *A*, discussed earlier. Recall that a Maniac *d* is one where the letter suddenly takes off at an acute angle to the right. It indicates a person who can lose emotional control, who can suddenly go off the deep end. People who exhibit frequent and severely rightward Maniac *d*'s are known to be extremely dangerous.

In sample *A* all the *d*'s are maniacally rightward. In sample *B* we find no maniac *d*'s. The writer of sample *B* intentionally inclined some of his *l*'s, not realizing that he should have inclined only the *d*'s to simulate the writing of the Zodiac. We conclude the writer of sample *B* intentionally inclined the *l*'s because a large space precedes them, revealing that he paused to calculate what he would do next and was not writing spontaneously at these points.

Another clue you may have picked up is the increase in the size of the word *Zodiac* in sample *A*, indicating that the writer feels big about himself and wants this name to stand out. Since the real Zodiac always signed his name in his notes, in addition to always beginning them with "This is the Zodiac speaking," we can assume he liked calling himself this name.

The writer of sample *B*, however, wrote the word *Editor* larger than the word *Zodiac*, and thus we deduce that what was important to him was that his letter would get to the editor and be published. Instead of emphasizing himself, as the real Zodiac always did, he was giving all the stature and importance to the editor.

13. A study of one thousand convicted rapists revealed a preponderance of which slant?

Among convicted rapists there is a preponderance of leftward slanters. (This does not mean, however, that if you're a leftward slanter you're a convicted rapist!) An inability to properly express real feelings is one of many psychological problems that frequently occur in this group.

YOU ARE THE GRAPHOLOGIST: SOLUTION

Who Burglarized Grandma Bessie's Home?

Once again, here are portions of the three High-Tech Security guards' statements from the burglary case described in the beginning of this chapter. Can you spot the guilty party now?

Davis

ON ROUTE 7 AND 8 UNTIL MIDNIGHT I SPOKE TO JIMMY TUCKER BEFORE I PUNCHED OUT FOR ABOUT 10 MINUTES. THEN I LEFT AND WENT HOME. I DID NOT COMMIT THE BURGLARY AT THE OSTLER HOUSE.

Nicholas

AND THEN I WENT HOME FOR THE NIGHT. I WAS NOT ANYWHERE NEAR THE GREENFIELD AREA THAT NIGHT. I AM NOT FAMILIAR WITH THE PLACEMENT OF ANY ALARMS ON ROUTE 13.

Carter

AND I ONLY DRIVE ROUTES 4, 5, 9, + 13 ON THE WEEKENDS I DON'T KNOW ANYTHING ABOUT WHAT HAPPEENED AT THE OSTLER HOUSE OR GREENFIELD AREA. I DIDN'T COMMIT THE BURGLARY

The guilty party is Nicholas.

Did you notice a change in slant when Nicholas wrote, "I was not anywhere near the Greenfield Area that night," and, "I am not familiar with the placement of any alarms on Route 13"? He lost his largely stable, rightward slant in these sections, becoming very vertical or leftward on key words ("not . . . near . . . not familiar . . ."). This means his subconscious mind was pulling away from the feeling, from what he was writing. His subconscious, which knew that the truth was different from what he was writing, distracted him enough so that he lost control of his slant in these areas.

Here's How the Story Actually Unfolded

I told Mr. Watson that Nicholas looked the most guilty from his statement because of the highly visible, abrupt changes in the slant of the writing in key phrases.

A few months later, Watson called to inform me that Nicholas had just been caught red-handed breaking into a home he was supposed to be guarding. So now High-Tech is going to have guards guarding the guards on a regular basis.

11
BASELINES

Baseline Quiz

Before you start reading about baselines, once again please take the following quiz designed to see how much you may already know about the subject without realizing it.

1. Who's feeling more up, *A* or *B*?

A.

who's feeling more up today?

B.

who's feeling more up today?

2. Who's moodier, *A* or *B*?

A.

who's moodier?

B.

who's moodier?

3. Who's feeling suicidal, giving up, *A* or *B*?

A.

who's feeling more suicidal, giving up?

B.

who's feeling more suicidal, giving up?

4. What makes a writer's hand go up or down, as in all the preceding examples?

Answers

| 1. A | 2. B | 3. B | 4. His brain. |

93

Introduction to Baselines

"Baseline" refers to the imaginary line upon which we write on a blank piece of paper. Does the writing go uphill, downhill, stay level, or go up and down? The answer to this question describes a writer's baseline.

What does the baseline reveal?

We can think of each line of writing as a road on the way to reaching a goal. We start at the left, which is the past, and go along the line, which is the present, and end up on the right side of the paper at our goal, the future.

By looking at our baselines, graphologists can see a number of things such as general moods; attitudes about reaching our goals; attitudes toward the past, present, and future; and the kind of mental energy we apply to life's situations.

Where does the baseline come from? What makes our handwriting go up or down or stay level?

Is it the paper that causes it? The pen? Is it our hand? Our brain? Well, what makes some people slump over, while others sit up straight? Why do some walk with heads down or heads held high? Why do we walk quickly or slowly? Why do we act the way we do?

The answer to all of these questions, including what makes our handwriting go up or down or stay level, is that it is dictated by the way we're feeling. It's our brain that decides whether or not we're feeling uplifted or depressed.

Types of Baselines

Let's take a look at a number of different baselines, and see what they mean.

Straight Baseline

The straight baseline reveals someone who is stable in outward behavior, even-keeled, level. This is the baseline of someone who exerts a degree of control over his outward moods. It takes enormous mental control to write straight across the paper, and this reflects the consistent and controlled behavior exhibited by the writer, at least on the surface.

Overly Straight Baseline

If yes, what recommendation did you make?
On January 31, 1986, did Chief Deputy Warden
move plaintiff Davis to some cell other than

A naturally straight baseline (as shown in the previous example) is to be distinguished from the rigid, overly controlled baseline in this example. An overly controlled baseline is one that looks as though it were written with a ruler (and may have been!). The sample shown here reveals overcontrol to compensate for an inner fear of loss of control.

Remember: It's a red flag if someone always uses a ruler to write; it's a red flag if someone writes *as if* he used a ruler but didn't, and it's a red flag if someone refuses to write unless he has lined paper. All these people can be scary because outwardly you cannot tell that anything is wrong with them. They behave, superficially, as if they're very much in control, when actually they feel one step away from losing it.

Those who write as if a ruler were actually used when it was not are perhaps in the worst shape of all. It takes an exceptionally long time to write this way. These writers feel that if they loosen up even a little bit, they will fall completely apart.

True Ascending Baseline

this is an example of true ascending base line that goes all the way to the last letter.

A "true" ascending baseline is one that goes uphill all the way to the last letter and does not drop off at the ends of the lines. This is one of the most positive traits a person can have in all of graphology. Studies of successful people in all types of careers show that over 90 percent of them have uphill writing.

Uphill writing means healthy mental energy and indicates someone who wants to stay busy, active, and constantly on the go, involved in many activities simultaneously. Someone who writes with a true ascending baseline is a great person to have on your ball team!

This trait does not necessarily mean optimism. You could be feeling depressed and pessimistic and still be writing uphill. It simply means you'll put just as much energy into your depression as you do into your good moments. It means you put healthy mental energy into everything.

False Ascending Baseline

this is an example of a falsely ascending baseline because the last word or letters on a line drop at the end.

The falsely ascending baseline is one where the lines rise but then fall down at the ends. This indicates a quitter. It is a sad baseline. Here the person starts off with great gusto, great excitement, then gives up right at the end. This is the person who can't wait to get it going, buys all he needs to make it happen, enrolls in the class in order to become this or that, and then quits before making it. This person is like a fire that burns brightly, then just as quickly goes out.

The same quitting trait could show up in a level baseline:

You could have the same trait in a level baseline .

This person, seemingly in control of his moods, doesn't get too excited as he works toward his goal. But he, too, gives up before he reaches his final destination.

Convex Baseline

this is an example of convex

A convex baseline is one where the writing starts to fall in the middle of each line. This trait is much rarer than a false ascending baseline. The person who writes this way is the classic quitter, and quits at the halfway point. It is important to determine at what point on the baseline the person quits. Some people quit halfway (convex baseline), while others do so at the last second (false ascending).

Partial Ascension

I'm going to wear my blue dress .

A partial ascension is where a word or phrase suddenly rises off the line. This indicates an elevated or hysterical feeling about the word or phrase that goes up. In the example above, the writer gets some sort of emotional high or elevated feeling regarding "blue." The sample does not tell us, at this point, why the writer feels this way about "blue." She may like the color or associate it with someone she loves, just to name two possibilities.

Descending Baseline

this is a descending baseline. IT goes downhill.

A descending baseline occurs when a majority of the lines are going downhill. With the exception of children (most of whom write downhill until adolescence), downhill writers are usually negative people. They look on the down side of things. There's something wrong. These people are often fatalists, people who are on a "downer," cynics with an attitude of defeat and disillusionment, constant disappointment.

Suicidal Baseline

this is an example of the suicidal base line when only a few lines in a page will suddenly fall.

The suicidal baseline often indicates suicidal feelings. The person who writes this way may give up suddenly and unexpectedly, and can also be accident prone. This baseline trait is seen regularly in suicide notes (in fact, the suicidal baseline was given its name by graphologists studying thousands of these notes), as are unstable writing and signs of unhappiness, some of which we will discuss later.

Be careful to distinguish the suicidal baseline from the false ascending baseline. In this sample only a *few* lines on a whole page of writing suddenly crash down on the right margin. Believe it or not, this is a much more serious trait than having the ends of most or all of the lines crashing down.

With the suicidal baseline, the writing might stay level or go uphill in general but then, out of nowhere, one or two lines crash down on the right margin. The reason this is scarier than the other descending baseline is that this person doesn't give you warning of his tendency to suddenly get deeply depressed and just give up. If someone is depressed and giving up all the time, we can predict it. If someone gives up only God knows when, we can't predict it, and it's far more serious. It's like a dog that bites. If it always bites, you'll be on your guard. But if the dog is nice most of the

97

time, you might be petting it one day and be surprised when it suddenly bites you.

Suicidal people usually kill themselves on impulse. Out of nowhere they get a sinking feeling that they cannot control; they "fall off," lose it all. These people subconsciously set themselves up for a fall.

Following is a sample from an actual suicide note. Notice the suicidal drop on the third line:

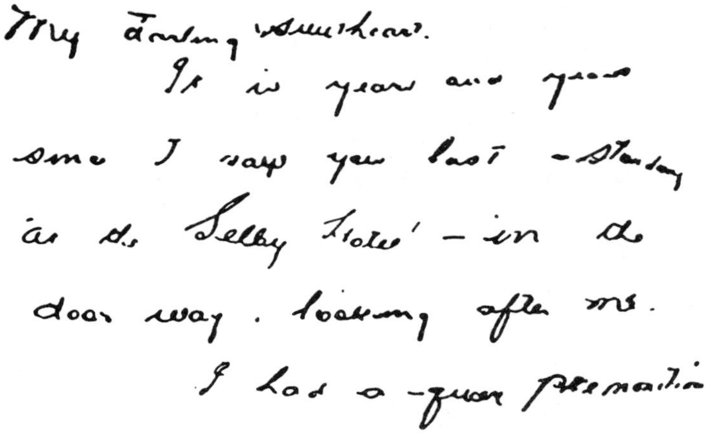

[handwritten suicide note sample]

People who commit suicide successfully tend to write the shortest suicide notes. People who mean to kill themselves seldom write rambling notes about ". . . how you did me in . . . I never meant to hurt you . . . doing this because I love you . . ." The types who are unsuccessful in their suicide attempts usually write long notes and manage to be "saved" just in time.

It's also interesting to note that families of suicide victims often have great difficulty in accepting the fact that their loved one really killed himself. They would rather believe that their loved one was murdered. A suicide is embarrassing to the family and a source of great guilt for those who feel they could have prevented it or are somehow responsible for it. Often these family members will seek out a handwriting expert, saying, "He couldn't have killed himself! This can't be his handwriting!" or "Someone must have *forced* him to write this note!"

Partial Descension

[handwritten example: and I'll wear my violet dress.]

A baseline with partial descension indicates a sudden sinking feeling associated with the word that suddenly fell down. In the example above, we could conclude that "violet" is a depressing thought for the writer for some reason.

This type of descension is not to be confused with the suicidal baseline, where the descension comes only on the last word and/or words, or last letter and/or letters of a word at the end of a line.

Concave Baseline

[handwritten example: this is an example of concave]

Remember, we can think of each line of writing as the road to reaching our goals. So the person with a concave baseline starts off with high enthusiasm and in the middle thinks, "I don't know if I should've undertaken this. Maybe I should give up." But as the end is in sight, the writer manages to achieve his goal, to "rise to the occasion." He likes beginnings and endings but sags in the middle.

Erratic Baselines

this is an example of an erratic base line.

Erratic baselines indicate moodiness. The bouncier the baseline tends to be, the more moody the writer. These people laugh and cry easily, are temperamental, are always up and down.

These people may seem the most unbalanced, but since they show their ups and downs so much, they're actually much less likely to end up in a mental institution than, say, someone who keeps the baseline rigidly straight. It's healthier to let it all hang out than to hold it all in until one day it explodes.

Incoherent Baseline

in control of my life again I would like to work so I can be independent and not have to depend on anyone else to support me

An incoherent baseline indicates a writer who is mentally deranged. Someone who cannot keep his lines in a coherent spatial pattern is unable to stay within any kind of a line or pattern of society. The person is "spaced out," as they say, just out of it. This type of person is referred to as a sociopath.

The Universal Concept Associated with Baselines

As discussed earlier, the interpretation of baselines comes from the universal concept of Up versus Down.

Please recall that not only graphology assumes that uphill is good, downhill is negative, and level is neutral. The English language (and languages around the world) applies these same connotations.

Here are a few more expressions for up, down, and level, in addition to those listed earlier:

DOWN (associated with depression, fatigue, dishonesty, gloom, and pessimism)	LEVEL (associated with calmness and outer stability)	UP (associated with hopefulness, ambition, honesty, activity, motivation, and success)
Low man on the totem pole. *Low* life. In the *depths* of depression. *Low*-down good-for-nothing. *Down*trodden of the world. *Low*-grade quality. Lie *down* on the job.	On an *even* keel. *Level*headed. Do one's *level* best. *Even*handed. It's on the *level*.	*Rise above* it. Reach for the *stars*. I can *top* that. Thumbs *up*. Chin *up*. *Up* and coming. *Jump* for joy.

Pop Quiz

1. Who doesn't like his father, *A* or *B*?

A.   B.

The answer is *B*. Notice that the last name crashes downhill in *B*'s writing, which is indicative that there's something wrong with the writer's attitude about his last name. This may translate to an attitude about the writer's father, from whom the last name usually comes. However, if the last name were something awful-sounding, embarrassing, or associated with an unpopular ethnic group, then the disfiguration of it might be due to distaste for the name itself.

2. One of the two writings below is that of Albert Einstein, and one is that of the sinister Russian monk/hypnotist, Rasputin. Which one is by Rasputin?

Sample A   Sample B

Sample B is by Rasputin. Although very influential at the court of Czar Nicholas II and Czarina Alexandra, Rasputin's insidious ambitions and nefarious deeds eventually brought about his own downfall.

Baseline Tidbits

Tidbit #1

A number of studies conducted several years ago investigated the effect of having an uphill writer work alongside a downhill writer. Would the uphill person bring the downhill writer up? Would the downhill writer bring the uphill person down, or would nothing occur?

The researchers found that, more often than not, the downhill writer brought the uphill writer down. It's easier to tear a house down than to build it up.

Tidbit #2

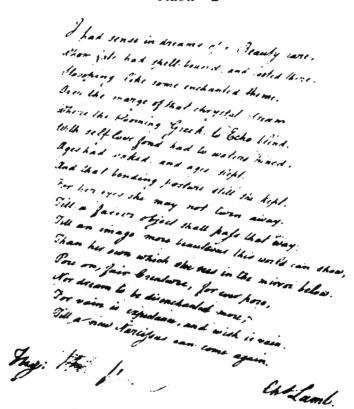

If all the lines of a sample of writing are evenly and equally downhill, like essayist and critic Charles Lamb's writing above, it means, in addition to all the rest of the downhill traits, that the writer has been depressed for a long, long time and learned to live with it. You cannot write so evenly downhill unless you've been doing so for an extended period of time.

12

MARGINS

"If Grandma was in Miss McElfresh's class she'd get marks off for not leaving proper margins."

YOU ARE THE GRAPHOLOGIST

Who Embezzled $62,000 from the Dentist's Office?

Dr. Foster, a dentist in Phoenix, calls you because his accountant has just discovered that someone in his office embezzled $62,000 from him over the past three years.

Here are Dr. Foster's descriptions of the three employees who could have embezzled the money from him:

1. Millie works in Dr. Foster's back office, doing bookkeeping and billing. She's forty, blonde, divorced with two children, and is always having trouble with men. She looks a little slovenly at times, never seems to be able to make ends meet, and her children always seem to be getting into trouble at school.

2. Rhonda is a dental assistant. She is a nice twenty-eight-year-old girl from the ghetto. Rhonda has risen from a poverty background by working hard, coming in early, and having no qualms about working overtime. She has a boyfriend who can truly be classified as a deadbeat, and others in the office suspect him of being involved with drugs.

3. Connie, twenty-four, is the front-office person. She is demure, friendly, quiet, and neat. Connie has worked for Dr. Foster longer than the other employees. She keeps a Bible at the corner of her desk and attends church regularly, although no one knows her that well because she never reveals much about herself.

Cartoon reprinted with special permission of King Features Syndicate, Inc.

You instruct Dr. Foster to have the three employees write a description of anything and everything they have to do with the company's money on the days they work. They should describe any knowledge they have or recommendations about how to improve the accounting situation, and they should end with a sentence like, "I did (or did not) embezzle the money from Dr. Foster."

A few days later you receive the three suspects' statements. Can you spot the guilty party by looking at the final lines of each of the three samples below?

Millie

to have it be just one person's responsibility. I think this will be an improvement over all of us handling it in the office. I did not embezzle the money from Dr. Foster.

Rhonda

Since there is not any cash that we deal with. If Marvin picks it up I don't know it that cuts more. I did not take any money from Dr. Foster or anyone else.

Connie

Even though she only comes in twice a week. Maybe Rhonda could help out as well with it. Something should be done. I didn't steal the money from Dr. Foster.

After you read this chapter, you will have learned some key clues that will allow you to solve this particular crime. At the end of the chapter, you will find the solution and learn how the culprit was actually caught by the authorities.

Margin Quiz

Before you start reading about margins, let's see how much you already know about them without realizing it.

Each of the following samples represents a letter written on a blank page. Please look at the four below and answer questions 1 through 4.

A. Even All
Around

B. Overly Wide
Left Margin

C. Overly Wide
Right Margin

D. Too Wide All
Around

To answer the following questions, choose the correct letter for the samples above:

1. Who's more future-oriented?

2. Which person is clinging to the past?

3. Which person plans ahead and is interested in aesthetics, outward appearances, beauty, design, and symmetry?

4. Which person has to be surrounded by four solid walls?

Let's do some more.

E. Left Margin
Widening as It
Descends

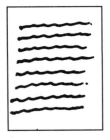

F. Left Margin
Narrowing as It
Descends

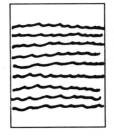

G. Narrow
Margins on
Left and Right
Sides

5. Who wrote the slowest?

6. Who wrote the fastest?

7. Who doesn't leave room for other people?

More yet:

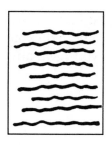   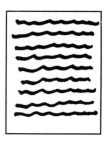

H. Uneven Left
Margin

I. No Margins at
All

J. Wide Upper
Margin

K. Narrow Upper
Margin

8. Who fills every waking moment of his life with activity?

9. Who's in jail?

10. Of *J* and *K*, one person is writing to the President of the United States and the other to a personal friend. Which one is writing to the President?

And the final questions:

  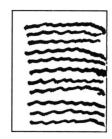

L. Wide Lower
Margin

M. Narrow Lower
Margin

N. Crushed Right
Margin

11. Who delays the inevitable?

12. Who is dangerously impulsive?

13. Who is avoiding the future?

Answers

1. B	5. F	8. I	11. M
2. C	6. E	9. H	12. N
3. A	7. G	10. J	13. L
4. D			

Explanation of Margins

A blank piece of paper represents life itself, and what you do on that blank page represents how you interact with other people and with life around you. Where do you choose to start your margins? Do you have large or small margins? Do you have any margins at all?

Because we write from left to right as we move across the page, the left represents the past, while the right represents the future.

Of the top and bottom of the page, which represents the past? The top. That's because, as we write from left to right, we are also moving from top to bottom:

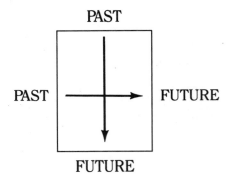

So the top is the past (again, reflecting where we came from), and the bottom is the future (where we're going).

Ideal Margins

The ideal adult margins, based on graphology, would be to have the left margin wider than the right margin, so that on an average 8½″ by 11″ page, you would naturally indent 1 to 1½ inches on the left side and go pretty far to the right side of the page without crashing into it. This would be a healthy left/right balance, meaning you have a healthy relation to the past and future.

Let's look at the meanings associated with the various margins shown in the quiz.

Margins Even All Around

You can control your left margin because you can choose where you start each line of writing, but you do not always know how long the last word on the line is going to be. Someone who is also controlling his or her right margin must write more slowly. There's no way to write quickly and make every word end in the same place.

Therefore, people who keep their margins even all around are most interested in the visual effect. They actually see the paper as almost like a work of art. They are extremely appearance-conscious and interested in beauty, design, symmetry, order, and balance. Everything has to be aesthetically pleasing to these people. To make that happen is to be very detail-minded and, of course, to give up spontaneity in the process. Such people plan everything ahead to the *n*th degree.

Overly Wide Left Margin

Since the left represents the past, the person who has a very wide left margin is subconsciously putting up an imaginary barrier between himself and the past. This trait is almost always an indication of someone who's had a terrible past from which he is eager to flee.

Overly Wide Right Margin

If you stop yourself short of the right margin, it means you are putting up imaginary barriers as to how far you can get in life.

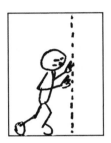

When you are moving to the right, you're moving toward your goals and the future. When you stop too soon at the end of your lines, somewhere in your subconscious is a little voice saying, "Uh-oh. I have to stop. I have to return to the left, to the past and the familiar. This is as far as I can go." You're putting up a stop sign, a roadblock, an imaginary wall.

Margins Too Wide All Around

Writing with margins that are too wide all around is abnormal. It looks more like a column or a poem. If you ask someone to give you a page of his ordinary writing, the person should not put the writing smack dab in the middle. This sort of person needs to be protected by four solid walls. He cannot make it on his own. He doesn't relate to his environment in a normal manner or fit into society in an average way.

Remember, the way you put yourself down on paper tells how you interact with life around you, and a person with this trait is displaced. He does not use the space properly. This is social maladjustment.

Left Margin Widening as It Descends

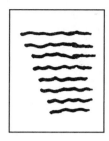

A left margin that widens as it descends means rapid and spontaneous writing. If you're writing quickly and spontaneously, you will leave wider and wider left margins as you descend the page. In your haste to make a point and/or reach a goal, it becomes increasingly difficult to take the time to move all the way to the left side of the paper as you return from the right margin.

Left Margin Narrowing as It Descends

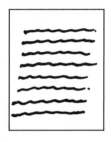

If someone were writing on an airmail flyer, and the writing started to get smaller and smaller and the left margin narrowed, the writer would obviously be running out of room. In that case, scrunching the writing all the way to the edges of the paper would be a practical and necessary adjustment.

But if someone's left margin typically narrows on page after page, this means a tendency to start out brave, going toward the future, but eventually retreat to the past and what is familiar. As this writer proceeds, he becomes more fearful and apprehensive about the future. He is losing spontaneity.

Narrow Margins on Left and Right Sides

Some people write all the way to the side on both the left and right, leaving no side margin whatsoever.

This trait indicates one who leaves no room for other people. Such a person doesn't see things from other people's point of view. Many times in the workplace there's an employee who's always having trouble with the other employees. That person often has this type of margin. He takes up all the space and doesn't see himself properly in relation to his environment. The person leaves no room for the rights and opinions of others.

Uneven Left Margin

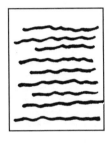

Please take out the sample you were directed to write at the beginning of this book, and look at your left margin. If you're like 99.999 percent of all literate people who write from left to right, you will automatically have made a straight left margin when writing to someone else. It is the only graphological trait we all do in common. These are all examples of straight left margins:

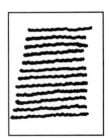

The left margin represents "the line of society." Each time we begin to write a line, we get to choose where to start that line on the left side of the paper. Thus, each time we return to the left margin, it's up to us whether we're going to align the next word below the line above or we're going to get "out of line." Since we usually can't control where a line of writing will end, it is normal to have a more uneven right margin.

110

That small percentage who do not have a straight left margin are those people who cannot conform to society's standards. They do not "toe the line" of society; they do not adapt or fit into a framework or structure. An uneven left margin means waywardness, hostility, one who gets "out of line." These are also people who, quite expectedly, would not do well in a strict nine-to-five job; they cannot discipline themselves to "stay in line."

No Margins at All

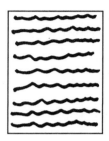

By a writer who uses "no margins at all," I mean someone who writes this way page after page. Obviously, if someone writes like this because he has only one piece of paper on which to write a great deal, that's a matter of practicality.

Writing with no margins, filling every inch of the paper, indicates someone who feels he must fill every waking moment of his life with an activity. It means compulsively busy, leaving no stone unturned. God forbid that the writer should leave one little part of the page without a word on it. God forbid that he should leave one moment of life not planned for! Very often such people have miserly natures as well. Since the writer has no left margin, this person also leaves no room for the rights or opinions of others, as in the case of narrow margins on both sides.

Wide Upper Margin

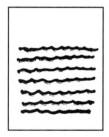

Graphologists can tell how formal or how informal you feel toward the person you're writing to by how low or high on the paper you begin the letter. The lower down on the page you start, the more you tend to have formal, respectful feelings toward the person to whom you're writing. You waste more paper to show respect, and you "lower" yourself down on the page.

Narrow Upper Margin

In contrast, a narrow upper margin means you are feeling more familiar than formal toward the person to whom you are writing. By starting high on the paper, you don't "bow down" or "lower yourself" to show respect.

Wide Lower Margin

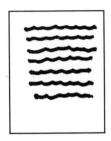

A wide lower margin results when someone stops writing long before reaching the bottom of the page even though he has more to say and continues on the other side of the paper or on another page. You have already seen that on a blank page the left represents the past and the right represents the future, respectively. You have also seen how the top and bottom of the page also represent the past and the future. Thus, this writer is stopping short of reaching his goals, just as someone who stops short of the right margin. This trait is a sign of fear of the future and avoiding going ahead.

Narrow Lower Margin

A narrow lower margin is just the opposite. This sample is meant to represent a writing sample where the writer wrote all the way to the right side and bottom of the paper until there was no room left, then probably turned the page over before he or she finally got another sheet.

This means someone who delays the inevitable. Such a person is so eager to express himself that he feels it would take too much time to turn the paper over or get another sheet. So he keeps writing until there's absolutely not an iota of space left.

Crushed Right Margin

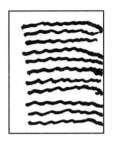

A crushed right margin is a warning sign! It's like the old sign that reads:

Some people, in writing a page, find themselves saying over and over again, "Whoops! I forgot the end of the paper was coming!" This is very serious.

It means dangerous impulsiveness. People like this bash their heads into the wall and do it again and again. They don't learn from their mistakes. They don't have the sense to say to themselves, "Hey, wait a minute. You know, the paper ends, and I have to accommodate." They don't say it because they don't care or think about it!

Right-margin crashers are often people who have accidents, perhaps driving off cliffs. If you know someone who's accident-prone, get his or her handwriting. Very likely it will have impulsive right margins. These people do not see the wall coming, even though it's the same stone wall, so they keep crashing into it. They're so impulsive they don't look before they leap, don't plan ahead.

These are also the people who do things they later regret: "Gee, I know I said that, but I couldn't control myself at the time. I lost my head!"

A good rule of thumb is: If a person crashes this way more than twice per page, it's time to get out of his way.

The Universal Concepts Associated with Margins

Several universal concepts are used in interpreting margins. They include Left versus Right, High versus Low, Wide versus Narrow, and Straight versus Crooked.

You've already seen a number of everyday expressions associated with the concept of Left versus Right. Here are some expressions associated with the other concepts:

HIGH	LOW
Don't act so *high* and mighty. Don't put yourself *on a pedestal*.	*Bow down* to show respect. *Lower* oneself down.
WIDE	NARROW
Separates himself from the past. *Wide* margin of error.	A *narrow* miss. A *tight* fit. A *marginal* defeat. A *margin* of success.
STRAIGHT	CROOKED
She *toes the line* of society. Gets *in line*. Stay *in line*. *Straighten* up! Fall *in line*!	Sets a *crooked* course. *Doesn't stay* on course. Gets *out of line*.

Margin Tidbit

Would you like to have some fun with margins in a slightly different form? If so, please get an 8½″ by 11″ sheet of paper, and on that page draw a wheel. That's all I can tell you. Draw the wheel before you read the next paragraph!

Did you do it yet? If so, read on.

Where did you put your wheel on the page? The normal place to put it is in the middle of the paper. If you *didn't* put it in the middle, regardless of the wheel's size, it means you don't feel confident, you don't feel on your center. Even if the wheel is just off to the left or right a little bit, it's still not in the center.

Then it is desirable to have perspective. A flat circle is usually indicative of inferior artistic skills and/or seeing things one dimensionally. Showing dimension means you're able to see all sides of an issue and/or you have artistic ability.

Next we look to see whether you drew spokes. If so, they should be symmetrical. If there are five spokes on the left and four spokes on the right, you're not feeling organized and balanced.

The sturdier the wheel, the better. The bigger the wheel, the better, unless it is *too* big. Example:

Good Size

Too Big

The more solid the lines, the better. Also, there should be a hubcap in the middle; there should be a center.

Drawing a wheel is a form of a common psychological test, such as those where the therapist might ask the patient to draw a house, a tree, and a person. The manner in which the patient draws these things reveals a great deal about his attitudes, home life, work, and himself in general. Graphologists call such interpretations of graphic movement graphology; psychologists call it psychological testing and therapy.

Pop Quiz

1. You've asked a person to give you a sample of his handwriting, and this is what you get. Is the writer socially adjusted or maladjusted?

Before you read a single word of a sample, you should look at the overall placement of the writing to see whether the writer integrates normally with his environment and other people. Here the writer is putting the writing in a strange place. In these extreme instances, the writer is frequently physically odd in appearance, as well as odd in behavior and social adjustment.

It doesn't matter that each word looks normal and the spelling is correct. The fact that the writing is placed abnormally on the paper means, of and by itself, that the writer is abnormal, displaced, and not behaving like the average person. Often the writer appears as out of kilter as his behavior, such as having an unusually long beard or strange clothing or bizarre jewelry.

115

2. Which person, *A* or *B*, will get further in life at this time?

A.    B.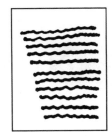

B will get further in life at this time. Even though *B* isn't writing uphill, he's going all the way to the right side of the paper (and not going downhill). While *A* is writing uphill, a trait associated with healthy mental energy and success, he stops his sentences way short of the right margin, which cancels out the positiveness of the uphill writing.

It doesn't matter if you have everything going for you. If you put up imaginary barriers as to how far you can get in life, then you're your own worst enemy! In studies of success in life, graphologists have found that people whose right margins stop way short of the right side of the paper never make it the way they should. Even if they're somewhat successful, they could be that much more so if they didn't stop themselves short.

3. Based on the use of the margins, which writer doesn't follow the rules but makes his own rules?

Sample A

> *It is also clear that with your help, we can see this through to a final victory. Your support has been critical to the battle we have already won -- and slowly, step-by-step, we are winning.*

Sample B

> *There is no charge for design typesetting, paste-up or basic camera. In cases where an advertisement in a special charges, the advertiser will be billed at cost.*

The answer is *A*. Why? Because the writer ignores the left writing margin and writes right through the vertical line as if it didn't exist.

This margin means the writer goes outside the boundaries that are given to him. He flaunts his desire not to stay within the limitations set before him by making his own rules, setting his own limitations. Remember that the left margin represents the "line of society." When we don't respect it, when we ignore it and make our own margin, it means we feel beholden only to our own rules, not society's.

Why did person *A* bother to choose stationery with a lined margin on it and then completely ignore it? Do you know whose writing this is? Can you think of a public figure who made national headlines in the late eighties for breaking the rules of the land?

Here's a hint: What this man did was to make himself the law. He didn't care that he wasn't supposed to lie to Congress, or go behind people's backs and sell arms to Iran and the *contras*, and pocket the money.

Yes, this is the writing of Lieutenant Colonel Oliver North, who was convicted of obstructing Congress, destroying government documents, and accepting an illegal gratuity in the form of a security system for his home.

4. The writer of the paragraph below said he didn't believe in graphology. He was then challenged to write a page of true statements and to stick in a factual lie, which he agreed to do. Can you find the lie that occurs somewhere in the following paragraph?

It takes many years of practice in discerning falsehoods in written statements before one can do this quickly and easily. So if you didn't get this right away, don't be too hard on yourself.

The first thing to do when looking for a lie is to hold the page away and look at the left margin to see if something moved out of alignment to the left. Also, look at the spacing to see if it suddenly gets too wide or too narrow in any particular area. Remember that rapid and spontaneous writing causes the left margin to widen and move farther to the right, not to the left. Also, spontaneous writing stays even in its spacing and doesn't suddenly get too wide or too narrow.

Did you notice that the spacing got wider on the third and fourth lines? Now look at the left margin on the third and fourth lines. Which line juts out farthest to the left?

117

The bottom line, the line that starts with the word *born*, juts out the farthest. Remember, when you are writing quickly and spontaneously, your left margin will move to the right, and as soon as you lose spontaneity, you pull to the left. So the lie probably occurs in the line beginning with the word *born*. Can you find it now? (*Hint*: Something doesn't slant to the right in that line.)

Did you notice that the number *2* doesn't slant to the right as much as the other part of the writing?

Kimberly was, in fact, *not* born on July 28. The writer fessed up that she was actually born on July 18.

YOU ARE THE GRAPHOLOGIST: SOLUTION

Who Embezzled $62,000 from the Dentist's Office?

Once again, here are the samples from the three suspects who work for Dr. Foster described at the beginning of this chapter. Can you now guess who the guilty party is?

Millie

to have it be just one person's responsibility.
I think this will be an improvement
over all of us handling it in the office.
I did not embezzle the money
from Dr. Foster.

Rhonda

since there is not any cash that we deal with, If
Marvin pick it up I don't know it that cuts more.
I did not take any money from Dr. Foster or anyone else,

Connie

EVEN though she only comes in twice
a week. Maybe Rhonda could help
out as well with it. Something should be done.
I didn't steal the money from Dr. Foster.

The guilty party is Connie. When we look at all three statements, we notice that the last line of Connie's starts farther to the left than the lines above it do. Remember, when you lose spontaneity, you suddenly pull back to the left.

Also remember that when someone lies or subconsciously withdraws from what he is writing, he rears up and/or pulls to the left.

Here's How the Story Actually Unfolded

When I reported to Dr. Foster that Connie was lying in her statement, she became the focus of the investigation. It was soon discovered that she had established a bank account at the same bank as Dr. Foster and was occasionally depositing his checks into her own account. She was arrested and ultimately convicted of the crime.

Thus, Connie, who had worked the longest for Dr. Foster and who seemed so religious, turned out to be the one doing this most "ungodly" deed!

13

SPACING

Who Stole $52,000 from the All-Night Supermarket?

You receive a call from Mr. Hanks, the head of an investigative firm. Hanks has been hired by Waldo's Incorporated, a chain of all-night supermarkets, to investigate a recent theft of $52,000 from the vault of one of their stores.

Mr. Hanks tells you that the theft occurred during the 10:00 P.M.-to-6:00 A.M. shift on a particular day, and that the company has concluded it was an inside job. Sixteen people worked that shift—far too many suspects to put under surveillance. He has heard that you can look at somebody's handwriting and determine whether a person is honest, specifically whether or not he or she is telling the truth. Mr. Hanks comments that such an ability would be very useful at this time because he has no idea where to even begin. Although, like most people, he remains skeptical, he's willing to give graphology a try at this point and would like you to help him narrow the field.

You direct Mr. Hanks in the procedure of having all suspects sit down with plenty of unlined paper and a ballpoint pen and asking them to write what they were doing the entire night of the theft. They should write what they saw, who they were with, and whether or not they committed the crime.

If any of these sixteen people are guilty, you'll know it from their handwritten statements.

The sixteen statements arrive at your office a few days later. After many hours of scrutiny, you conclude that none of these sixteen people appears to be the guilty party. However, you are able to find one particular clue that will later prove to be very useful.

On the following page are portions of three suspects' statements. Can you find the significant clue?

Cashier A

I stocked the frozen food section between 4 & 5 a.m. I cashed out registers 3 4 and 5 before leaving and put approximately $2700 into the deposit slot in the safe. I left at 6.

Janitor

and there was a pill in the darey ile which I cleaned up. I put away the cart and put the trash in the back, and then I left work at my usual time of 6:00 in the Morning.

Cashier B

and when my break was over I was on chekout #5 until it was time for me to go home at 6. I have no knowlidge of who took the money.

After you read this chapter, you will have learned enough to find the key clue. At the end of the chapter, you will find the solution and learn how the culprit was actually caught by the authorities.

Spacing Quiz

Before you start reading about spacing, please take this little quiz to see how much you already know about the subject without even realizing it. Please look at the four samples and answer the questions below.

Sample A

And I think we should do it soon.

Sample B

And I think we should do it soon

Sample C

And I think we should

Sample D

And I think we should do it very soon.

1. Who can't get close to other people?

2. Who has uneven thinking?

3. Who is uptight and narrow-minded?

4. Who is confused?

Answers

1. C	2. A	3. D	4. B

Explanation of Spacing

Spacing refers to the distances between letters, words, and lines of writing.

Spacing tells how the writer feels toward other people, about his social behavior, and whether or not he thinks fluidly—his intelligence.

Each word you write represents you, the ego. Where you choose to put the next word represents where you subconsciously choose to put other people in relation to yourself.

Do you choose to put words or people right next to you? Or do you choose to keep them at a distance?

words close together   words   far   apart

What is considered "normal" spacing?

The space between words and lines varies with the size and speed with which you are writing. Looking at many writings over time will give you an idea of what the average person does most of the time.

"Normal" is really just the absence of *abnormal*. If the spacing doesn't look unusual, then it's normal. When the spacing gets too wide or too narrow or somehow appears odd, it falls into the realm of "abnormal."

For example, the following sample appears normal:

I always try to do the right thing.
Sometimes I fail; sometimes I succeed.

And this sample would be considered abnormal:

I always . try to do the
right thing. sometimes
succeed; sometimes I fail.

123

Meanings Associated with Specific Spacing Patterns
Overly Wide Spaces Between Words

this   is   overly   wide   spaces

The pattern in this sample should look strange to your eye. Each word looks normal, but the distance between the words is abnormally wide.

Putting a great deal of space between words is akin to putting a great deal of space between yourself and others, and means paranoia. People who write this way cannot get close to other people. They are suspicious and apprehensive of the motives and intentions of others. They cannot trust anyone. If you want to be their friend, they want to know why. They cannot get intimate. They hold you at arm's length.

Overly Wide Spaces Between Letters

this is overly wide

The spacing between the letters in this sample is abnormally wide. This is extremely strange and abnormal because so few people do this. Anytime you see a writing that is abnormal, it means that the writer is abnormal (provided that you are normal enough to know what normal looks like!).

In this instance, the writer is making each letter represent himself instead of each word. The abnormal distance he puts between each letter symbolizes the abnormal distance he puts between himself and other people. So this person is socially isolated. The fact that the writer sees himself as a letter, and not a word, further reveals how abnormally detached he is.

Overly Narrow Spaces Between Letters

this is overly narrow spaces between letters .

Does this sample look as strange to you as the preceding one? It should look *less* strange because it is statistically more common and is therefore more normal.

On your scratch paper, please try writing like this sample, and see how it feels.

When someone writes one letter abnormally close to the next letter, it means the person is feeling extremely uptight and narrow-minded, not open. He is automatically in a more tense posture, because when one is loose and relaxed, the handwriting will automatically broaden as a result.

Closely Spaced Letters with Overly Wide Separations Between Words

this   is   closely   spaced   letters   with

Wow! This person has real social problems!

When letters are closely spaced but words are separated widely, this is a double negative whammy. The narrow spaces between letters reveal an extremely uptight individual, and the overly wide spaces between the words represent a person who is also extremely paranoid and incapable of intimacy. This is truly a socially maladjusted person.

Cramped Letters *and* Cramped Spacing Between Words

this is cramped spaces between letters and between words .

Everything is close here. Remember, when letters are too close, it means uptight and narrow-minded. Narrow spaces between words indicate that the writer does not keep a proper distance from others. The result is someone who is narrow-minded *and* invades your space.

People have an imaginary territorial boundary, which most of us observe. For example, studies of people sitting in a restaurant facing each other have shown that there is an imaginary line down the middle of the table that each observes: "I don't put my coffee or cigarettes on your side, and you don't put yours on mine."

Writers like the one in this sample often stand too close to other people, touch them when they talk, pat them on the back. You're always backing off from them. Or they'll ask personal questions they shouldn't. They get nosy, encroach upon your space, ask how much you paid for things, and the like.

It comes from a compulsive need to be physically close to others—crammed together, just like their words.

Tangling Lines

this is tangling lines and tangling letters as well, sometimes too tall, too.

Tangling means confusion. As one letter overlaps another letter or word, so one thought is overlapping another thought. The more severely lines are tangled, the more severe the confusion.

Uneven Spacing

this is an example of uneven spacing. Wide and

Sometimes uneven spacing is a result of the writer's struggling with what he is writing. Notice that when you know exactly what you're going to write, your writing is even and flowing. It's only when you stop to think what to say next—which adjective to use, how to spell a word—that your writing starts faltering and loses rhythm.

If a handwriting is continuously lacking in good rhythm, with some words close together and others far apart, it is a sign of inferior intelligence or of the intelligence not functioning well at the time. Remember, "functioning intelligence" means how intelligently the person is behaving at the time, not how he scores on an IQ test.

Uneven spacing is symptomatic of uneven thinking, of inferior intelligence at the time of the uneven writing.

Generally Large Spacing Between Letters, Words, and Lines

this is generally wide spaces everywhere

If you are writing very fast, you're going to cover more territory than if you're moving slowly. And if your writing is also big, then everything is going to be larger.

Wide spacing means broad-mindedness. The faster, the more open, the looser the writing, the faster, more open-minded, and looser the individual. This trait is also revealing of generosity of spirit, an openness of attitude, a letting loose.

The Universal Concepts Associated with Spacing

The interpretation of spacing *between the words* involves the universal concept of Wide versus Narrow.

Here are some expressions from everyday language that show these common meanings:

WIDE (*associated with distance, separation, detachment*)	NARROW (*associated with closeness, uptight qualities, lack of privacy*)
Keep your *distance*. She was acting so *distant*. It's *impossible to get close* to her. His manner was so *detached*. Let's go our *separate ways*. *Separation* of powers. Hold *at arm's length*. Widen the *gap* between them.	*Invading* your space. *Encroaches* on my territory. *Get off* my back. You're *stepping on my toes*. *Narrow* one's focus.

The interpretation of spacing *between the letters* involves the universal concept of Loose versus Tight. Here are some examples from everyday language:

LOOSE (*associated with open-mindedness*)	TIGHT (*associated with closed-mindedness*)
Very *broad*-minded. *Loose* and uninhibited. *Open*-minded. *Free* and easy. *Generosity* of spirit.	How *narrow*-minded can you be? He sure is *uptight*! Keep it *to yourself*. *Loosen up*, will you? She's so *tight*-lipped!

Pop Quiz

1. Which writer got a better grade on this essay answer?

Sample A

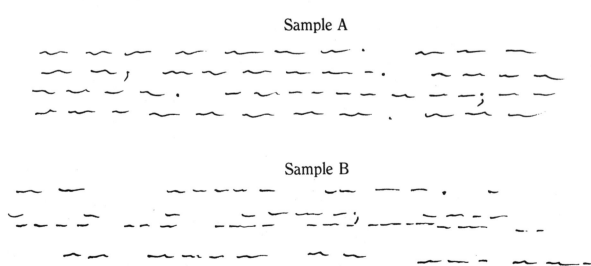

Sample B

127

A got a better grade on this test. The even spacing between the letters, words, and lines indicates that he knew exactly what he was saying; the thoughts and words came out smoothly.

In contrast, *B*'s essay contains wide then narrow spaces between the words, with no particular pattern. Thus, we know that this writer was struggling with the content. The words were not coming out freely; he did not know what the answer was as well as *A* did.

2. Below are statements from two suspects in a crime. Both people claim to have been with Jeff Harotian on the night of February 1, 1982. Who's lying? How can you tell?

Sample A

On the night of Feb. 1, 1982, I was with Jeff Harotian the whole time.

Sample B

On the night of Feb 1, 1982, I was with Jeff Haroten.

A is not telling the truth. The wide space before the name "Jeff Harotian" indicates a loss of spontaneity; *A* paused to think of what name to write. The name was spelled the same way it was in the question, so we must presume that it was spelled correctly.

In *B*'s sample, however, we see that the writer paused *after* the name Jeff and before the last name Harotian, which is faltering and misspelled. Thus, *B* appears to have lost spontaneity while trying to think of the correct spelling of Jeff's last name, and not before the first name. He didn't have to pause to think of whom he was with, but rather how to spell the last name.

Who Stole $52,000 from the All-Night Supermarket?

Did you find the significant clue in the handwritings of the three suspects presented at the beginning of this chapter? It's in the sample written by the janitor.

Take a look at the part of the janitor's statement that says, ". . . and then I left work at my usual time of 6:00 in the morning."

and then I Left work at my usual time of 6:00 in the Morning.

Did you notice the big spaces before "my" and before "6:00," the time he wrote that he left? These unusually big spaces reveal that the janitor lost spontaneity as he was about to write about the time he left work. Why did he stop at that point? Did he forget how to spell the word *my*? Or perhaps he forgot the "usual time" that he leaves work? It's doubtful! More likely he stopped to think because he *didn't* actually leave at what he calls "my usual time of 6:00 in the morning." What would you do with this information?

Here's How the Story Actually Unfolded

I called Mr. Hanks and said I was sorry but I couldn't find the guilty party. I mentioned, though, that I felt the janitor was probably lying about the time he'd left work on the night in question.

A day later I got a call from Mr. Hanks, who told me, "When we confronted the janitor and said we thought he hadn't been truthful about the time he'd left that night, he made an interesting confession. The janitor said the daytime manager had come in two hours earlier than usual and let him go home early. The daytime manager had, on one or two occasions, let the janitor go home earlier and had warned the janitor not to tell anyone, since it might look like favoritism, and the company would take a dim view of someone being paid for two hours work he didn't perform.

"So," continued Hanks, "we now have another suspect, the daytime manager, and we're going to meet with him."

Later, several members of the company and the security firm met with the daytime manager and asked him why he had not come forward to say he had been present during two hours of the graveyard shift in question. The daytime manager denied that he had been present or that he had come in early that morning.

The janitor was then brought into the meeting and asked to repeat what had actually happened that morning. The janitor was excused, and the company officers stated that it was their belief that the daytime manager was the thief, and that they were about to launch a full investigation.

Later, through an attorney, the daytime manager agreed to make restitution of the money if the company would agree not to press charges against him.

14
PRESSURE

"You don't have to press down so hard."

"But I really MEAN what I'm writing!"

Pressure Quiz

Once again, please take the following quiz to see how much you already know about the subject.

1. One of these people is a follower and one is a leader. Who is the leader?

A.   B.

Your coliemn is very   *Your questions of*
                             are interesting to
                             Coots asks all the

2. In which subject did Johnny get the worst grade?

I took math, science, speech, + history.

Cartoon reprinted with special permission of King Features Syndicate, Inc.

3. Who is more nervous, *A* or *B*?

A.

Can you see who is more nervous?

B.

Can you see who is more nervous?

Answers

1. B	2. Speech	3. A

Explanation of Pressure

Pressure is the amount of force you exert while writing—how hard or soft you press on the pen or pencil. This is best assessed when the writer has used a ballpoint pen.

To see how pressure is measured, please use a ballpoint pen to write this sentence on your scratch paper with *very light pressure*: "I like graphology, and I will use it the rest of my life."

Now write the same sentence with heavy pressure, pressing down hard.

Finished? Now turn your scratch paper over, and feel the writing from the other side of the page. If you did indeed vary your pressure, one area should feel much bumpier. Which one?

The area where you used heavy pressure is bumpier. Now, looking at your sample right-side up, is the heavy-pressured writing or the light-pressured writing more angular? Again, it should be the heavy-pressured writing. In fact, the two samples should have a very different look overall.

What Pressure Reveals

If you're relaxed, do you think you're going to be writing lightly or heavily? Lightly. If you're feeling very intense, are you going to be writing gently or hard? Hard, right?

Pressure reveals the amount of mental energy the writer is currently using in his life. It can also reveal the strength and intensity of the writer's appetites and desires, and the degree to which he can respond to them. And it can indicate for which particular words and/or phrases the writer lacks intensity or feels an increase of it.

Pressure is an "unfixed" graphological trait, meaning that we don't always write with the same pressure. The amount of pressure you use may change frequently depending on your immediate mood. On the other hand, you may be a person who writes with the same pressure nearly all the time. A graphologist will only know this by asking you or by looking at several samples of your writing over a period of time.

Most people write with medium pressure most of the time, which means they are feeling "averagely" intense.

When you're not writing with medium pressure, your writing pressure is one of the following:

- Heavy
- Too heavy
- Light
- Too light
- Uneven

Let's see what each of these means.

Heavy Pressure

Heavy pressure means the writer is bearing down, feeling intense. He is feeling resolute, assertive, more aggressive than passive. It also means feeling active, energetic, vital, alert, forceful, and sometimes it means pugnacious.

People who write with heavy pressure most of the time are self-assertive, determined, and resolute. They're usually very dynamic people who seek to impose their will on others.

The key words for heavy pressure are *intense* and *aggressive*. You cannot exert heavy pressure unless your muscles are contracted. When do we contract? When we're tense, angry, anxious, determined, forceful.

Pressure That Is Too Heavy

Do you think it would mean something positive or negative if your baby-sitter pressed down so hard that he or she tore the paper? What emotion would he or she be feeling?

This would be a very negative sign. Overly heavy pressure means profound frustration. And profound frustration and fear are what usually lead to violence. As the person is eaten up with frustration, so he devours the paper. So beware of anybody who's pressing hard enough to tear the page or who makes cross-outs on mistakes that rip through the page. By the way, this handwriting sample of pressure that is too heavy is that of the infamous British killer Jack the Ripper.

Remember that pressure that is too heavy at the beginning and ending of strokes is called clubbed stroking, as we saw on page 80. This indicates the potential for cruelty.

Light Pressure

other night. It was fun
Catching up on recent events.
From time to time, we get

Remember how you felt when you wrote with light pressure? Assuming you are physically healthy, light pressure means feeling passive. When you exert little force as you're writing, you've got a light touch, are lacking in intensity, feeling gentle or calm, perhaps more spiritual than aggressive, a follower rather than a leader. Sometimes light pressure can be the result of physical sickness, which is an area of graphology I won't address in detail in this book.

Pressure That Is Too Light

Your column is very

If the pressure is too light, do you think that trait means something positive or negative?

It means something negative: spinelessness. It means that if I tell you to go jump off a cliff, you jump; you have no will of your own. If your pressure is too light, you are overly timid, submissive, and wholly lacking in willpower, vitality, or intensity. Again, we're assuming the writer is physically healthy.

Uneven Pressure

And of course I was worried sick, and I didn't know

On your scratch paper, please try writing with uneven pressure. Bear down heavily, then lighten up, then bear down again, and so on.

Now how did you feel when you went from heavy to light to heavy to light? Did you feel stable?

Probably not. Uneven pressure is associated with the worrier. The energy doesn't come out evenly. You can think of it like pacing. Have you ever watched a worrier pace? He paces determinedly in one direction, then slows down, stops, turns, begins moving, then paces determinedly again. It's always in jerks and starts. That's exactly the pressure pattern of the worrier.

So uneven pressure also means nervousness. The more nervous you are, the more uneven your writing will be. The happier, calmer, healthier, and more centered you are, the smoother your writing will be.

Healthy and Normal Writing Pressure

To know what healthy and normal pressure is, first you have to know what downstrokes and upstrokes are. A downstroke occurs anytime your hand moves down.

When you're making a *y*, this is the down-stroke:

When you're making an *h*, this is the downstroke:

An upstroke occurs anytime your hand moves up. Handwriting is full of down-strokes and upstrokes.

If you're a normal, healthy adult, one of these directional movements, either up or down, should be slightly heavier than the other. Take a moment to look at your own writing and decide: Are your upstrokes heavier in pressure, or are your downstrokes heavier?

If you're normal and healthy, your downstrokes should be slightly heavier in pressure than your upstrokes, like this:

Ray

If your upstrokes and downstrokes are of equal pressure, or if the upstrokes are heavier than the downstrokes, then something is definitely wrong physically.

Healthy writing pressure, then, is even overall, with the downward movements being slightly heavier than the upward movements.

Why are downstrokes heavier than upstrokes in a normal, healthy person? It has to do with the fact that downstrokes require the muscles of the hand to contract, and upstrokes require extension of the hand muscles, as well as with the relative strength of those muscle groups.

Ask anyone who's ever wrestled an alligator! It's far easier to hold an alligator's mouth shut than it is to hold it open. The most powerful muscles in an alligator's jaw are those used for contraction, for grasping its prey and holding on until it's dead. The extension muscles, which open the jaw, are relatively weak. Their only job is to put the jaw back into position for the choppers to do their work.

Your hand works on the same principle. When you need hand strength, it's to hold on to something. You don't need the same kind of strength to open up your hand. The downstroke, because it uses the contracting muscles, is naturally stronger and therefore produces a heavier mark on the paper. If you happen to be writing vertically, as on a blackboard, for example, then gravity further makes downward movements easier and heavier.

In some writings you will notice that people take the normal pressure pattern to an extreme. Thus, they may exert extra-heavy pressure on the downstrokes or use very light pressure on the upstrokes.

Very Heavy Pressure on the Downstroke

Pressing overly heavily on the downstrokes means self-determination to an exaggerated degree. As the stroke goes down, it's moving toward the writer, like pounding his chest. The overly heavy downstroke can be likened to an exclamation mark or to a judge pounding a gavel on his desk.

Very Light Pressure on the Upstroke

I wanted to be certain

Although it's normal to be slightly lighter on the upstrokes, some people are so light that the stroke almost disappears, as you see in this sample. Try writing this way. On your scratch paper, please try to write the word *wanted* as in this sample, with barely any upstrokes.

Now how did you feel? What do we associate going "up" with in life? Success . . . hope . . . ambitions . . . dreams . . . We say, "reaching for the stars," "looking up to something," "aspiring to great heights."

Being too light on the upstroke means a weakness of inner strength and conviction. A person with this trait either doesn't know what he is reaching for or doesn't have the strength of conviction to go after it.

The Universal Concepts Associated with Pressure

The meanings applied to the pressure of a writing come from the universal interpretations given to the concepts of Hard versus Soft and Heavy versus Light.

Once again, we need only look to expressions in everyday language, around the world, to see these common meanings:

HEAVY/HARD (*associated with intensity, aggression, forcefulness, determination*)	LIGHT/SOFT (*associated with gentility, passivity, calm, lack of aggressiveness*)
Heavy-handed.	*Light*-hearted.
Bear down.	*Light*-headed.
Pressure tactics.	*Light* conversation.
Hard-headed.	Don't make *light* of it.
Putting *pressure* on him.	*Soft*-hearted.
Press ahead, *press* on.	*Lighten* up.
Press forward.	*Ease* up.
Force yourself.	Take it *easy.*
Put some "*oomph*" into it.	Takes things *lightly.*
Hard-fought.	Takes the *pressure off* him.
Hard-line.	He's *softening* up.
Throwing your *weight* around.	*Light* on her feet.
Feels so *strongly* about it.	A *light* meal.
Rules with an *iron* fist.	We travel *light.*
Hands of *steel.*	*Lighten* the load.
So *hard* on him.	*Gentle* touch.
Hard to please.	A *light* weight.
Hard-core.	Go *light* on her.

Pressure Tidbits

Tidbit #1

Pressure that is too heavy *or* too light is associated with mental illness. Both types of pressure are extremes, and as we have seen, anytime the writer goes to an extreme, it means something negative. In one case, the person is overwrought with frustration; in the other case, the person doesn't have enough mental intensity to properly engage in life's activities.

Tidbit #2

The next time you're feeling angry, try writing with very light pressure. If you can do it, you won't be angry anymore.

There's a wonderful relaxation technique for times when you are in an agitated or enraged state. If you can possibly force yourself to take a pen in hand and make soft, round figure eights in slow motion like this:

within about thirty to sixty seconds you will automatically slow down your heart rate. Of course, you will often be so uptight you'll probably be doing something like this:

Still, this is one of the most wonderful, relaxing techniques there is. It also mimics the movement of a fish swimming. Have you noticed that more and more hospitals and doctors' offices are putting in fish tanks? That's because they have noticed that if you watch a fish swim, your heart rate slows down. It has a very calming effect.

Tidbit #3

Usually the combination of heavy pressure with a rightward slant is made by unforgettable, go-getter types. They express a wealth of emotions readily and with fervor, and cannot be taken lightly.

Tidbit #4

A partiality for bright colors is found most often among heavy-pressure writers, and a preference for the lighter pastel shades among light-pressure writers.

Tidbit #5

There are two machines that measure handwriting pressure. One is the graphodyne, invented by Klara Roman, and the other is the electrographodyne invented by Clarence Tripp at the Huntington Hartford Institute in New York.

Tidbit #6

Sometimes your pressure can be influenced by the implement you write with, and the implement you write with is often a matter of choice. I have come to some conclusions about people who have a definite preference for the type of writing implement they wish to use. The following observations are based on thirty years of my own experience.

- *The felt-tip pen user* wants to make the biggest impression with the least amount of effort. He wants to be noticed, to do things in a big way, but doesn't want to expend much energy in the process. It's impossible to assess pressure with the felt-tip pen user because this pen produces large quantities of ink as soon as it hits the paper. For this reason, and because people often make unnatural letter breaks when using it, the felt-tip pen is the worst implement to use if you want your handwriting analyzed.
- *The old-fashioned nib pen* is not seen much these days. Usually people who do prefer it wish to draw attention to their writing. Because of the nib pen's impracticality, we could also say these users will go to great lengths merely to be different.
- *The pencil* is used for a variety of reasons. Some people simply prefer its un-inky look; others feel they are more dexterous with the pencil. Some people like it because it's cheaper and cleaner than a pen. Still others enjoy the erasability it affords because they are perfectionistic and enjoy the privilege of correcting their errors, and still others prefer it because they are fearful of permanence. It's interesting to note that a study of convicted embezzlers found that the pencil was their number one choice!

   Because the lead in a pencil becomes duller as you write, thus thickening the stroke, it also is not a good implement by which to judge pressure.
- *The ballpoint pen* is the most frequently used writing implement, and the easiest by which to judge pressure. Those who prefer a fine-tipped ballpoint are often sticklers for clarity, precision, method, and details, and they generally like things conspicuously clear.

Tidbit #7

Did you know that if you sign a document with a felt-tip pen, the document can be thrown out of court? The reason is that when you use a felt-tip pen, you leave no pressure, as you would ordinarily do with a ballpoint pen, and therefore it's impossible to tell what sort of pressure pattern you have. We can't see where you bear down, where you lighten up, what particular habits you have in connecting your letters. Therefore, from a technical standpoint, a document signed with felt-tip pen could be challenged.

Tidbit #8

I have also noticed that members of certain professions definitely tend to prefer specific types of implements. For example, salespeople often prefer big, bold felt-tip pens. On the opposite end of the scale are people who work with small details for long periods of time, such as accountants and bookkeepers. These people usually prefer fine-point pens or finely sharpened pencils. People who prefer their own pen, and who like to write with it only, are usually fastidious people who might have a monogrammed handkerchief in their pocket or purse.

Pop Quiz
Which writer is more dangerous to society?

Sample A

Sample B

The answer is *A*. While *A* and *B* both have highly unstable slants, *A* also has very heavy pressure, which means he's going to act out all his instability with enormous intensity and aggression. *B* is lacking in pressure and thus is lacking in the mental intensity with which to act out his instability.

15
SIZE

Size Quiz

Please take this "little" Size Quiz designed to show that you already know about the subject without realizing it.

1. Do big people necessarily have big writing?

2. Who is the hermit, *A* or *B*?

A.

B.

have been recognized in similar which a short time ago fell Italia.

3. Who likes more subdued colors, *A* or *B*?

A.

20' to complete / would stop + return to complete
Actual date 2-9-89
Previous med use: Navane, Cogentin, Ascendin
c/o "sleeping spells", disorientation, eye pressure
told she has had abnormal EEG since 1980 (Jen)
R/o seizures, epilepsy

B.

4. Who's more unstable, *A* or *B*?

A.

B.

5. Who does things in a big way, *A* or *B*?

A. B.

de Libre et Civilisé.

J. Foch

Can't remember when I've enjoyed a group of people more — Louise's good friends — and Sabrina is just great.

Answers

1. No.	2. B	3. A	4. B	5. A

Explanation of Size

In this chapter, size will refer to whether the writing is large or small. More specifically, size may be categorized as large, overly large, medium, small, or overly small (microscopic). The best way to determine whether a handwriting is large or small is to study many different handwriting samples done on the same size paper, and decide, by comparison, what constitutes "average," "large," and "small." After seeing a variety of samples, you'll be able to know this at a glance.

Does a person always use the same writing size?

Some people write big all the time; others write small all the time; and still others write large sometimes and small at other times, depending on their mood. Thus, size is an unfixed trait.

When determining the size that a writer uses, take into account the size of the paper the writer had to use. If you're analyzing a postcard, it's possible that the writer is using much smaller writing than he normally would. This is another reason why, whenever possible, graphologists want to see several different writing samples over a period of time and under different circumstances.

Meanings Associated with the Size of the Writing

If the blank paper represents the writer's total environment, then whether a person is expansive or restrained with his writing tells whether he reaches out or pulls back from his surroundings and other people. So the size of the writing reveals whether a person is feeling socially extroverted or introverted, and how that person relates to his or her environment. The size of writing also tells us about the writer's present capacity for concentration.

Large Writing

This is large writing

As a rule, large writers are feeling socially extroverted, expansive with their movements, and unwilling to concentrate or confine their energies to small details.

Large writing requires the writer to make expansive and sweeping movements with his hand, and the result is an easily noticeable script that attracts attention. Being socially extroverted means wanting to be noticed by other people, and this is what large writing accomplishes.

People who write with large letters that sprawl across the page are also showing their need for space in life. These people need to go many places and cover extensive ground, and they do not wish to confine themselves to a limited territory. Because they are interested in their environment and in moving around in it a great deal, large writing also means they're not in the mood to concentrate or confine their attention to a small area.

- The desire to appear big and important—Some people write large because of a subconscious desire to gain the approval of others. Wanting to distinguish themselves from the masses, they make themselves bigger than life around them, desiring to top others in accomplishment. This type of large writer makes an unconscious association between bigness and greatness. His large writing is saying, "Look at me. I'm big and important. I'm impressive, and I want you to know it."
- Extravagance—Some large writers are flamboyant people who lean toward the lavish, the ceremonial, the luxurious. This interpretation is based on the letter size and how it affects the amount of writing per line and per page. Thus, when prodigality results from large writing, it is often the sign of a wasteful extrovert.
- Big planners—Some people who frequently write big do so because they tend to see the "big picture." They usually perceive matters on a grandiose scale and may undertake what other people consider overwhelming projects.
- Showing off—Another underlying reason for large writing may be the need to show off. Those who "bloat that others may take note" are usually fancy dressers who gesture broadly, take big steps, talk loudly, and seem to burst forth upon the scene. They just want to be noticed!

Overly Large Writing

This is overly

The person whose writing is overly large possesses the same characteristics as someone with large writing, but to a much greater degree. This person *demands* to be seen and heard. As he consumes the paper, so the writer overruns his boundaries and knows no limits.

Remember that whenever you *over*do something, it's to compensate for an intense inner feeling of the opposite. The writer who overdoes the size of his writing makes huge letters in compensation for an inner feeling of smallness and/or unimportance. Overly large letters symbolically demand that you take notice, as they unabashedly sprawl across the page. This means the writer is obsessed with a need for attention and is willing to go to great lengths to obtain it. Exhibitionism is rampant among overly large writers.

The person who writes this way is usually restless and wayward, full of excessive vitality, and prone to behave in a hyperactive manner. Send a person who writes very large to the store for a can of peas, and he or she will most likely come back with three bags of groceries!

Anyone who continually displays an exaggeration in his handwriting will exhibit a corresponding extreme in behavior. This behavior is generally the consequence of obsessive thinking. The person with overly large writing, then, displays obsessive tendencies by the need to use oversized writing and call attention to himself.

Medium-Sized Writing

This is medium sized

If a writing is neither "big" nor "small," then you are looking at the work of someone who is feeling normally social and who has an average ability to concentrate.

Medium-sized writing is the rule and not the exception. Most people write with average size most of the time, varying only at moments of great mood shifts.

Small Writing

this is small sized writing

Small writing most often means introversion. To produce small writing, you have to confine the movements of your hand and fingers to a limited area. The person with small writing is not reaching out expansively toward other people. Instead, he is holding himself tightly to a limited space that, for the time of the small writing, includes only himself.

There are several reasons why someone might confine his writing movements to a small area, and thus reduce expansion toward his environment and others:

- *Introversion*—Introversion is the tendency to direct one's interest upon oneself rather than on external objects, people, or events. So both concentration and feelings of introversion involve shutting out external stimuli, and both result in restricted movements by the hand and fingers. However, feelings of introversion do not necessarily imply that a person also feels like concentrating. A person who is feeling withdrawn and inwardly directed may write with small-sized letters because he wants to be alone and is not interested in what is going on around him. A person who feels introverted most of the time may be a hermit. As the hermit decreases his involvement with the outside world, he symbolically confines his movements on the paper. He is an "island unto himself."

- *Concentration*—Many people who have large or average-sized writing sometimes find themselves writing smaller than usual because they are in the mood to concentrate. When you concentrate, you shut out external stimuli (your environment and other people), and this enables you to zero in on your immediate thoughts. As your mind narrows its focus, the hand automatically limits its movements, and small writing results.

- *Small self-image*—Somewhere between 5 and 10 percent of people whose writing is perpetually small feel small in importance. They see themselves as inferior and indicate their shrunken self-esteem with letters that are small and weakly made. They become introverted and meek as a result of their feelings of inadequacy.

- *Economy*—Only about 1 percent of people who write perpetually small are confining their movements because they do not wish to waste paper. These writers are usually compulsively economical in all facets of their life.

Overly Small (Microscopic) Writing

this is overly small writing

Remember that an extreme in handwriting represents a corresponding extreme in personality. Microscopic writing is definitely an extreme; few people write this way.

People who are confining their writing movements to an inordinately small space on the paper are shrinking within themselves and/or concentrating to an exaggerated degree. On your scratch paper, please try writing with overly small letters as in this sample.

How did you feel? You can't write microscopically and retain legibility unless you are concentrating very intensely, excluding outside stimuli completely.

For the person whose writing is microscopic, then, there is nothing in his world at the moment except himself, his thoughts, and his writing. So, at the time of the microscopic writing, this writer is exceptionally introverted, deep within himself, tuning out the entire world.

There are two distinct types of people who write with exceptionally tiny writing: deep thinkers and disturbed persons.

Deep Thinker

144

The truly deep thinker becomes intensely introverted in order to descend deep within himself and satisfy a quest for personal knowledge. The preceding sample is the writing of Albert Schweitzer, who shunned society and decided to live with his family among primitive people.

Disturbed

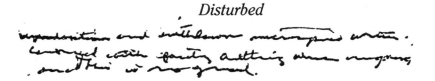

The second type of microscopic writer is truly disturbed, unproductive, and withdrawn. The distinction between this type of writing and the writing of a "deep thinker" is that the writing of the deep thinker is legible, while the disturbed person's writing usually is highly illegible or distorted.

The disturbed writer retreats into his own world and does not function on an average level. He is completely cut off from normal environmental relationships.

Making a "Bigger Deal" About Size

Now let's go beyond the approach of the other trait chapters and see how far a graphological trait—in this case, size—may be taken into account. So far we've been exploring the meanings of Big versus Small in terms of whether the handwriting's overall size is big or small. But the concept of Big versus Small can be applied in many more ways to a handwriting, to give us much added information. For example, we can look at Big and Small in terms of the writer's self-image, intelligence, past or future orientation, and more.

Self-Image

Which Sally Johnson, *A* or *B*, feels bigger and more important when in public than she does when in private? (*Hint:* A writer's personal pronoun *I*, as you probably remember, is his or her personal self-image, while the writer's signature is his or her public self-image.)

A.

I can't wait to see you. Take care.

Sally Johnson

B.

I can't wait to see you. Take care.

Sally Johnson

The answer is *B*. Notice how Sally Johnson wrote her signature in huge letters, while her personal pronoun *I* is small. In this sample, we see that big is associated with pride, confidence, success, and feelings of self-worth.

145

Remember this question from the Science Quiz?

Who has a higher IQ, *A* or *B*?

A.   B.

   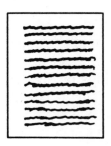

B has a higher IQ. Here we can think of size in terms of an increase or decrease as the word is written. If the letters in a word grow smaller, it's associated with higher intelligence, and if the letters get bigger, it's associated with lesser intelligence.

Past or Future Orientation

Who's more future-oriented, *A* or *B*?

A.   B.

B is more future-oriented. Here we're looking at size in terms of how much space is left on the right or left side of the paper. If the left margin is bigger than the right margin and the right margin is normal and not too wide, it means that the writer is future-oriented. A person who leaves a wider space on the right and clings to the left is past-oriented.

By the way, you can hear this past/future orientation in the way people talk. Past-oriented people are always talking about yesterday: "Oh, you should've seen what I did . . . I've got to tell you a story about . . . My mother always did it like that . . ." But, if they're future-oriented, and they hug the right margin, they're probably saying things like, "This project will be done in September . . . We have a meeting next Tuesday . . . I can hardly wait until we . . ."

How the Writer Relates to Other People

Who puts a great deal of space between himself and others?

A.   B.

The answer is *B*. Here we're looking at size in terms of the amount of space between words. If you put the words close together, you want to be close together. If you put big spaces between the words, you want to keep people at a great distance from you.

Feelings about Specific People or Things

This interpretation is based on sudden enlargement or sudden decrease in size of a certain letter, word, or phrase.

Dear Bill, Sally, Jack and Fred.

If something suddenly enlarges a little bit, it means the writer holds it in high regard, has big feelings for it. If something decreases in size, it means the writer has a diminished or smaller feeling about that which shrank. And, of course, we can get even more sophisticated and ask whether a word got *too* big or *too* small, as opposed to *slightly* bigger or *slightly* smaller.

I really love you!

I hope you've started to see that the hidden meanings on just this one concept of Big versus Small are infinite.

The Universal Concept Associated with Size

Once again, the interpretations graphology makes for universal concepts such as big and small are the same as society gives to these concepts all over the world. Here are a few additional expressions for big and small in our everyday language:

BIG (*associated with success, importance, showing off*)	SMALL (*associated with brevity, feelings of smallness and inadequacy*)
A *huge* success.	She felt too *small*.
Big-hearted.	*Short* and to the point.
Big and important.	*Short*-tempered.
Walk *tall*.	*Shrunken* ego.
A *giant* in his field.	*Short*-lived.
Monumental works.	Came up *short*.
Big deal!	Was *reduced* in stature.
He comes on so *big*.	It was a *petty* matter.

Remember that the process of examining this universal concept of Big versus Small in greater depth can be done with any trait to get a wealth of information. For example, with the concept of Left versus Right, we can look not only at whether the

147

letters lean to the left or right, but also to see if the writing shifts to the left or right on the paper, and whether the ending strokes reach left or right.

Size Tidbits

Tidbit #1

An exceptionally high percentage of scientists, composers, authors, and mathematicians write with small-sized letters most of the time. This fact seems logical, since these types of professionals spend a good deal of time alone in deep concentration.

Tidbit #2

An exceptionally high percentage of actors, salespeople, and politicians write with large-sized letters a good deal of the time. This makes sense, since these types of professionals spend a lot of time doing things requiring extroversion and involvement with other people.

Tidbit #3

Do you recall this question from the quiz at the beginning of this chapter?

Who's more unstable, *A* or *B*?

A.   B.

B is more unstable. Instability in any trait is not good. Writers who change their letter size frequently on the same sheet of paper cannot decide whether to behave introvertedly or extrovertedly, and consequently their behavior is confusing and off balance.

Remember, however, that some variation in slant, sizing, spacing, and so forth is to be expected. It is where there is too much variation, or too much uniformity, that we become concerned.

Tidbit #4

You learned that people who write with large-sized letters are usually active extroverts who need a great deal of space in which to move around. You also learned that, as a general rule, the smaller the writing, the greater the introversion and capacity for concentration.

Some people, however, who write with large-sized letters are able to concentrate on small details as well as a writer with small-sized letters. In these instances the middle letters will either be small in comparison to the other letters or the writing as a whole will be uniform and easily legible.

If a child or adult has been writing normally, but his writing suddenly becomes microscopically small, this is a red flag meaning he is deeply troubled and unhappy. He should receive help at once. Life seems so unbearable that he is retreating into a world of his own and locking himself out of a normal existence.

Tidbit #6

With much love

mkgandhi

In the movie *Gandhi*, Mahatma Gandhi was made out to be a politician, spending a great deal of time before the masses. In fact, if you read his biography, you will find that was not the case. He was a loner, and he spent most of the time hour upon hour alone in meditation, which is what his handwriting above would say.

Tidbit #7

writing as many of you as we can. Your vote is important if our government is to represent all the people.
Cordially,   Adlai E. Stevenson

Here is the writing of Adlai Stevenson, who lost his presidential bid to Dwight D. Eisenhower. His writing and signature are both small, indicating an all-around introvert. Remember, if the writing is small and well formed, it indicates a person who can concentrate on small details for long periods of time as well. Stevenson's introverted tendencies may have been his political downfall. While he was highly intelligent, honest, straightforward, competitive, and hardworking, he was too introverted to communicate well with the public and just couldn't reach out enough. Of all the world leaders whose handwriting is available for analysis, not one has been an introvert.

Tidbit #8

A small percentage of people suddenly enlarge a letter somewhere within a word. For example, this occurs with the letters *k* and *d*.

I have discovered that lod luck only a state of mind as described in following verse I found.
If you think you are beaten, you are,

This trait is associated with defiance, and in highly unstable writing it also indicates severe, uncontrolled feelings that often erupt into violence. As with the Maniac *d* in the chapter on slant, the writer doesn't know when his mind, and then his hand, will lose control. In an otherwise stable writing sample, this trait warns of the writer's potential for unexpected violent behavior.

Pop Quiz

1. Which employee did the boss (the writer) fire?

Copies to: Jack, John, Joe, and Jim.

Joe was the person who was fired. The clue is that the author made the *J* in "Joe" so much smaller than the other three names. The name is also running downhill, so we know the boss not only thinks less of Joe but is also depressed about him.

2. What can you say about the following writer based on the words getting larger and farther apart toward the bottom of the page?

We finished the blueprints around mid-night last night. Our ideas include: three car garage; terraced lawns, up and down; maids

The writer is tiring of writing, losing his ability to concentrate. If your writing begins to get larger after writing only a few lines, at that moment you had a low attention span, a short tolerance for concentration. If your writing always gets larger quickly, then you always tire quickly.

Bear in mind, though, that there are numerous reasons why you might lose your desire or ability to concentrate on a given sample. For example, the sleeping pill you took may be beginning to take effect; your lover may have just arrived and you're anxious to finish the letter; or you may detest what you're writing, which makes it difficult to continue.

3. What can you say about the writer of this sample, where the writing is growing increasingly smaller?

We finished the blueprints around midnight last night. Our ideas include: three car garage; terraced lawns up & down; maid's

You guessed it! This writer became increasingly involved and interested in what he was writing, and probably could have gone on writing for quite some time. When you increase your concentration, your writing simultaneously becomes smaller. Of course, there is one other possible reason that you might start to write very small: you're running out of paper and have a lot more to say!

16
SPEED

Speed Quiz

Before you start reading about speed, see how you do on this itty-bitty quiz.

1. Who wrote faster?

A.

fasta

B.

faster

2. Which person appears more cautious, patient, and a better baby-sitter at this time?

A.

Ill laga was Tea
Jeshua were th
one at the Best
I ~~liked~~ liked ...
I called the
The lady said

B.

Dear Rod,
Today you don't
you glad? I bet you
going to the hospital
of yours. Take care and

Answers

1. A	2. B

Explanation of Speed

In graphology, speed refers to how fast or slowly you write.

The speed of a writing tells how quickly an individual thinks and acts, the person's intelligence level, and his degree of spontaneity and honesty.

Normal Speed

In characterizing speed as "normal," there is a basic rule for adults: No adult with average or better-than-average intelligence should write slowly most of the time. And, if he does, it's a sign of guarded behavior and calculated responses. The writer goes slowly lest he give himself away by acting spontaneously. Writing that is usually very fast reveals one who is usually very fast in thought and action, is often impatient, hates to wait for anything, and will find shortcuts whenever possible.

Speed is one of the traits graphologists look for when they're screening handwriting for integrity or discernment of falsehoods. Whenever someone slows down, he has lost spontaneity and begun calculating his responses to a greater degree.

How to Determine the Speed of a Sample

Let's see how graphologists know how fast or slow a sample was written, without having watched the person write. Please use a clean sheet of scratch paper, and draw a line horizontally across the middle. On the top half, please write the following sentence very slowly and deliberately. Then, on the bottom half, please write the same sentence as fast as you can.

I want to know how it feels to write slowly and quickly, and I'm going to do it right now.

Now look at your two sentences, and use them to answer the following questions:

1. Which sample is sloppier?   Slow   Fast

2. Which sample takes up more space?   Slow   Fast

3. Which sample has *i* dots and *t* bars far to the right of the stem?   Slow   Fast

4. Which sample omits details?   Slow   Fast

5. Which sample replaces dots with slashes and dashes?   Slow   Fast

6. Which sample has more rightward traits overall?   Slow   Fast

7. Which sample is more squiggled?   Slow   Fast

The answers to all of these questions should be *fast* writing. So, in summary, the signs of speed in handwriting are the following:

1. Fast writing tends to be sloppier than normal.
2. Fast writing tends to take up more space than normal.
3. In fast writing, *i* dots and *t* bars are far to the right of the letter stem, because the writer doesn't want to take the time go back to the left to cross and dot them.
4. Fast writing tends to omit details in order to save time.
5. In fast writing, slashes and dashes replace periods and dots because stopping to make dots takes too long.
6. Fast writing tends to have more rightward trends, since that's the direction the writer is going. The faster someone is writing, the more each line, the letters, and the *t* bars and *i* dots will pull to the right.
7. Fast writing tends to squiggle because squiggling is faster than articulating the letter shapes.

Speed in Conjunction with Some Other Traits

1. What can we say about Claudette Colbert's writing below?

What size writing does she use and what speed? Here we see generally large and fast writing. This is a special combination. A large, fast writer is a very animated and outgoing individual who will risk making a fool of himself. A study of three generations of people recognized as war heroes showed a preponderance of this combination in their writing. These people were courageous, did things in a big way, and were quick in thought and action.

2. What can we say about Fregoli, Italian variety star?

L'Arte è Vita e la
Vita è Trasformazione

Fregoli

Paris 12 febbraio 1911

Fregoli was a famous Italian master of disguise. This sample of writing is large, angular, rightward, heavy, and fast.

Large means outgoing, extroverted, attention-grabbing. Angular means aggressive and hard-driving. And recall that fast writing means someone who is always in a hurry, is impatient and dislikes waiting, and will find a shortcut if there is one. Heavy means assertive and intense, and a person who exerts heavy pressure with a rightward slant is all the more demonstrative and dynamic.

When we put all of these together, we have an unforgettable individual who is extroverted, hard-driving, intense, competitive, and impatient. This is a strong and powerful person who will leave his mark on society.

Fregoli's signature is fascinating; it looks like a disguise. It looks like someone with a cape around himself.

The Universal Concept Associated with Speed

The meanings attached to writing speed come from the universal concept of Fast versus Slow. Once again, we need only look to expressions in everyday language to see these common meanings:

FAST (*associated with intelligence and spontaneity*)	SLOW (*associated with lesser intelligence and guarded behavior*)
Quick-minded. Catches on *quickly.* *Fast* in thought and action. *Fast* friends. *Quick*-witted. *Smart* as a whip. *Quick* on the uptake. *Fast* and loose. *Quick* assets.	*Slow*-minded. *Slow*poke. Going in *slow* motion. *Slow* to comprehend. *Slow* down, be careful. *Take your time.* Grinds to a *halt.*

1. Which writer wrote much faster?

A.   B.

B is faster. Even though both writers wrote quickly, as denoted by all the signs of speed in their writing, the round writing is inherently faster than angular writing because angular writing requires coming to a point and, therefore, a stop.

Notice that we could also say that heavier-pressured writing is slower than lighter-pressured writing. Angular writing requires greater use of force of writing pressure. Therefore, light and round is faster than heavy and angular.

2. Where is the writer telling a lie?

The writer became very slow when she wrote, "I knitted the booties myself." Notice that everything got very round, very tight; all the *t* bars and *i* dots were right over the stem. That sudden loss of spontaneity suggests the writer isn't telling the truth.

17
ZONES

Zone Quiz

Before you begin reading about zones, please take a moment to answer the following questions.

1. Which writer has his head in the clouds and lives in a fantasy world?

A.

hilly

B.

hilly

2. Which writer is more childish?

A.

flowery

B.

flowery

3. Which writer is more restless?

A.

hilly

B.

hilly

Answers

1. A	2. B	3. B

The Three Zones

The chapter on slant (Chapter 10) introduced three zones in handwriting. They are the upper, middle, and lower zones:

Models for Interpreting the Zones

We can think of the three zones in handwriting in basically three different ways: using Freudian terms, expressing time, and describing body image.

The Freudian Model

We can apply Freud's theory of id, ego, and superego to the three zones. In graphology, the *id* is represented by the *lower zone*:

Freudian psychology says we are born with just an id, which houses the libido. The id says, "I want pleasure, and I want to avoid pain. Feed me, and I don't want colic, and please change my diaper." That message reflects the pleasure/pain principle, and supposedly it stays with us all our lives.

In graphology, the *ego* is represented by the *middle zone*:

At about the age of three, according to Freud, the ego develops. This is when the child looks in the mirror and says, "Hey, I'm a person. I'm a separate entity. That's me!" Then the child becomes very "me, me, me-ish."

In graphology, the *superego* is represented by the *upper zone*:

At about the age of seven, in Freudian psychology, the superego develops. Another term for the superego is "conscience." That's when the child realizes, "Uh-oh. There's not only me in this world. I can't always have just what I want to have. I have to worry about other people, too."

The Time Model

We can also think of the three zones in terms of time:

- The *lower zone*, which is associated with the id, the basic drives we are born with, becomes the *past*.
- The *middle zone*, which houses the ego and develops next, becomes the *present*.
- The *upper zone*, which holds the superego, becomes the *future*.

The Body Image Model

Finally, we can also project our body image into the three zones. Whenever there is a vertical figure or symbol that can be segmented into three parts, human beings tend to project their body image onto it. For example, please look at this treble clef and point to its head.

If you're like 99 percent of people, you just pointed to the top of the figure. If I asked, "Where's the waist?" you'd probably point to the middle, and if I asked, "Where are the feet?" you'd probably point to the bottom.

Now if I take the word *hay*

and ask you, "Where's the head?" you'd probably point to the *h*. If I asked you, "Where's the waist?" you'd probably point to the *a*. And if I asked you, "Where are the legs?" you'd probably point to the *y*. That's the idea of the body image model.

So we project our body image this way:

The Upper Body in the Upper Zone

The Middle Body in the Middle Zone

The Lower Body in the Lower Zone

General Description of the Three Zones

Upper zone/superego/the future/upper body
Middle zone/ego/the present/middle body
Lower zone/id/the past/lower body

Drawing from all three of the models, we can summarize the broader meanings attached to each zone:

- The upper zone, in general—the superego—is the realm of the mind. It represents thinking, fantasy, imagination, ideas, illusions, philosophy, and sometimes religion. It is what we associate with the head. What does your head do? It thinks, it creates, it imagines, it hopes.
- The middle zone, in general—the ego—is the platform between the upper and the lower zone, and it represents one's daily life. As you'll see in a moment, graphologists can tell whether or not a writer is currently happy by the way the person writes his middle zone. The middle zone also reveals what the writer thinks of himself in relation to other people. It may show one person to be an egotist and another to feel small and insecure.
- The lower zone, in general—the id—represents the world of instincts, urges, longings, and desires. The lower zone reveals the writer's attitudes toward his home life; body; basic drives for sustenance, money, health, and sex; and the world of his libido.

Balance of the Three Zones

Remember this question from the beginning of this chapter?

Who's more childish, *A* or *B*?

A.   B.

flowery   *flowery*

The answer was *B*. What is it about *B*'s writing sample that makes it look more childlike? It's all middle zone. This is how children write, with a dominating middle zone. Somewhere in adulthood, though, we are supposed to find a balance between the three zones.

In graphology, the "perfect" balance of zones for a healthy adult is a middle zone approximately half the size of the upper and lower zones, and the upper and lower zones equal in length, within a given word. For example:

graphology

In other words, if the upper zone were one inch tall, the lower zone would be one inch long, too, and the middle zone would be about one-half inch.

160

Some people do not have this "perfect" zone balance all the time. Let's see what it means if any one of the three zones dominates.

Dominating Upper Zone

Dominating Middle Zone

Dominating Lower Zone

Dominating Upper Zone

A dominating upper zone is a writing where the upper zones are decidedly taller and/or fuller or more elaborate than the lower zones.

This trait indicates someone who lives in a fantasy world at the expense of reality. This person is top heavy. He is full of heady ideas with little basis in support.

People like this are theoretical over practical. They are seldom at a loss for an idea, plan, or scheme, but there's no basis in reality. By the way, the above sample is that of Senator Ted Kennedy.

The wilder the imbalance—that is, the more dominating the upper zone becomes—the more the person is theoretical over practical or, in other words, the more he lives in a fantasy world at the expense of reality.

In the sixties, studies were conducted to see how LSD affected handwriting. The studies found that the greater the frequency of LSD use and the dosage, the more the subject hallucinated and the more the upper zones began to dominate wildly. Graphology shows vividly when a subject is on a "head trip."

In certain professions, a slightly dominating upper zone can be very desirable. In those professions, such as consulting, creative writing, and advertising, being theoretical over practical is an advantage. But because the writer with dominating upper zones isn't practical, he is best in a situation where someone else will implement the ideas, while he provides creative inspiration.

Sometimes the upper zone dominates to an exaggerated degree:

get out of

This is totally abnormal, and the writer is not functioning normally in life. He is off in the clouds somewhere.

Dominating Middle Zone

Thanks for helping me through a really rough spot. I treasure the time we spend together just talking

The writer with a dominating middle zone is often described by others as egotistical, and immature like a child. This trait indicates someone who is overly concerned with outward appearances and matters of the immediate moment: "What will I wear today? Who will I have lunch with? How does my hair look?"

Writers with dominating middle zones are self-centered. What they see is today, right now, this exact moment. In this regard, they are like children, wanting instant gratification of their desires. For example, if a father promises to take his child to the zoo, but on that day it rains and they can't go until the next day, the child may have a tantrum. Tomorrow is too far away; it doesn't mean anything to the child. When an adult has a dominating middle zone, it indicates a very immature, childlike person who may have tantrums if he doesn't get his own way.

Companies that hire people who write with a dominating middle zone often find that these employees are unwilling to wait for a promotion or a raise; they're not as capable in delaying gratification, in putting up with a difficult situation now with the knowledge that doing so will benefit them later. They want what they want here and now, or they have to move on, which is where the self-centeredness comes into play. And they expect to be the center of attention and are usually overly conscious of their appearance. Caring so much what one looks like at the immediate moment is a very childish behavior pattern.

We appreciate your *(handwriting sample)*
thought for this, to
a rather special mile
in our life together.

The writer with a dominating lower zone is dominated by the material and the physical aspects of life, the basic drives. This person may be obsessed with one or more of the following: his body, the physical in general, money or the material aspects of life, and attitudes toward loved ones, family, or sexuality.

In studies of bodybuilders—people pumping iron every day and looking at themselves in mirrors continuously—graphologists have found a preponderance of dominating lower zones. In addition, people who are obsessed with monetary gain also have enormous lower zones. People who are in the process of a divorce, or who are worried about their home life, tend to have enlarged lower zones, as do those who are worried about their health and/or money.

Remember, graphology holds to the same principles as basic psychology in the supposition that whenever something is overdone, it is usually in compensation for a lack in that area. Thus, if you are subconsciously feeling insecure or lacking in physical prowess in some way, you may enlarge your lower zones, just as the weakling boasts too much of his conquests. So if the lower zone gets *too large*, it means the writer subconsciously perceives a lack in this area that preoccupies his thinking.

So now you may be asking, "When I see a writing with a dominating lower zone, how do I know whether I'm looking at someone who is obsessed with money or sex or bodybuilding? How do I know which obsession it is?" Graphology is a very big science, so as you learn more, you'll have more clues.

Specifics of the Upper Zone

Now you've read about what the three zones mean generally. Let's take a look at some specifics for each one.

Upper Loops That Come to a Point

Which writer is extremely tense, uptight, frustrated, a "Type A"?

A.

like

B.

love

The answer is *B*. On your scratch paper, please make an upper loop that comes to a point, as it does on the *l* of *love* in *B*'s writing sample.

Did you do it? How did your muscles feel—relaxed or tight? They should have felt tight because you cannot make a point without freezing your hand at the top of the loop. If you don't freeze at the top of the loop but keep your hand relaxed, the shape will come out rounded instead of angular.

Do you think the meaning associated with pointed loops is going to be hard or soft feelings? (The softer emotions are love, tenderness, sympathy, etc. The harder emotions are anger, fear, anxiety, worry, tension, etc.)

The meaning associated with this trait is the harder emotions. These are the emotions that cause constriction. If you put an angle where roundness should be, you've picked up anger, tension, frustration, anxiety, worry. Someone with upper zones that come to a point as in *B*'s sample, feels frustrated, angry, tense, alone at the top of the heap.

The same thing that causes someone to put an angle where roundness should be causes what we refer to as Type A behavior. And if all the upper zones are pointed, you are looking at the work of a very uptight individual.

Ballooned and/or Malformed Upper Loops

Which writer is probably psychotic, distorts reality, hallucinates?

A.

B.

The answer is *A*. Look at the second *h* in the word *thought* in *A*'s sample. The loop crosses too high, so it looks like a balloon floating on a string. This trait means psychosis. Whenever you see malformations, or any kind of distortion of the shaping of loops (unless you're looking at calligraphy, which graphologists don't analyze), it's a psychotic projection onto paper. Twisted thinking produces twisted writing.

When I started studying handwriting, I wasn't really sure what it means to be psychotic. I knew that one major difference between a psychotic and a neurotic is that a neurotic knows he has problems. The neurotic says, "I'm such a nervous wreck! I'm so neurotic!"

One of the doctors with whom I was doing research in a mental hospital offered to show me what a psychotic is. So we went into a room and sat down with a male "psychotic" patient. The doctor showed the patient a series of cards with geometric shapes on them. After he showed the patient a card, the doctor would put the card face down and ask the patient to draw the shape he had just seen.

When he showed the patient, for example, a picture of a triangle and then asked the patient to draw it, the patient didn't draw a triangle. He would draw some bizarre heptagon, or other weird shape. When the doctor would show him a circle, it would come out a distorted square, and so on.

The doctor later explained to me that, just as the patient does not observe the geometric shapes the same way we do, so he doesn't perceive circumstances, events, or life itself in the same way. So if you say, "I love you," to a psychotic, he doesn't necessarily hear "I love you." The psychotic doesn't interpret his environment in the same manner we do.

So when you see handwriting that looks as abnormal as *A*'s sample, with its abnormally shaped loops, you'll know this is an individual who's not perceiving life in the normal manner (provided, again, that *you're* normal!). His point of view is misshapen, distorted.

Here is the writing of a person adjudged psychotic and confined to a mental hospital:

mate and that they would have a good financial life, have a nice home and only 2 children and live a happy and peaceful life of which they are as she

Too Many Retraced Upper Loops

Which writer is a liar? (*Hint:* If you're lying, will you be looser or more uptight?)

A. *thoughts*   B. *thoughts*

The answer is *B*. Retraced letters are produced when the pen goes up and down the same stem.

A Looped h   *A "Retraced"* h

Do you remember which letters we were taught to retrace in the cursive Palmer method? They are the small *d* and the small *t*.

If you see a Palmer handwriting that is perfect in all respects, then retraced *d*'s and *t*'s are normal, and you're looking at a very traditional and conventional person. However, this is extremely rare. Most adults do not write with 100 percent Palmer writing; they've changed at least some aspects.

If the handwriting is not 100 percent Palmer, then more than about 35 percent retraced upper loops is considered too much retracing. What does it mean to be a retraced writer?

You can answer that yourself if, on your scratch paper, you draw a series of looped *l*'s, first looping them widely, like *A*, then making a series of retraced *l*'s, like *B*.

A.   B.

Now, if you were lying, do you think you would be writing more like *A* or *B*?

You would be writing like *B*, because to write like *B* means to be totally uptight. If you're writing naturally, your hand is going to swing and produce loopiness. As soon as you're inhibiting something, holding something back, not being forthright and open, you tighten up. Your body tenses up, and one of the results is retracing of letters.

If 35 percent or more of the upper zones are retraced, it indicates one who is inhibiting natural instincts to the point of lying.

Stick-Figure Upper Zone

Who is more direct, efficient, gets right to the heart of the matter?

A. *hit the*   B. *hit the*

The answer is *B*. Ah, that rare moment when there's something *good* to say! A "stick figure" refers to a letter that has no lead-in stroke. We originally are taught to make lead-in strokes on beginning letters in cursive writing. Here's an *h* with a lead-in, and one without:

h   *h*

Lead-In   *No Lead-In*

A lead-in stroke is not really a necessary stroke at all. It's just as clear to read a letter without one as with, and usually more so. Many people, as they hone their writing style, have eliminated lead-in strokes, either consciously or unconsciously.

Cursive handwriting with few or no lead-in strokes means intelligence, directness, efficiency, and speed. If you think fast, you will write fast, and making stick figures affords you one of the easiest means possible to do this.

Breaks in Upper Loops (and Elsewhere)

Which sample suggests that its writer is cracking up, falling apart, breaking into pieces?

A.

Dear Friend —
You will be
Seeing more of me
Soon in -
"Let's Make Love"
Marilyn

B.

Dear Friend
You will be
Seeing more of me
soon in -
"Let's Make Love"
Marilyn

The answer is *A*, the handwriting of Marilyn Monroe. The trait under scrutiny here is one where a person could do harm to himself, as well as possibly to another. You could save lives by knowing this trait.

Here is an example of an abnormal break in a loop:

Here is an example of an abnormal break in an *m*:

This is abnormal because the break doesn't occur between the letters, *but in the middle of the letter*. The hand comes off the paper, leaving a break or hole in the formation of the letter itself.

Abnormal breaks in letters mean falling apart emotionally, cracking up. Just as the letter is falling apart, so is the writer. It means acute mental anxiety, going to pieces, cracking up.

Do you see the breaks in the *d* in "Friend?" Did you notice the break at the top of the *s* in "soon?" How about the breaks in "Marilyn," such as in the middle of the *M*, and on the upstroke of the *l*?

Again, as with any trait in graphology, breaks must occur frequently throughout an entire page for them to be serious, and not just on one or two letters. In Marilyn Monroe's case, breaks are occurring everywhere. This means acute mental anxiety, and this person requires immediate help.

(REMINDER: You may suddenly start making breaks in your writing for the first time in your life after reading this section. Don't worry about it. You're simply sensitive and susceptible and should start writing normally again in short order!)

Breaks in the Upper Loop Only

Which writer perceives a problem, or lack of wholeness in his upper body?

A.

B.

The answer is *B*. If all the breaks in a sample of writing were only in one zone, such as in the upper zone only, but all the other areas had smooth loops, this would mean acute mental anxiety the writer associates with his upper body.

For example, people who have cancer in the upper part of their body sometimes project the sense of sickness they feel into the upper parts of their handwriting. This isn't true of everyone who has an upper-body problem, but it does occur in many instances.

It is important to note that the part of the writing that will be affected depends on where the writer perceives a problem to be. If you had to make three horizontal lines and divide this body into upper, middle, and lower areas, for example, where would you divide it?

When you've decided where you would divide it, then decide whether each body part in the following list goes in the *upper*, *middle*, or *lower* body.

- Heart
- Thalamus
- Liver

- Thymus
- Lungs
- Spleen

The point is that we can't look at a break in a certain part of a letter and *automatically assume* that person has an anxiety problem associated with a particular organ, because we don't know where he perceives that organ to be.

All we can really say is, "It appears that you have acute mental anxiety associated with a problem you perceive to be in your upper body." For one person that might be a tumor in his chest; for another it might be bronchitis, or it might be an earache.

In this case, *B* is a heart attack victim who died the day after he wrote this sample. This sample is illegible because the man was unable to physically articulate the letters. If you look closely at the first line, though, you will see that the upper letters are broken, with holes in the upper loops throughout. This man knew he had a serious heart condition and felt acute anxiety associated with what he perceived to be his upper body.

Specifics of the Middle Zone

Once again, the middle zone represents your daily life, the immediate moment, the present. Let's look at the specifics.

Undersized and Poorly Formed Middle Zone

Which writer is more unhappy, anxious, not functioning smoothly?

A.

And we then can move quickly if all goes well.

B.

ad in the L.A. Times got more from two fl un conversation telling me

The answer is *B*. If you want to know how happy someone is in the present, on a day-to-day basis, you look at the middle zone. When it's undersized and poorly formed, do you think it's going to mean the writer is happy or not?

Not happy. The more poorly formed the middle zone, the more unhappy the person. When you're at your calmest, happiest, and most centered, the handwriting flows. When things are problematic, when you're anxious or unhappy, your handwriting is usually obstructed, and you find it harder to write.

In *B*'s sample, you see a middle zone that is squished, uneven, and poorly formed. That's how the person feels about his daily life at this moment—not happy. To know if this is just a momentary condition, or if it's pretty much the condition of his life, you have to see several samples over a period of time.

If the middle zone is also very small in comparison to the upper and lower zones, it means that the writer's daily life does not live up to his expectations and dreams.

Tiny and Well-Formed Middle Zone

Which writer concentrates on small details for long periods of time better than the other writer? (*Hint:* which writer's sample looks more like that of a bookkeeper or scientist?)

A.

B.

The answer is *B*, who is actually Friedrich Nietzsche.

Oh dear! Here's something good to say again! Where do you find writings that look like *B*'s? In the handwriting of bookkeepers, engineers, scientists, researchers, writers, teachers.

People who write with small, well-formed middle zones can concentrate on small details for long periods of time. Because the middle zone here is *well* formed, meaning letters are clear and even in all respects, we don't attach the adjective *unhappy* to this particular sample.

By the way, *A* is the writing of sculptor Aristide Maillol.

169

Specifics of the Lower Zone

In general, do you remember what the lower zone represents? The id, the past, the lower body. The lower zone represents our basic drives, which include our attitudes regarding our bodies, health, home life, love life, sexuality, and monetary comforts. Now let's look at some specifics of the lower zone.

Long Lower Zone

Which writer is feeling more restless?

A.   B.

hilly   *hilly*

The answer is *B*. The writer with a long lower zone is usually restless and in constant need of variety and change. The longer the lower zone, the more restless the writer. Graphologists have found these people to be the job hoppers, the mate hoppers, the people who change homes and circumstances in their life more frequently than others

Conversely, people who have the greatest longevity on the job usually have normal-sized lower zones. They are not overly restless.

Large-Looped Lower Zone

Which writer is lacking as much money and/or sex as he would like?

A.   B.

who is lacking in money and play?   *who is lacking in money and play?*

The answer is *B*. You can think of large lower-zone loops as pouches to be filled. Remember, you bloat up where you subconsciously feel a lack. So this could mean a healthy sexual appetite, or a big drive for the physical and material.

This trait doesn't necessarily mean a "good lover" or anything like that. When I first started teaching that a big lower zone meant a big appetite, a woman in one of my classes at UCLA raised her hand, furious, and said, "I thought you said a big-looped lower zone meant, you know, that a person has a really big sex drive, you know . . . a lot. Well, let me tell you, I went out with this guy just because of his big lower zones—and wow! What a dud!"

170

So please don't get it in your mind that bigger means "better." As a matter of fact, when you're sexually satisfied, you normally won't enlarge in the lower zone. If you're totally satisfied, there's no need to bloat up to compensate for anything.

Twisted, Bent, or Reversed Lower Zones

Who has "deviant" sexuality?

A.

hey

B.

hey

The answer is *B*. There's a great deal to say about this area. Graphological interpretations are based on the same tenets as psychology, so that, for example, in psychology "normal" sexuality used to be considered the ability to maintain a one-to-one heterosexual relationship. Everything else was considered "abnormal." Today, however, "normal" sexuality is simply defined as the ability to maintain a one-to-one sexual relationship, as long as it is not with a child, a dead person, an animal, and does not include bizarre fetishes.

But who's to say what is "normal" and what isn't, in reality? For the time being, however, let's go along with this original definition, because an introductory book such as this cannot hope to teach fine distinctions in sexual "deviation."

So "normal" sexuality would show up in the lower zone as normal shapes—any kind of a straight line that isn't too short or too long, or any kind of loop formation that goes to the left. If the writer is reversing, bending, or twisting, it indicates feelings of abnormal sexuality. Let's look at a few examples.

Normal   *"Versatile" (Deviant)*

hey hey hey hey hey   *hey hey hey hey hey*

If we were to cover up the lower zones in the preceding sample, the handwriting would look fine, normal. It's the lower zones that are bizarre, with the loops reversed and twisted.

Such loops represent "versatile" sexuality. We're not absolutely sure what type of sexuality we're looking at—promiscuity or someone who only does it with his German shepherd or whatever.

On the following page is another example of twisted lower zones, written by Pope John XXIII when he was cardinal:

Graphologists have done countless studies of people who are believed to lead celibate lifestyles and find that an overwhelming percentage have abnormal lower zones. We don't know whether they started out with abnormal lower zones, or whether they developed them as a result of their choice of lifestyle.

But if we were to go just on the handwriting, it seems that celibacy, if indeed the subjects really were celibate, is not a normal psychological condition of humans, because such a high percentage of the lower zones are abnormal in celibate people. Another possible conclusion might be that a large percentage of the people attracted to a celibate lifestyle have abnormal sexuality to begin with.

Try Your Hand at Analyzing Zones

Take a look at the writing of former New York Mayor John Lindsay:

Do the lower zones dominate in any particular place? Yes, they become the longest on the words *City*, *York*, and *Lindsay*. Wherever lower zones become especially long the writer is feeling restless, in need of variety and change in regard to whatever he's writing when his lower zones suddenly become elongated.

So here we know that John Lindsay, in regard to his public self-image (which is his signature) and in relation to the words *City of new York* suddenly becomes restless. Without knowing the man, we might say, "Gee, Mr. Lindsay, you're feeling particularly restless and in need of variety and change, and it has something to do with New York City and your public self-image."

And Lindsay would say, "Well, gee! I'm resigning as mayor of New York City!"

And do we get any other subconscious clues as to how he feels about New York City in a way that we haven't been taught yet? Look at the way he wrote "new York." Can we get any psychological clues there? Yes. He didn't capitalize the *N* in New York, revealing lack of respect and feelings of smallness toward the city.

On the other hand, he *did* capitalize a word that he shouldn't have. That word is *Era*, which obviously doesn't take a capital. Whenever you put a capital where a capital shouldn't be, and you know when to capitalize or not, it means that subconsciously you're giving stature or importance to the word or phrase that was miscapitalized.

So Lindsay, by capitalizing the word *Era*, is showing that a new era is extremely important to him. It looms large in his mind, much larger than "new York." So if we put everything together, the man is saying, "I'm looking forward to a new Era, and that new Era doesn't include new York City."

Universal Concepts Associated with Zones

We've just looked at the sources of the meanings associated with the upper, middle, and lower zones. Once again, we can look to expressions in everyday language to see the common meanings ascribed to these three zones.

UPPER (associated with the mind, mental processes, ambition, hopefulness)	MIDDLE (associated with the ego, the self, the here and now)	LOWER (associated with desires, needs, security, sexuality, home life, health and body)
Has a real *head* on his shoulders. Aspire to great *heights*. Put your thinking *cap* on. Let's get together and *brain*storm. *Mind* over matter. Use your *head*. A *heady* move. On a *head* trip. A *tall* order to fill.	*Self*-centered. Only thinks of him*self*. Can't see beyond her*self*. Has to be the *center*. Only sees what's *right in front*. The world *revolves around* her.	From the *depths* of my soul. From the *bottom* of my heart. *Down* and dirty. Get *down*. Let's settle *down* and marry. Buckle *down* and get to work. Putting *down* your roots. *Down* with the flu. Get *down* to business. *Down* to earth. *Longing* to see you.

Zone Tidbits

Tidbit #1

When graphologists take written statements from suspects in a crime, sometimes what gives the culprit away is that he or she will be writing loopy and then, all of a sudden, in a phrase we'll see sudden retracing:

At 4:00 pm. I began my usual closing routines. I
→ *didn't see nothing unusual at all.* ←
→ *And I don't know who did it.* ←

The writing may get small and tight, as a psychological reaction that occurs because the writer is suddenly feeling small and uptight. You might observe a similar phenomenon on your next Valentine's Day card written to someone you really can't stand but feel compelled to pretend otherwise:

and I hope your family
is in wonderful health!
→ *I really love you! Will you*

Tidbit #2

As you've learned, the lower zone has a tendency to dominate in people who are obsessed with their bodies and/or health. In the writing of hypochondriacs, graphologists often find the combination of dominating lower zones with an uneven, wavering pressure pattern (the worrier). Additionally, the writing of hypochondriacs contains components of compulsive use of space (obsessive qualities) and too many underlines and exclamation marks (tendency toward exaggeration).

Tidbit #3

We can get hidden clues from the lower zones, too. Joe writes a thank-you note to all the girls in the office who bought him a birthday present. For whom was Joe feeling something "special"?

Dear Lilly, Sally, & Suzy

Did you get it? Sally, definitely. Lilly and Suzy don't appear to be in the running.

So the longer the lower zone, the more restless the writer feels at that point. And if the lower zone suddenly elongates or bloats on key words, look at what the person is writing there for additional information.

Pop Quiz

1. Which person is more direct and efficient and wrote much faster?

A.
B.

The answer is *B*. *B* has stick-figured lead-ins and looped ending strokes. The lead-in stick figure saves time because it takes more time to loop up and then back to make the *h*. But it doesn't take any more time to loop a *y* than to stick-figure it, because you have to come around to the right and up to start the next word in any case.

2. Did the writer become more, or less, outgoing between samples *A* and *B*? Do you think something good or bad happened between these two samples of writing?

Sample A

Sample B

Something bad. From sample *A* to sample *B*, the writing got smaller, more leftward, and the upper zones became twisted.

Between writing sample *A* and *B*, this person's face was tragically disfigured in a fire. Before the accident, the writer had rightward, round, big, loopy writing.

After the accident, the writer became a recluse. The whole personality changed, and the writing became leftward and twisted. The twisted letters in the upper zone in this sample correspond to the feelings of being twisted or deformed somewhere in the upper body.

What could cause the upper-zone letters to be twisted like this? Could something physical cause it, in the same way Parkinson's disease makes a person's hand shake and, therefore, makes his writing shake? Is there a difference?

Yes. The difference is that if your body is shaking, your entire handwriting will then shake. But if just one part of your handwriting is misshapen, deformed, or shaky, and the rest is not (as in sample *B* above), then it cannot possibly be anything physical. Rather, it has to be a psychological projection onto the paper that something is "wrong" or "twisted" or "shaky" in the part of your body that corresponds with that part of your writing.

Thus, in this instance, the actual scars on the writer's face did not cause the deformity in the upper loops, but the *feelings* of being twisted and deformed in the upper body were projected into the corresponding area in the handwriting, and the upper zones became deformed as a result.

It's important to add, however, that if a person does not *see* himself as deformed, he will not project anything unusual into his writing.

18
PRINTING vs. CONNECTED WRITING

Printing-vs.-Connected Writing Quiz

Before you read about printing versus connected writing, please take this little quiz to see how much you already know.

1. Which way does the Palmer method teach us to write? Like *A* or like *B*?

A.

improved during
The quick bro
over the lazy d

B.

he quick brown
Fox jimped over

2. Who wrote faster, *A* or *B*?

A.

I wrote faster.

B.

I wrote faster

3. Who wrote faster, *A* or *B*?

A.

inattentive

B.

inattentive

4. Who looks less intelligent?

A.

inattentive

B.

inattentive

5. Which writer is more likely to be a man?

A.

We are very busy betw in little league & john a team, and jeff the now that Shannon

B.

I am talking on behal have to work anywhere a week to make reason

Answers

1. A	2. B	3. B	4. A	5. B

Ways to Handwrite

There are three basic ways to handwrite:

1. Printing

Printing

2. Connected or "cursive" writing (the way we were taught in school)

Cursive

3. A combination of printing and cursive (or what we call disconnected or "print-writing")

Print – writing

This chapter will answer the following questions:

- What does it mean if you print?
- What does it mean if you write cursively?
- What does it mean if you use some combination of the two?

Printing

Now we are in

In printing, each letter is separate, and there are no connecting strokes.
There are three reasons why you might print:

1. You print because your cursive writing is illegible, in which case you print out of practicality, common sense, and consideration for others.
2. If your cursive handwriting is legible but you still prefer to print, then it is because you do not wish to reveal your real personality to others.
3. Or you print only certain words or phrases on occasion when you wish them to stand out, or when you really don't want to say them and are overcompensating.

Let's take a deeper look at each of these reasons, to see where they come from.

1. Printing Because Your Cursive Writing Is Illegible

To understand why many people's cursive writing is illegible, let's consider the following questions.

Who tends to print more often, men or women? And why?

You probably already knew that more men print than women. When I first participated in a study of this back in 1974, ten times as many men printed as women.

Why do so many more men print than women?

Is it because men just don't have the finger control to be as legible as women? No, it's not. If that were true, men would not outnumber women in the fields associated with fine muscular movement, such as brain surgery. The reason more men print than women can be traced back to the beginning of learning to handwrite in school.

Back when we learned to write, at age five, six, or seven, why were we first taught printing rather than cursive writing?

It is because printing is but a series of downstrokes, which rely on contraction of the muscles. The most difficult movements for a child of that age to make are those requiring a combination of contraction and extension, called "fine motor movements," which are the movements required for connecting one letter to another. These movements are very difficult for children between the ages of five and eight, although some are more adept than others.

The average girl in this age group, however, is approximately two years ahead of the average boy in fine motor skills. In the gross motor skills, however, involving such activities as kicking a ball, socking a ball, and other playground activities, the boy is two years ahead. If you've ever taught elementary school, as I have, you'll know that these same little boys, whose handwriting looks spastic, can be sturdy little athletes out on the playing field. And the average girl, who has no difficulty with her handwriting, often feels awkward and lost on the playground.

So from the beginning, the average boy dislikes handwriting because he's not good at it. In fact, many children hate handwriting for a number of reasons. First of all, we force children to write with big, black, thick pencils that have no erasers—a huge two-by-four that even adults would hate. Then we give the children lined paper to write on where the lines are two inches apart. So we have a little tiny hand wrestling with a great big club, trying to make ridiculously huge movements that look nothing like real handwriting, and the child knows it.

On top of all this, somewhere around the age of seven after the child has supposedly mastered printing, the teacher says, "OK, boys and girls, now we're going to stop printing because we're going to learn a brand new way to write, called cursive writing!"

The average boy, who's had so much trouble with printing, now has to learn a new, different way of writing that calls for him to make difficult round movements. No wonder he gets it in his mind that he hates handwriting.

As soon as the average boy is out of elementary school, at approximately age twelve, he goes to junior high school, and suddenly his handwriting is no longer graded on his report card. So he thinks, "Oh, heck! I'm going back to printing because it was easier!" And many boys do this for the rest of their lives.

We find that boys who go on to use cursive writing probably were good at it from the beginning, and those who had a hard time with it, who disliked it, go on to printing. Even though the boy catches up with girls in the fine motor skills around the age of nine or ten, it's already in his mind that he hates handwriting, so he doesn't even try anymore.

When someone tells me he always prints because his handwriting is illegible, I always ask for a sample of his cursive writing anyway. If the cursive handwriting really is illegible, then the person prints out of practicality and consideration for the reader.

But more often than not, the cursive writing is as legible, if not more so, than the person's printing. In this case, the person prints because it feels better to him. This writer doesn't want to join his letters together.

2. Printing to Avoid Revealing Your Personality

If your cursive handwriting is legible but you still prefer to print, then it is because you do not wish to reveal your real personality to others. Thus, this reason for printing describes a person who has acceptable handwriting but still wishes to print.

Since we can write so much faster cursively than with printing, why would someone prefer to print all the time? The reason is that the person subconsciously wants the extra time. He does not want to reveal himself simply and spontaneously through writing (which is what cursive writing allows). He wants to have time to think, to calculate, to consider his effect on others.

Graphologically, what sets us apart from one another are our connecting strokes. Our individual personality, what makes our handwriting uniquely our own, is seen through our connectors. No two people have the same connecting pattern. This is why a printed signature on a check or will is not a legal or valid one. It is also through the connectors that we can make so many graphological interpretations, such as whether a writer is sociable, aggressive, or dishonest. So subconsciously, printing is one of the most effective ways to hide your personality from others.

The obvious exception to this interpretation is anyone who has an occupation where printing goes hand in hand with his work, such as an architect, an engineer, or a member of the law enforcement community. For these types, who may use a certain print style on plans, blueprints, and forms, printing soon becomes an ingrained habit. Their specific style of printing is usually easy to identify.

3. Printing Only Certain Words or Phrases

Someone who prints only certain words or phrases on occasion does so when he wishes them to stand out—or when he really doesn't want to say them and is overcompensating.

Have you ever been writing a letter, and all of a sudden you wanted to print? It happens to a lot of people. Let's say you're reading a letter and come to a passage where it's suddenly printed:

I can't tell you how much I LOVE you.

Ask the writer, "Why did you print that?" and the writer says, "To make it stand out." Do you believe that? Why didn't the writer make the word *you* stand out instead?

Usually, whenever you have a subconscious desire to print suddenly, it means you have taken out your feelings, have stopped the flow, have suddenly wanted to slow.

This might be acceptable. It depends. You have to look at other clues. For example, did the slant change? Did it get too big or too small?

Connected or "Cursive" Writing

Cursive

For a person to qualify as a connected writer, at least 80 percent of his letters must be connected.

Connected writing means that the writer is highly sequential in thought and action; he doesn't want to stop. The word *cursive* comes from the Latin for "running" and applies only to handwriting.

People who are highly connected writers are highly connected thinkers, sequential in thought and action. They are more likely to attempt to follow an orderly procedure and may feel disoriented if they have no definite plan of action for achieving their goals. When they set up a list, they'll want to complete step four on the list before they go on to steps five or six. Highly connected writers are the logical thinkers who leave as little as possible to chance. And they usually rely on practical methods more than on hunches.

A Combination of Printing and Cursive
(Disconnected or "Print-Writing")

Who wrote faster, *A* or *B*?

A.   B.

inattentive   *inattentive*

The answer is *B*; the person who wrote with print-writing wrote faster than the person who connected all his letters.

When I was a student of graphology in Germany in 1962, my German graphology professor once said, "Ov course you know zat zose ov you who print-write and do not connect all your letters, ov course you're going to write much faster zan zee stupid Anglo vay, where zey haf all zee letters connected and never stop as zey write."

I was thinking, "How could someone who keeps stopping write faster than someone who never stops?" So, like an idiot, I raised my hand and asked this.

"OK, you inferior species," my professor said, "Ve're going to haf a race!" And he made me come up, and he made someone else come up, and we had to write a word, something like *inattentive*. I was supposed to write it completely connected, while the other person was to use print-writing. We both had to be legible, which the class would judge.

The professor said, "Ready, set, go!," and when I finished writing the word:

inattentive

I turned and looked over, expecting to see my opponent still writing. But he'd beaten me! And he was leaning against the board next to his version of the same word, looking very bored!

inattentive

Can you guess why he beat me so badly? What is the difference in the way we both wrote the word? The difference is that he dotted his *i*'s and crossed his *t*'s as he went along. When he got to the end of the word, he was done, whereas when I got to the end of the word, I had to go all the way back to the beginning of the word to dot my *i*'s and cross my *t*'s, and then go all the way back to the end of my word to start the next word to the right:

Me   *Him*

inattentive   *inattentive*

Write word. ⟶   Write word. ⟶

Go back for *i*'s and *t*'s

⟵

Go to next word. ⟶

If you use print-writing (or disconnected writing), you mix together aspects of printing and cursive. When you get to the end of a word using print-writing, you've already dotted all your *i*'s and crossed all your *t*'s, and are ready to go right on to the next word.

People who do print-writing are of two types, depending on when and where they lift the pen within a word:

1. Those who write with efficient breaks
2. Those who write with inefficient breaks

Print-Writing with Efficient Breaks

To qualify as an efficient disconnector (print-writer), you must meet the following criteria:

you either stop to dot an *i*:   *paint*

or you stop to cross a *t*:   *mation*

or you stop after a downstroke to start the next letter on a downstroke.

So this is an efficient break: *m attentive*

And this is an inefficient break: *m attentive*

Do you see the difference? In the second example, the writer stopped on a downstroke to start the next letter on an upstroke. He had connectors on the *n* and *a* but didn't connect them to each other. He stopped just to make another lead-in stroke. That's *in*efficient breaking.

If you incorporate your *i* dot into the lead-in to the next letter, that's *super-efficient*:   *m*

It's super-efficient if you stop to cross a *t* and the *t* bar becomes the lead-in to the next letter: *atten*

And it's *also* super-efficient if you do it with one continuous movement, not lifting the pen: *atten*

Writing with efficient breaks (efficient print-writing) means intelligence, speed, efficiency, directness, simplification. People who write this way do not like to go to excess. They don't like phony frills and want to get right to the root of things.

If you write with cursive writing and not with efficient breaks, does that mean you are inefficient?

inattentive

No. Even though you may write with perfect Palmer handwriting, and therefore have no efficient disconnectors in your writing, that does not mean that you are not efficient. To know that, we have to look at the speed and simplicity of your stroking.

However, if you are an efficient print-writer, you usually are intelligent, efficient, direct, succinct, and so on. But don't think that you have to write this way to be efficient. A lot of Palmer method writers are brilliant, too.

Print-Writing with Inefficient Breaks

Who looks less intelligent?

A.

in atten tive

B.

in atten tive

The answer is *A*, as you know from the last section, as *A*'s writing contains inefficient disconnections.

Inefficient breaks in the writing mean the writer's mind is wandering. You know how we say someone "gets off track" or "loses the thread of what he was talking about" or "stops and starts in his work"? Such writers can't focus, can't keep their mind on what they are doing.

Here's an example of the way an inefficient disconnector might think. Let's say an inefficient disconnector has just returned from taking his dog to the vet:

YOU: So, how's Fido?

INEFFICIENT DISCONNECTOR: Oh, thank you for asking. I just took him to the vet, and you know what? On the vet's little stand was this beautiful vase, and I'd seen it before at Sears, so I'm going to buy it for my mother, and did you know that my mother's anniversary is coming up? They're driving up to the mountains for a week. I can't wait to take a vacation, too! And I've just got to get my car fixed!

We all know these types of people. Look at their handwriting, and I promise you, nine times out of ten, you're going to find inefficient disconnectors. It's just fragmented thinking, starting and stopping and starting and stopping and starting.

When children write this way, the teacher says the same thing: "You know, Johnny just can't keep his mind on his work. He does some work, then looks out the window and he's gone, a real daydreamer."

184

By the way, this trait does not necessarily indicate a writer who would score low on an IQ test; he might score very high. This person just can't keep the thread going. And the more frequently the writer disconnects inefficiently, the more disjointed his thinking.

Printing-vs.-Connected Writing Tidbits

Tidbit #1
Among professions that graphologists have studied, the most common profession for highly connected writers is scientists. People in the arts tend to be the least connected, on average.

Tidbit #2
You may have noticed that when people become very old, one of the first aspects of their handwriting to break down is the connectors. The writing of the very elderly often looks like that of very young children. Both groups find it very difficult to make connectors between letters. It is very much like the Jungian concept of the circle of life, in which humans begin and end our lives in a similar state of helplessness.

Tidbit #3
Cursive writing as a system of writing was developed and taught long before we developed our print manuscript style, which came as the result of a twofold problem: (1) very young children couldn't write cursively because they lacked fine muscle control, and (2) we wanted a style that was easily legible.

It's not surprising that, because we teach it in the opposite order, most people envision that printing came first and then along came cursive writing. But it is just the opposite.

Pop Quiz
1. Who's more dishonest, *A* or *B*? (*Hint:* Who is revealing the least, hiding the most?)

A.

WHO IS LESS REVEALING?

B.

who is less revealing?

A is more dishonest. We know that one reason for printing is that the writer doesn't want to reveal his real personality to others. Still, there's some personality revealed in *B* because there are upper, middle, and lower zones in the writing. But when someone chooses to print in all capitals, there's only one zone to assess, and therefore less is revealed.

When someone chooses to print in block letters all the time and this kind of writing is not required in his or her work, this signifies dishonesty:

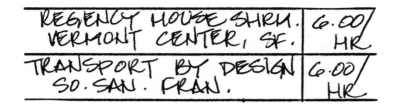

REGENCY HOUSE SHRU. VERMONT CENTER, SF.	6.00/ HR
TRANSPORT BY DESIGN SO. SAN. FRAN.	6.00/ HR

VIOLENT BEHAVIOR,
fact THAT SHE/
TRYING TO SCRATCH, i'
ING WITH ALL HER STRENT!
MY ATTEMPTS TO Hand-

2. Who's more dishonest here? (*Hint:* Again, who is revealing the least, hiding the most?)

A.

THIS IS BLOCK PRINTING

B.

THIS IS SEGMENTED PRINTING

B is more dishonest than *A*. *B*'s writing sample is an example of what is called *segmented printing*. In segmented printing, the letter pieces don't touch each other. So, although both *A* and *B* are block printing, the fact that *B*'s writing is also segmented makes it that much more dishonest and nonrevealing.

It's almost as if the writer were just making little chicken scratches. Watch out for these people! Segmented printing is absolutely identified with criminal tendencies.

3. Who is unreliable, unstable, and unpredictable?

A.

*who is unreliable
and unstable
and unpredictable*

B.

*WHO is UNRELIABLE
and unstable
AND UNPREDICTABLE*

The answer is *B*. *A*'s writing is print-writing, which, you will recall, is a sign of efficiency, directness, and intelligence. *B*'s writing, however, should not be confused with print-writing; it is called *mixing of styles*. In this case, the writer prints one word, then cursively writes another word, and goes back and forth between printing and writing with no particular pattern.

Mixing of styles is a strong indicator of antisocial tendencies. Just as such writers cannot make up their mind how they are going to write, so they cannot make up their mind how they are going to behave. These people do not want to stick to a predictable behavior pattern and instead are impulsive and without structure, without rules of conduct. They are wayward.

19
CONNECTING STROKES

Explanation of Connecting Strokes

Connecting strokes are the little pieces that connect one letter to another in a cursively written word. If you always print, then you have no connecting strokes.

Types of Connecting Strokes

There are four basic types of connecting strokes: garlands, arcades, angles, and threads. Let's look at each of these, using the word *fore*:

Garlands
A garland connects the letters with an underhand stroke, and it is primarily what we're taught in the Palmer writing system.

Arcades
An arcade connects the letters with an overhanded stroke.

Angles
An angle connects letters using angles.

Threads
A threaded connecting stroke is really no connecting stroke at all. It's just a little squiggle, so that you can barely read the word.

Connecting-Strokes Quiz

Before you read about each type of connecting stroke, I'm going to show you that you already have a sense of what each means. Please answer the following questions:

1. Which of the four types of connecting strokes shown above looks the most open, friendly, and sociable?

2. Which looks the most aggressive?

3. Who's the sneakiest and the most devious?

4. Who has the most to hide; who's covering up something?

Answers

1. Your answer should have been garlands. Garland connectors mean the writer is feeling open, friendly, and sociable.	3. Your answer should have been threads. This type of threaded connecting stroke correlates to sneaky, devious, evasive behavior.
2. Your answer should have been angles. Angled connectors mean the writer is feeling aggressive and tight, because you have to tense your muscles to make angles.	4. Your answer should have been arcades. Arcades are comparable to someone putting an arm up over his head to hide or to defend himself.

Most likely, you got these right because your common sense guided you.

"Ideal" Connecting Strokes

If you are a connected writer, the ideal connecting system would be 75 percent garlands, with the remaining 25 percent of the connectors mixed between angles, arcades, and threads. What you don't want to see is a handwriting that is 100 percent of any one of the four types of connectors, because, once again, anything to the extreme means an overcompensation for something that is lacking.

Now we'll take a more in-depth look at the varieties of garlands, arcades, angles, and threads that people use.

Garlands

all the exercises in this book.

Garland connectors mean the writer is friendly, sociable, ready to establish a link with others, affectionate, flexible, and communicates easily. People who work best with other people are garland makers. More women than men make garlands.

Clothesline Garlands

Which writer makes a show of his goodness?

A.   B.

goodness   *goodness*

The answer is *B*, because the writer flattens out, or makes a show of, the garlands so that they appear as straight lines between the letters. This means one who makes a show of his goodness. It doesn't mean the person *isn't* good, just that he lets everyone know it!

Droopy Garlands

Which writer feels a great weight upon his shoulders?

A.   B.

a great weight   a great weight

The answer is *A*, the writer with "droopy" garlands. This type of garland is made by writers who feel a great weight upon their shoulders, someone or something pushing them down with a heavy load. You might call this type of garland maker the martyr or the victim. This person feels oppressed, burdened, overloaded, weighted down.

What if only a few words contain droopy garlands? What would that mean? It would mean that where the garlands drooped, the words were depressing to the writer or that the writer felt weighted down by what he thought at the time the words drooped.

Sham Garlands

Who *pretends* to be nice, is a sham, is underhanded?

A.   B.

*I am a   I am a
sham.   sham.*

The answer is *B*. The following interpretation applies only to American writing, because for some reason a large percentage of Europeans, especially the French, make shams.

The sham garland is when you make an *m* look like a *w*, a *w* look like an *m*, a *u* look like an *n*, and an *n* look like a *u*. Thus, an *m* and an *n*, which are supposed to be made overhanded:

m   n

are made underhanded instead:

m   n

We can apply the expression *underhanded* to convey the meaning of sham garlands. Sham garlands mean the writer gets people to do things for him by

190

manipulating them with calculated kindness. Garlands mean "niceness." But if you use garlands where they do not belong, you make people think that you have their interest at heart when actually whatever you're doing or saying is really for your own personal gain.

Arcades

*person . for him
Also, I'll fill
out a form for me*

Arcades indicate a desire to cover up, a desire for formality, control, to pretend to live by a rule rather than live one's own life. This person has a concern for appearances and tradition, but it's a facade, a self-protective gesture. Arcades are associated with giving lip service rather than sincerity. The arcade maker is the hypocrite who has something to hide.

Big Arcades

Who wants to show off more?

A.

who

B.

who

The answer is *A*. When arcades get too big, they reveal a tendency to show off in order to hide the real self. Remember, whenever you overdo, it's to compensate for a lack. So people who really flourish their writing, who come on too big, are compensating for an inner feeling of just the opposite—smallness.

Often you'll see this kind of arcading among actors and actresses, people who feel that they're bluffing. It means pretentiousness, putting on a front to hide what's really there.

Arcades with Angular Twists

Who has a "twisted" mind?

A.

Thanks

B.

Thanks

The answer is *B*. This type of twisted, deformed writing is symptomatic of

191

psychosis. The person should not be walking the streets. Twisting shapes, any shapes, means twisted, aberrant thinking, someone who is potentially dangerous. This person is not functioning the same way you and I are. He is "bent out of shape," a crooked, distorted, twisted thinker.

Angles

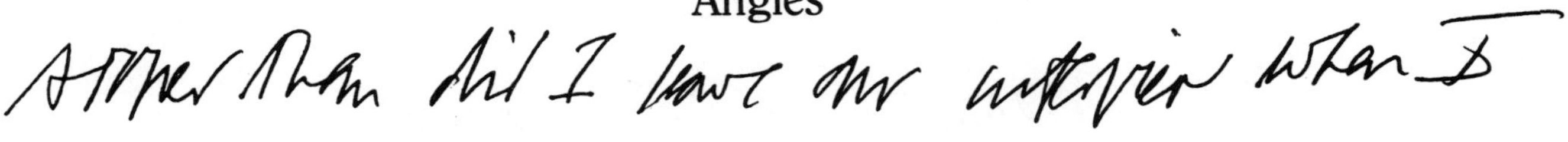

[handwritten line]

Angles are associated with aggressive individuals, people who are hardworking, competitive, determined, serious about their work, and not easily influenced. These people will try to impose their will on others and on their environment, and they seldom deviate from their purpose. This trait is also associated with stubbornness.

Overly Angular

Who's more uptight and tense?

A. *[handwritten]*   B. *[handwritten]*

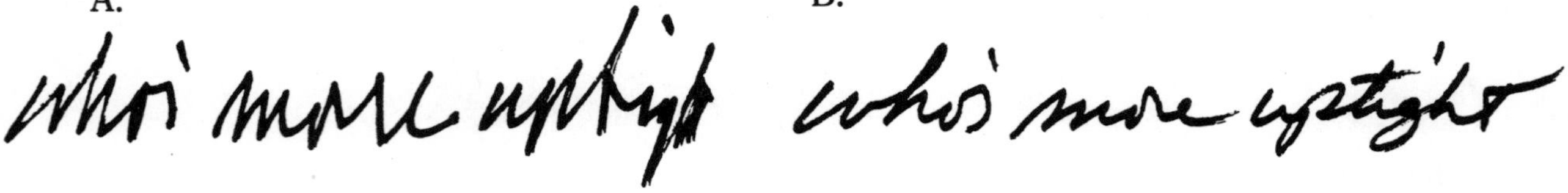

The answer is *A*. Please try to write this way. Imitate the following sentence, full of angles, on your scratch paper.

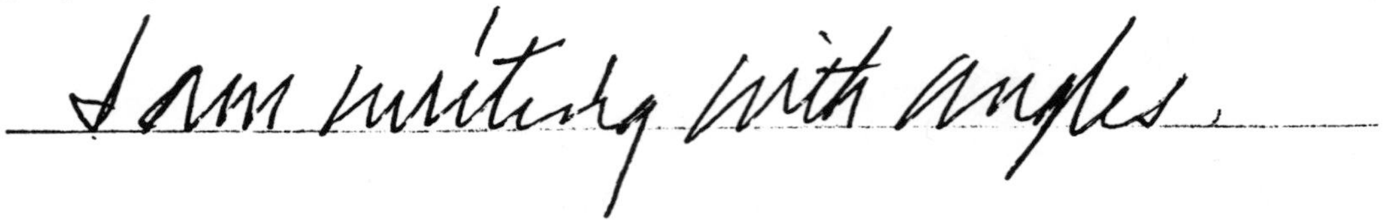

[handwritten: I am writing with angles.]

Now feel the other side of the paper where you wrote your sentence. Did you write with heavy pressure or light? If you wrote with angles, it should be very heavy. How did you feel as you wrote? You should have felt intense, aggressive, competitive. When graphologists take writing samples of desperate people at gambling tables in Las Vegas, they find incredibly heavy pressure and angularity. (Let me tell you, it's no small feat to get a handwriting sample out of someone who won't take his eyes off his money or his cards!)

192

Now, having *some* angles in your writing is very good. The most productive people, the most fertile minds, have angularity in their writing. In fact, research shows that the most productive people have close to 50 percent angularity in their writing.

It's when the writing is *too* angular and devoid of roundness that it signifies an uptight, rigid, tense, totally inflexible person. And someone cannot be truly brilliant if he is too uptight and narrow-minded to let anything else in.

Overly angular writing means everything just described for angular writing *plus* extreme rigidity, inflexibility, uptightness, tension, a rubber band ready to snap. A person can't stay this way too long before breaking.

This is the heart attack candidate described as the Type A person to the max. Someone with overly angular writing is about to burst a blood vessel. He is angry and a professional opponent, who will argue with you about anything. It's uncomfortable to be around this person; you sense how uptight he is and heaven help whoever's around when this volcano erupts!

Threading Quiz

Before you begin reading about threading, take this little quiz to see how much you already know.

A. *Something happened today and*

B. *Something happened today and*

C. *Something happened today and*

D. *Something happened today and*

Samples *A, B, C,* and *D* all contain threading in some form or another within the word. Threading is where the letters are squiggled together in an unintelligible manner.

1. Which writer is communicating the least, is revealing nothing, and you wonder why he bothered writing at all?

2. Which writer lets you in just so far, then shuts the door at the end?

3. Which writer is unhappy in his daily life?

4. Which writer is the happiest, is communicating in the best, most expedient way?

The answers to these questions are contained in the following explanations of threading.

Explanation of Threading

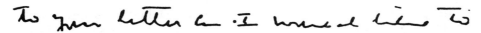

Threading is just squiggling out the letters so that the reader can't see what they really are, as in the example above.

People thread for many reasons. They thread for speed. Or they thread because they don't know how to spell a word and therefore squiggle out the writing so no one will know that they don't know how to spell the word. People also thread when they're feeling dishonest or sneaky or small about something and subconsciously don't want others to see what they're saying.

Threading Due to Fatigue, Unhappiness, Laziness or Sneakiness and Evasiveness

1. Which writer is communicating the least, is revealing nothing, and you wonder why he bothered writing at all?

The answer is C.

When you get tired, you stop wanting to articulate letters because it takes more energy to write legibly than illegibly. If you see a sample where the writing started out neat and small, then got larger, sloppier, and more threaded, you can conclude the writer was getting tired. It's akin to starting to slur your words when you get tired.

If the entire writing is threaded from start to finish, then the writer may be horribly tired. He may be terribly unhappy, or may be feeling totally evasive and noncommunicative.

Why would anyone bother to write anything if no one could read a word of it? Such a writer may be noncommunicative and doesn't stop to realize that no one could read a word of what he's just written, in which case he's impractical, lazy, and inconsiderate. Or, for some reason, he doesn't really want to make clear what he is writing about and may be feeling totally evasive and sneaky.

It's amazing, when graphologists assess written statements to discern falsehoods, that when someone starts to lie and gets sneaky and evasive, one of the many things the writer may do is to start to get squiggly and become illegible in those words and phrases about which he is lying. At the root of total illegibility, however, is usually grave unhappiness.

Threading Only at the End of Words

2. Which writer lets you in just so far, then shuts the door at the end?

The answer is *A*.

Something happened today and

Threading only at the end of words means the writer is devious by way of omission. Such people can manipulate not by what they say but by what they leave out. When you ask them why they didn't tell you about a meeting they had without you, they say, "Oh . . . well, you never asked me."

Threaders can be sneaky. They know how to wiggle out of difficult situations, and foist them on others with ease, if need be. This trait is also called the diplomatic ending because these people will let you in just so far, then shut the door. They are legible to a point, and then they suddenly slip away.

As a general rule, this type of threading also indicates someone who is impatient and in a hurry.

Threaded with Disappearing Middle Zone

3. Which writer is unhappy in his daily life?

The answer is *B*.

Something happened today and

In this sample, the middle zone is threaded. The middle zone represents what? It represents the writer's daily life and the present moment. If the middle zone is small and poorly formed, it means unhappiness with one's daily life. As the letters are small and without shape, so the writer's life feels small and without distinction.

This trait also means inconsideration, because the person is writing in a way that makes it difficult for others to read, so he is not considering the reader. Once again, the root of inconsideration is usually immense unhappiness.

Threading for Speed

4. Which writer is the happiest, is communicating in the best, most expedient way?

The answer is *D*.

Something happened today and

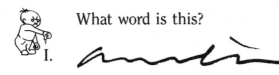

What word is this?

I.

You can't tell? Can you tell, then, what word this is?

II. *anything*

It's the word *anything*, which you could read this time, correct? Here's the rule. If you thread as in sample II and maintain legibility—and this is the key—then you are threading for speed. This trait means intelligence, efficiency, and a quick mind.

But if you thread for speed as in sample *I*, and if you leave an illegible word, then you've accomplished nothing. This means inconsideration, unhappiness, and inefficiency.

To know the difference between threading for speed and threading out of unhappiness, you must ask whether the word is legible. Since threading is fast, why not do it if you can get away with it? Our goal in handwriting is to write as simply, efficiently, and quickly as possible while remaining legible.

Threading for speed with legibility is associated with fast-minded people of higher intelligence who are busy and have executive potential. Most often you'll see this trait on words ending in *ing*.

Try Your Hand at Analyzing Connecting Strokes

What can you say about Ollie North based on the type of garlands he makes? And what handwriting traits does he have in common with Jackie Kennedy?

> You have made it possible to mount a defense against a persecution that has already spent more than $50 million. Equally important, you have helped me to protect my family from a very real and persistent terrorist threat.
>
> If there is any way that you can help us again now, on the eve of sentencing, we will be forever grateful.

North makes sham garlands, so we can say he manipulates people with calculated kindness. He makes people think that he has their interest at heart when actually whatever he's doing is really for his own personal gain.

Ollie and Jackie—We should get them together! Notice how similar their handwriting is? First, they both have leftward slants, which means that they tend to repress their real emotions, to think one thing and say another. Then they both write very slowly and have stylized writing, meaning they tend to calculate their responses and guard their behavior. And, finally, we need only look at the clubbed strokes to know we have a match here!

This sample comes from a letter in which Ollie was asking his supporters for more money for his defense.

Universal Concepts Associated with Connecting Strokes

The meanings given to the four types of connecting strokes come from the universal connotations associated with the concepts of roundness, angularity, overhandedness, and squiggling. Here are some expressions from everyday language that show the common meanings:

garlands	*arcades*
GARLANDS (Roundness) (*associated with openness, friendliness*)	**ARCADES** (Overhandedness) (*associated with formality, control, covering up*)
Let me *extend* my heartfelt thanks. Let's *link* arms. *Reach out* and touch someone. Let's establish a *link*. There's a *connection* between us.	What a *cover-up*. She tries to *hide* the facts. I'll *put on* that I'm happy. I *need to protect* myself.
Angles	*thread*
ANGLES (Angularity) (*associated with sharp-mindedness, tension, determination, steadfastness*)	**THREADS** (Squiggling) (*associated with deviousness, sneakiness, evasiveness—when with illegibility*)
He's always got an *angle* up his sleeve. He's got a *point* there. They had a *pointed* argument. Let me come straight to the *point*. What a *sharp* mind! He's a hard-*liner*. She *won't bend* at all. Raised with a *firm* hand. Playing the *angles*. Knows the *angles*.	*Slippery* as an eel. *Sneaky* as a snake. *Slithered* away in the night. *Wiggles* out of it every time. *Slipped* right out the door. *Slipped* right through the cracks.

Connecting-Stroke Tidbits

Tidbit #1

Around 1980, the Mexican government, under President José López Portillo, forbade the teaching of cursive writing in all of its schools, both public and private. The children could learn only to print and nothing more. The reasons for this outrageous mandate have never been made clear. As a result, when we look at the signatures of those Mexicans who have emigrated to the United States and have never learned cursive writing, we find a faked, squiggled line. That's all they can do.

This is a very sad state of affairs. Mexico is the only country in history to go backward in time and deprive its people of an invaluable ability. The young people of Mexico now no longer can read or write cursive at all, nor can they sign their own names.

Tidbit #2

Notice where the threading occurs in the following paragraph. Decide which statement is untrue:

> I was definitely here on
> time. I worked all morning &
> stocked the entire room.
> I took lunch at noon as always.

In the word *definitely*, threading occurs only between the *n* and the *t*, where the *i* belongs. Because this is a commonly misspelled word and because there is no other threading in the word, we cannot immediately assume that the writer threaded here for any reason other than being uncertain how to spell the word.

On the other hand, in the phrase *stocked the entire room* we can barely read anything. Obviously, this is not because the person was likely to have had difficulty spelling these words. Notice there's a little wider spacing between these words as well, providing further clues that the writer is probably not being totally truthful here.

Pop Quiz

1. Who would make the better receptionist?

A.   B.

> received an offertion
> have until the end,

> and I would
> love working
> at this

B would definitely make the better receptionist. Remember that roundness (garlands) is associated with friendliness, sociability, desire to link up with other people. Those who do best meeting and greeting the public are generally the more garlanded writers.

2. Who's the harder worker?

A.

who's going to work harder?

B.

who's going to work harder?

B, who has the greater angularity and pressure, is the harder worker. People who put the most intensity behind their movements are generally the harder workers. *A*'s writing is round and slow, so *A* is not going to work as hard and quickly as the heavy-pressured, fast writer.

20
Signatures

"If you don't learn to sign your
name smaller it'll never
fit on checks."

Before you read further, please stop and, on your scratch paper, write your signature three times. If you usually have more than one signature, put them all down.

You'll have a lot more fun with this chapter if you do this now, before you learn what it all means!

Signature Quiz

Once again, please take a few moments to take this fun quiz before reading the chapter on signatures.

1. Who has negative feelings toward his father, *A* or *B*?

A.   B.

Billy Connor   *Billy conn*

2. How does Charles Garnier wish to be addressed?

3. Which writer's last name is an alias?

A.   B.

Andrew Jones   *Andrew*   *Jones*

Answers

1. B	2. As Mr. Garnier.	3. B

Explanation of Signatures
What Your Signature Reveals

Your signature represents your public self-image, which means how you behave in public, how you act around other people, your social persona.

The term *public self-image* also encompasses what you think of yourself in public, what you would like others to think of you, and what you *think* others think of you.

Public vs. Private Behavior

Not everyone acts the same in public (in crowds, in school, in business) as they do in private (in relationships, at home with family and friends).

There are people, for example, who feel fine in small groups, but as soon as they get into a public situation, such as at a party, they feel insecure.

Then there are people who come alive and shine *only* when they get to a party. They may have a social personality but on a one-to-one basis are very insecure and/ or dull.

Your Signature as Your Public Self-Image

Why does your signature symbolize your public self-image? Why is it analyzed any differently than anything else?

We use a simple psychological deduction to conclude that your signature symbolizes your public self-image. When you write sentences and paragraphs, you are communicating feelings and ideas. Your conscious focus is on these feelings and ideas and on communicating them. When you get to your signature, though, you're communicating something completely different; you are leaving your name, your self, your public identity on the page.

So if you are not the same person in public as you are in private, graphologists will be able to see this in your writing. How? By comparing your signature (your public self-image) with the rest of your writing (your real, or private, self-image).

When someone says, "You know, my signature looks nothing like the rest of my handwriting," what that person is actually telling you is that his public behavior is nothing like his private behavior; what you see is *not* what you get.

Interpreting Signatures

Take a look at some signatures with handwriting, and see if you can interpret what they mean by using what you've learned in the previous chapters. In this chapter I have interspersed famous people's writing with that of ordinary folks.

Remember that your signature represents your public self-image. The rest of your writing represents your real or private self-image.

Signature and Writing Are the Same in Appearance

[handwritten text] & charge the same to my account — very respectfully H B Stowe

If the signature is the same as the rest of the writing—that is, if the size, style, slant, pressure, spacing are pretty much the same, as we see here in Harriet Beecher Stowe's writing—then this means the person behaves the same way in public as in private. Such a person doesn't put on airs or change personalities when in public. What you see is what you get.

Signature Slightly Larger than the Writing

[handwritten text] Well, take care and be well. Say hello to the gang for me. We love you. Ann Myers

The size of this signature is just what graphologists like to see—slightly larger than the rest of the writing. If you have healthy self-confidence in public, your signature will be as large as, or slightly larger than the rest of your writing. This signature means healthy self-confidence in public.

Signature Much Larger than the Writing

*I swear to you there are divine things
more beautiful than words can tell.
Leaves of Grass — page 125.
Walt Whitman*

What's the first thing your eyes see with poet Walt Whitman's sample? His signature. This signifies someone screaming to be seen and heard. In actuality, a person with this trait feels small inside, and to compensate he comes on extra big, cocky, attention-seeking.

Remember the psychological principle that applies again and again in graphology: anytime a writer overdoes, it's to compensate for the opposite or for a lack. A person who constantly brags about his IQ doubts how smart he is. Someone who brags about her sexual conquests. . . .

When the average person meets this writer, the person sees someone who's coming on big and cocky. But the psychologically hip person knows that someone coming on this big is only acting this way to compensate for an inner feeling of smallness.

I've found that the most flamboyant and oversized signatures are found among people of the Middle Eastern countries, such as Iran, and in Mexico.

Signature Slightly Smaller than the Writing

*both of your parents will too!
Sean Hammond*

This sample is the opposite of Whitman's. A signature slightly smaller than the rest of the writing indicates insecurity. This person doesn't feel very big when he gets into public situations. He's shy, reserved, and would rather fade into the background, not get a lot of attention.

Signature Much Smaller than the Writing

*and hoping to see
you before long!
Phil Roach*

If you hold this sample away from you, what is your eye drawn to? The signature, right? It's so super small that it calls attention to itself.

This is the signature of someone who wants attention by being so obviously unobvious. An example: You're at a party where everyone is standing around talking together in a group, except for one person who is standing in the corner by himself. Who do you notice? You notice the one standing in the corner by himself.

This type of signature is equivalent to Walt Whitman's signature, except that the modus operandi is the opposite. Walt is going to come on very big and loud, making everyone notice him most obviously. But Phil Roach, here, is going off by himself. He still wants attention, but he wants to be unobvious about it.

Vertical Signature with Rightward-Slanted Writing

This person has a vertical signature, but the rest of the writing is rightward. Automatically we know that what you see is not what you get.

Remember that a vertical slant means a cool cucumber, one who is head over heart, in control, aloof, distant, difficult to get to know, above it all. It's the diplomat, someone who shows no emotion either way. That's this writer's public demeanor. But when he gets home, he's more rightward, a much warmer person.

Rightward-Slanting Signature with Vertical Writing

This sample is the opposite of the preceding one. This is the type of person who, when you meet him at a party, is very warm and expressive; his signature is round and rightward. He slaps you on the back, is very jovial. But at home he's colder and more unexpressive, as his writing is small and vertical.

Legible Writing with Legible Signature

George Deukmejian is a close friend and trusted adviser. His continued help as Governor is critical not only for California's success but also for our Nation.

Ronald Reagan

This sample of President Ronald Reagan's writing is meant to represent legibility. The script is legible, and the signature is legible. Remember that legibility means the writer wishes to communicate. (Again, this only applies to samples that were meant to be read by someone else.) So if the script is legible, it means you want to communicate your thoughts. If the signature is also legible, it means you wish to communicate who you are.

Legible Writing with Illegible Signature

This is probably typical of my various handwritings!

Karl Menninger md

Here we can read what psychiatrist Dr. Karl Menninger wrote, but we cannot read his signature. This combination occurs all the time, especially on checks. We can read everything until we get to the signature. This means someone who wishes to communicate his thoughts—legible script—but doesn't really wish to communicate who he is.

However, many people sign their names so many times a day that they don't have the patience to write it legibly. We have to take that into account. Thus, if you think a signature was illegible because the writer was in a hurry, then that's all it means, and it is not necessarily noncommunication.

This signature of the famous physician, "Karl Menninger MD," however, took a long time to write, so the illegibility has nothing to do with the fact that he was in a hurry or had signed his name many times. It's simply illegible. Thus, he doesn't really wish to communicate who he is!

Did you notice the clubbed stroking in his name?

Illegible Writing with Legible Signature

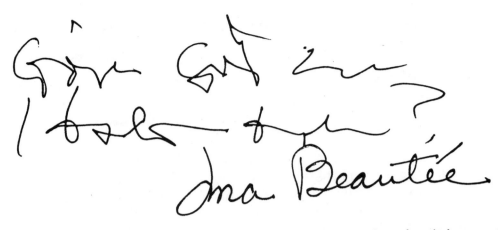

The signature here is "Ima Beautee." You won't see this too often, but it is meant to represent the situation where you can't read a word of the letter someone just wrote you, but you can read the signature. Here, the writer doesn't give a hoot about communicating her thoughts. She only wants to leave you with who she is. This is egotism to the max.

Illegible Writing with Illegible Signature

Can you figure out what this means on your own? This is the writing and signature of Napoléon III, nephew of Napoléon Bonaparte.

Illegible writing means the writer is not communicating his thoughts. When the signature is illegible, too, it means the writer is also not communicating who he is. So why did the person bother to write at all?

What could cause total illegibility? And what are the consequences of it? Illegibility throughout is caused by extreme unhappiness. The consequences are: (1) being inconsiderate to the poor reader, who must try to decipher the scribbles, and (2) being totally impractical and wasting time.

Total illegibility reveals a dysfunctional individual. You don't want to get a letter like this in the mail. (You wouldn't get a letter like this in the mail anyway, because no one could read the envelope.) It means the person is in the same state as his handwriting—profoundly unhappy and wholly noncommunicative.

Ascending Signature

What do you think of my writing — If you are interested in my candidacy please don't answer this publicly RFKennedy

In the late Senator Robert F. Kennedy's writing, we're looking at the difference between a signature that goes uphill and the rest of the writing, which does not. Kennedy's script is slightly concave in that it goes a little down and then rises, but the signature is very uphill. So Kennedy felt the most mental energy in regard to his public self-image. The energy and enthusiasm he felt was in his signature, so we know he felt good about his public self-image, and better about it than about his private life. By the way, did you notice what Robert has in common with Jackie, Ollie, and Karl Menninger? That's right: clubbed strokes galore!

Descending Signature

that I might have grown old with him.

Jacqueline Kennedy

Here she is again! What's descending here is Jackie's last name. The "ennedy" is written slightly lower than the "Jackie" part. Do you see that?

For someone like Jackie, who has such a tight hold over her outward behavior and doesn't show her real feelings, this drop in her last name is quite significant. The writing is so perfectly aligned and self-contained until she drops on "ennedy," which shows depression on it. This sample was written shortly after her husband was assassinated, which could account for the depression here.

You'll see this sort of thing all the time. Look at the following sample. Which of his names is the writer depressed about?

Jerry Brown
(Former Governor of California)

He's depressed about his last name, Brown.

Generally, unless you are an artist who is identified only by one name such as Cher or Ringo, your last name is the one that identifies you. We think of Nixon, McArthur, and Stalin, not Dick, Doug, and Josef. The family name is also the name used to identify people in business: Rockefeller, Ford, and Goldwyn are examples. In addition to these meanings, your last name can also represent your father or family.

Whatever part of the signature drops represents depression, disappointment, disillusionment, or negative feelings associated with that part of the public self-image. If the last name drops, it could signify depression about your public self-image in the business world, or it could signal negative feelings with your father or other family figures.

If your first name is downhill, in contrast to your last name, then you are depressed about yourself, feeling down on yourself.

Descending Signature with Uphill Writing

Here the writing is going uphill until psychiatrist Alfred Adler gets to his illegible signature, which is going downhill. The letter size in the signature is larger than in the script, so we know Adler feels public importance and stature, but the illegible and downhill qualities tell us that he doesn't want to reveal who he is and that there is depression, disillusionment, disappointment, and negativity associated with his public self-image as well.

Adler (a disciple of Freud's) was in disfavor with his peers at the time of this sample, which may account for these feelings.

Underscored Signatures

Harry Houdini
(Magician)

Roman Polanski
(Film Director)

Fidel Castro
(Cuban President)

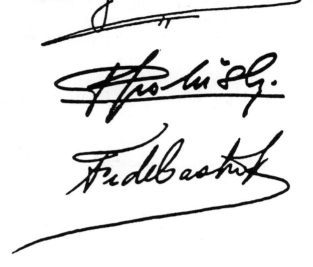

Underscoring means underlining. If you underscore your signature with a simple underline, which basically these three writers have done, it means healthy self-confidence, reaffirmation of the self. A simple underline is fine.

Once again, it's when you *overdo* that we see compensation for the opposite feeling. So if you write your name with too many underscores, such as:

it means you subconsciously feel a lack of public self-worth. This signature would be someone who is doubting her public importance and therefore trying to make herself look that much more important.

Overscored Signature

Mick Jagger
(Rock Musician)

Based on what you've learned about arcades, do you think an overscored signature is going to be something positive or negative?

It's negative. It is, in a sense, a giant arcade. It means total defensiveness, and a need to protect the self. It's also an egotistical type of signature in that it is as if the writer wants to put himself in a picture frame.

Overscoring stems from self-doubt and indicates extreme insecurity with your public self-image; it's a pretense, a cover-up. In some cases, as in this sample of singer Mick Jagger's, it may mean you emphasize your upper body or head in your public image.

Scoring That Obliterates or Plunges Through the Name

Frank Lloyd Wright
(American Architect)

Charles Garnier
(Architect of the Paris Opera)

Napoléon Bonaparte
(Early in his career)

Napoléon Bonaparte
(Late in his career)

M. Morrison
(Average Man)

These are samples of what graphologists call scoring, or obliterating part or all of a name with lines. Scoring reveals a subconscious desire to self-destruct.

Let's look at each of these signatures.

You're going to see that many people give away their profession by the manner in which they sign their name. Frank Lloyd Wright's signature looks like a blueprint, like a building. Do you see the structure and design in his signature?

Which of his three names is he obliterating? "Wright," so in this case the self-destructive part is not aimed toward the total self, but the last name. We don't know why. It might be that he hated the name Wright; it might be that he hated his brother; it might mean that he hated his father.

Whatever the reason, he is utterly obliterating it. The line that goes through Wright has a large barb, or tic (as it is called), at the end of it. This indicates that the writer had extreme anger, tension, and frustration in his body when he made that line. So not only is he crossing out the name Wright, but he's angry about it, too!

Now, if this man walked into a room, how would you address him, based on his signature, as "Charles" or "Mr. Garnier?"

Call him "Mr. Garnier." He is making it obvious that he doesn't like his first name at all. Not only did he not capitalize it, he abbreviated it, and it goes downhill, and he crossed it out with the stroke from his last name. Consequently, what he ended up doing was to frame the Garnier part of his name. Subconsciously he's saying, "I'm Garnier. Don't call me Charles!" Nevertheless, the fact that he did obliterate his first name reveals partial self-destructive qualities.

Napoléon's signatures are often seen in history books and are popular with autograph collectors because of their obvious graphic deterioration. You can see his rise and fall through his signatures.

The first sample was written near the beginning of his career, while the second sample dates from near the end. See the difference? One is clear, and one is self-destructive. He starts out "Napoléon Bonaparte" and ends up "Napoléon Blownapart"!

[signature: M. Morrison]

This last example is really unhealthy. If Morrison crosses out his last name, what's left? Just an *M*. This is suicide city. You don't ever want to see a signature like this!

Overly Large Capitals of Signatures

Barry Goldwater
(Former U.S. Senator)

Richard Nixon
(Former U.S. President)

Ronald Reagan
(Former U.S. President)

Jimmy Carter
(Former U.S. President)

These samples represent signatures whose capitals are inflated compared to the lowercase letters next to them.

This trait reveals someone who wants to be socially prominent, of enormous stature, and wants to stand out in public. Such people want to be famous and call attention to themselves. The bigger the capital, the greater the self-pride. If the capital is much larger than the rest of the letters next to it, it means excessive pride run away with itself. Here, the huge capital represents putting up a wall to the outside world.

Look at "Barry Goldwater," then at "Dick" (for Richard Nixon), and then look at "Ronald Reagan." In proportion to the lowercase letters in their names, which one has the most inflated capital of the three, in comparison to the rest of their name?

"Dick," right? His inflated *D* is outrageous, preposterous! This means something's wrong. It's a bluff. He comes on too big to hide an inner feeling of smallness. Even though Barry Goldwater's capitals are huge, the letters next to them are big as well, so the comparison between the capitals and the small letters is not as dramatic. The same is true of Ronald Reagan's signature.

Jimmy Carter also has a desire for greatness, as depicted by his oversized capitals, but notice the difference in the way he writes the rest of his name in comparison to the other signatures shown here. Carter's writing is very small and well formed, much more like the scientist than the politician (and, in actuality, Carter's background is in chemistry).

Wavy or Curved Underscore

Singer Kate Smith's signature has a wavy or curved underscore, indicating a sense of humor, feeling spritely, lively, silly, fun. Did you notice the period Kate put at the end of her signature? What do you think that means? It means, "The buck stops here," or, "After me, there is no more."

The Pedestal Underscore

Beethoven
(Composer)

Jane Russell
(Actress)

This underscore looks like a pedestal, and that's exactly what it means: that the writer thinks he belongs on a pedestal. It's a little bit of egotism.

Signature Placed at Left Side of Page

within our time frame. I look forward to your response.

Edgar Mose

When writing letters, some businesses use a format where everything, including the date, address, and salutation, starts at the left side of the page. If that is the case where a signature is placed on the left side of the page, then all we can say is that this person is following the standard business form and is probably involved in a business in some way.

If, however, the person chooses to place his signature on the left, and it has nothing to do with a business practice, it means self-doubt and insecurity about his public self-image. Remember that clinging to the left means feeling apprehensive about the future, clinging to the past and the familiar. Thus, if you're placing your public self-image on the left, you're feeling doubtful and insecure about your abilities in public.

Signature Placed in the Center

O l'autant plus qu'il peut même que je parte avant vous,

Charles,

Putting your name smack-dab in the middle of the page—as did Charles Baudelaire, the French poet and translator of Edgar Allan Poe, in this example—means that you want to be in the center of everything that's going on around you, to be left out of nothing. You want to be the center of attention, and if someone is talking in the corner, you want to know what he's talking about!

Benjamin Franklin

Abraham Lincoln

Placing your signature at the right side of the page is very normal and indicates that you adhere to the manner you were taught and are forward-thinking in regard to your public self-image.

Abe Lincoln's signature is an example showing how persons who reach greatness often have the simplest, most unadorned signatures.

Creative Signatures

In graphology we permit you to do all kinds of crazy things in your signature that, if you did them throughout your handwriting, would lead us to believe you were slightly bonkers. But if you do these crazy things only in your signature, we let you get away with it; and we'll call you "creative."

Olivia de Havilland

Look at where actress Olivia de Havilland says, "Merry, Merry Christmas!" What do we call those kinds of humps on the *M*'s? We call them arcades, and they mean putting on a show, pretentious, covering up, pretending to live by a rule rather than living one's own life.

Then on "Olivia de Havilland," the name is underlined, so she is self-confident. The *O* is rather bizarre, and the *de* is somewhat creative.

Noël Coward

The signature of playwright Noël Coward contains what graphologists call the "cent" sign in the middle of his name. See where he makes the *C* go through the *L* so that it looks like a dollar or cent sign?

As you begin looking at signatures, you're going to see that a lot of people actually make dollar signs in their writing. Here's the signature of Dwayne Schintzius, when he was a college basketball player being heavily recruited by NBA teams:

Obviously Schintzius associates himself with money, at least publicly, or he certainly has money on his mind to a great extent.

Edgar Allan Poe

This is one of my favorite signatures. I always loved Poe's works when I was growing up, and I couldn't wait when someone told me she had found his signature. I could not have been more shocked when I saw it. The man who brought us the gold bug, eyeballs beneath floorboards, the Raven, and other ghoulish things, has a flowery, beautiful signature! I would never have suspected it! And do you notice that he makes the capital *E* and capital *P* first and then knows exactly how much room to leave to add the *dgar*? This can be considered extremely odd and out of the mainstream.

Did you know that Poe spent the latter part of his life an alcoholic, in sanatoriums and institutions? The man went mad in later life.

Joe McCarthy
(Former U.S. Senator)

216

This is the signature of the Joe McCarthy who saw communists everywhere and started the witch hunts that spawned the "McCarthy era." Now, we could call that horrible, vicious scribble in his last name a "whip," or we could call it creative. It depends how you want to see it. I think it's a form of crossing out. It is obliterating part of his name.

Paul Santerre
(Seventeenth-Century Painter)

Might you guess that Paul Santerre is a painter? His first name begins with a paintbrush and palette. It's very artistic.

Walt Disney
Here are two Walt Disney signatures. Can you guess which one is really that of Walt Disney and which one was designed as a logo?

The signature on the right is the real Walt Disney signature, and the one on the left was designed for the Disney logo. Notice how the logo was made more legible and more childlike by increasing the size of the middle zone letters in relation to the upper and lower zones. And the angularity of Disney's real signature was removed, and more roundness—another feature of children's writing—was added. The circle *i* dot was retained, a writing feature found more often in children's writing than in adults'.

Musicians

What we see so often in the signatures of musicians and composers are large capitals accompanying a small, well-formed middle zone. This shows real diversity: On the one hand, the large capitals show a desire for greatness, to be seen, to stand out and be appreciated. On the other hand, the small writing means the ability to concentrate alone on small details for long periods of time.

Bruce Springsteen is a perfect example of this:

Here are a number of other musicians' signatures for your enjoyment. Note how many have large capitals and small, well-formed middle zones:

Luciano Pavarotti

Georg Solti

Leonard Bernstein

André Previn

John Williams

Jorge Bolet

Ronnie Milsap

Liberace

Mickey Gilley

Aaron Copland

Dave Brubeck

Billy Joel

Signature Tidbits

Tidbit #1

The crossing out of a President: Can you guess when President Nixon was forced to resign?

1968

1969

Early 1974

Late 1974

Notice how small Nixon's signature became in late 1974, when he was forced to resign. His signature was nothing but a long line with an *X* through it.

Tidbit #2

It's so interesting to compare President Reagan's signature from before he was shot in 1981 to his signature just a few weeks later. Notice how shaky the writing becomes, as well as the descending baseline on the first name.

Before Shooting

After Shooting

Tidbit #3

Remember this question from the quiz at the beginning of this chapter?

Which writer's last name is an alias?

A.   B.

Andrew Jones   *Andrew   Jones*

The answer is *B*. Notice the wide separation between the first and last names. Many times when someone has either changed his last name, or for some reason wants to disassociate from it, he will subconsciously leave an extra big space between his first name (himself) and last name.

Tidbit #4

When graphologists study the signatures of famous, successful people, they find that most of them have signatures that are very average looking. The people who have really made it in life don't have to put on airs or convince others of how big they are. Rather, they have simple, straightforward signatures. If you feel comfortable with yourself, you don't have to bloat up and impress others. You're comfortable just as you really are.

Lee A. Iacocca

As a side note, it appears that the head of Chrysler wants to be called "Lee," as this name is larger than his last name.

Here are some more signatures of famous people who don't need to puff up. (Do you think there is any difference in the way men and women sign their names? Interestingly enough there is absolutely no difference.)

MEN

Ed Davis
(Former L.A. Police Chief)

Gerald R. Ford
(Former U.S. President)

Lou Gehrig
(Baseball player)

Rock Hudson
(Actor)

Darrel Waltrip

Darrel Waltrip
(Race car driver)

Larry Bird

Larry Bird
(Basketball player)

Billy Barty

Billy Barty
(Actor)

Lorne Greene

Lorne Greene
(Actor)

Clayton Moore
The Lone Ranger

Clayton Moore
(The Lone Ranger)

David L. Wolper

David Wolper
(Producer)

Hugh Downs

Hugh Downs
(Newscaster)

Babe Ruth

Babe Ruth
(Baseball player)

Sincerely, George Bush

George Bush
(U.S. President)

Steve Allen

Steve Allen
(Entertainer)

Henry Valentine Miller 11/24/66

Henry Miller
(Author)

Donald J. Trump

Donald Trump
(Entrepreneur)

221

Jesse Jackson
(Politician)

Donald J. Bass
(Publisher, Sports Illustrated)

WOMEN

Martina Navratilova
(Tennis player)

Pat Nixon
(Former First Lady)

Marlo Thomas
(Actress)

Bernadette Peters
(Entertainer)

Vanna White
(Actress)

Mia Farrow
(Actress)

Thank you so much!

Erica Jong
(Author)

Bess Truman
(Former First Lady)

Bette Midler
(Entertainer)

Mamie Doud Eisenhower
(Former First Lady)

Eleanor Roosevelt
(Former First Lady)

Tidbit #5
Here are a few more famous people's signatures. What do you think of them?

Michael Dukakis
(Former Massachusetts Governor)

Ted Kennedy
(U.S. Senator)

Debbie Thomas
(Figure skater)

Elizabeth Taylor
(Actress)

Jane Fonda
(Actress)

Oliver North
(Marine Colonel)

223

Vidal Sassoon
(Entrepreneur)

Bob Hope
(Entertainer)

Scott Valentine
(Actor)

Donny Osmond
(Singer)

With Best Wishes

Martin Luther King, Jr.
(Civil Rights Leader)

Pop Quiz

1. Which of these five women appears to need the most attention at this time?

Dr. Toni Grant
(Psychologist)

Betty White
(Actress)

Rona Barrett
(Columnist)

Lady Bird Johnson
(Former First Lady)

Ingrid Bergman
(Actress)

The answer is Toni Grant, renowned psychologist who has had television and radio shows across the United States in which she dispenses psychological advice to her listeners. Now what do you think about her signature? Do we have a slight case of bloating here? And what does huge, grotesque, grandiose inflation of capitals mean? Hmmmm . . .

2. Which of these five men appears to need the most attention at this time?

William Shatner
(Actor)

Peter Falk
(Actor)

Jonathan Winters
(Comedian)

Richard Simmons
(Weight Loss Expert)

Ed Asner
(Actor)

The answer is Richard Simmons. Now, what do you think of Richard's signature, folks? Isn't it exactly what you'd expect?

3. Here are two Johns. One is John Hinkley and one is John Lennon. Can you guess who is who? (_Hint:_ Does an assassin feel in the center of all that's going on around him, or on the outskirts?)

A.

B.

John Lennon is _B_ (see full signatures on the following page). Notice that his signature is placed smack dab under what he just wrote, whereas _A_, John Hinkley, placed his signature so far to the right that it has nothing to do with the writing above it. This means one who is socially aberrant, not relating normally in public. It's spatially disassociated with what was written above, meaning one who sees himself not integrating with life around him (the rest of the words). Hinkley sees himself off to the side, not connected with reality.

Also, in some of Hinkley's postcards to Jody Foster, his signature took up the entire bottom half of the card and the writing above it was microscopically small. So what we have is a socially aberrant introvert with a desperate need for attention. How do you think he'll try to get it?

events follow in front steer
me down to levels not scrubbed
completely true promises we heard
ridicule the boy just standing
on borrowed lives waiting once
for a precocious teen exercise her
left wing narcissistic mate

John Hinckley

This is my story both humble and true
take it to pieces and mend it with glue.

John Lennon 1969, Feb.

PART IV
PERSONALITY CHARACTERISTICS

21

HIGH vs. LOW FUNCTIONING INTELLIGENCE

In Part III, we looked at handwriting from a graphological standpoint. That is, we checked out the writing size, slant, pressure, baseline, and so on, and determined what each of these aspects told us. In this section, we start out with a personality characteristic and then look for its corresponding graphological trait.

Obviously, in an introductory book, we cannot cover a great number of personality characteristics in depth. Thus, we will focus on four of the characteristics employers want me to look for when they ask me to examine the handwriting of a prospective employee: Is the applicant intelligent? Can the applicant work well with people, or is he or she best suited to working alone (that is, introverted or extroverted)? Is the applicant motivated and hardworking? Is the applicant honest?

Whether you're an employer or not, these are probably some of the same things you're interested in knowing about others so we've devoted a chapter to each characteristic.

In this chapter we'll concentrate on intelligence and examine the traits that indicate intelligence in a handwriting sample. As noted earlier in this book, this discussion does not necessarily pertain to IQ, as determined by an IQ test, but to the "level of functioning intelligence," which determines whether one is *using* his intelligence and is *acting* intelligently.

Functioning Intelligence Quiz

Once again, to show that without realizing it you already know a great deal about the handwriting traits that indicate the writer's level of functioning intelligence, please answer the following questions.

Pick the most intelligent person, *A* or *B*, in each of the following pairs:

1.

A.   B.

231

2.

A.

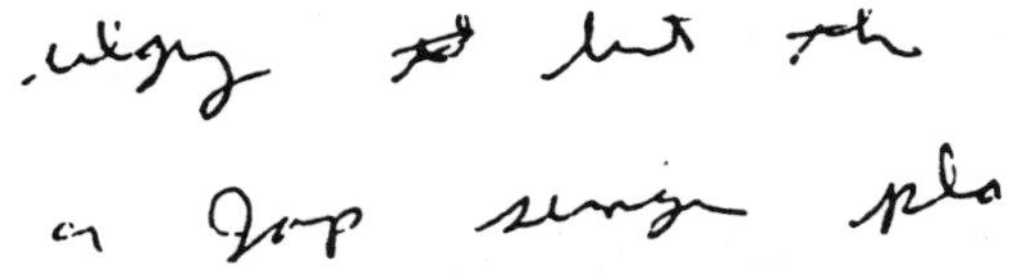

B.

very excited

3.

A.

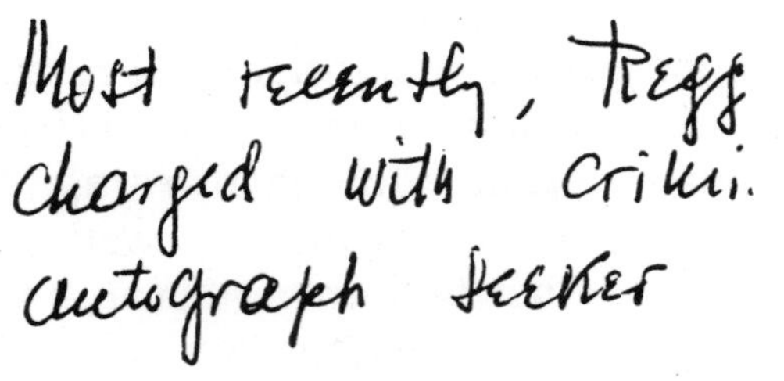
Most recently, Regg
charged with crimi
autograph seeker

B.

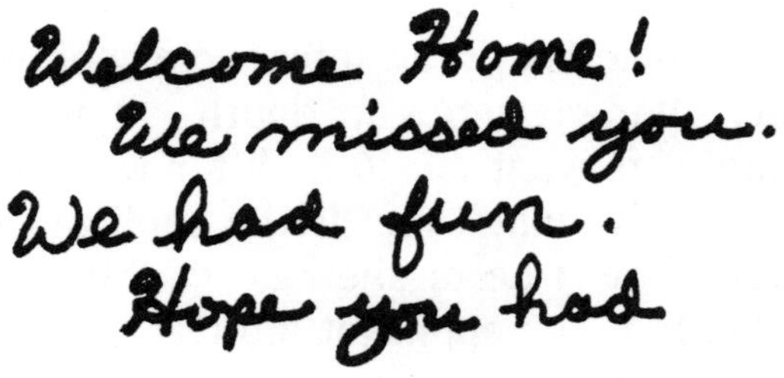
Welcome Home!
We missed you.
We had fun.
Hope you had

4.

A.

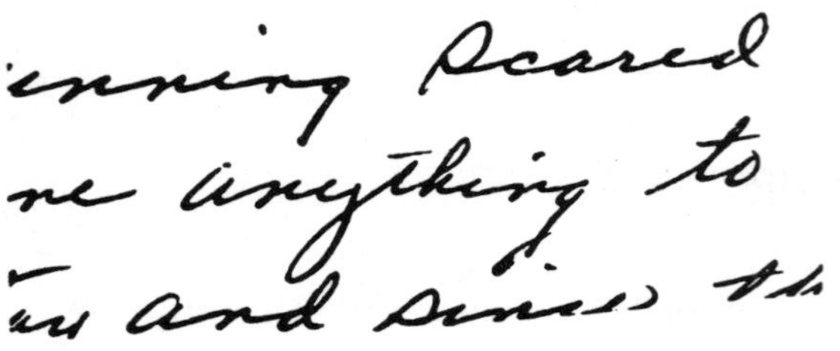
inning Scared
ne anything to
and since

B.

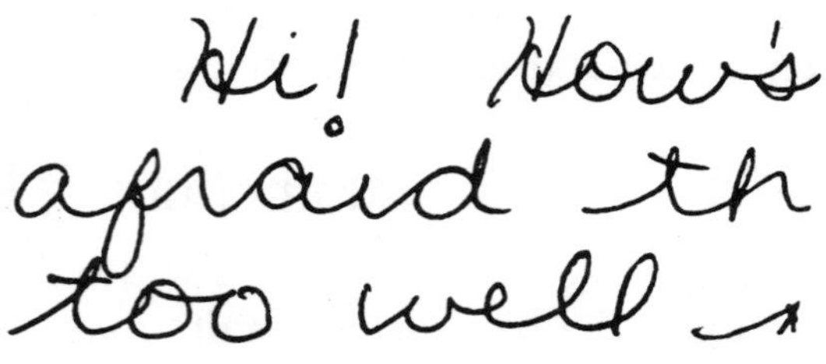
Hi! How's
afraid th
too well

Answers

1. A	2. B	3. A	4. A

Signs of Functioning Intelligence

The following two columns depict the differences between the signs of a high level of functioning intelligence and the signs of low level of functioning intelligence.

HIGH LEVEL	LOW LEVEL
High degree of legibility (capable of communicating).	Lack of legibility.
very excited	
Consistent form level (style), indicating the ability to adapt and behave consistently.	Lack of consistent form level.
don't need my words to at you're done. I just	
Presence of margins and pleasing layout (ability to structure oneself and awareness of life around oneself).	Absence of margins and conventional placements.
Mike, Design West, n Account, asked me see them on Wide	
Fast writing (ability to think and act quickly).	Slow, labored, overly neat writing.

233

HIGH LEVEL	LOW LEVEL
Simplified writing (efficiency, quickness, clear thinking), absence of all but letter essentials, stick figures, no unnecessary flourishes or elaborations.	Adorned, artificial writing or too many lead-ins.
The unfortunate shame inducing may overwhelm	*Thanks loax ! — 4 had a Nie*
Absence of overly round formations, and prevalence of angular and round connectors (receptivity in the garland, and aggression and hard work in the angle).	Overly round writing—found often among the slow-witted or among those who are too passive to use their brains to get ahead.
We will probably together though. It is fast this year.	*Day you e Rah the is*
Medium to small writing (ability to concentrate).	Overly large writing.
mini-readings are awa ne desiring them. Every service and special he rvice on the Second Su	*ALL GOOD / PUNT. WE*
Some originality in any aspect of the writing. Can include stick figures, efficient letter disconnections, changes in letter shape from schoolbook model that enhance speed, such as figure 8s, Greek *e*'s.	Rigid adherence to exact schoolbook model (lack of originality; blind adherence to tradition, right or wrong; refuses to think for self).
Most recently, Regg charged with criku. autograph seeker	*Welcome Home! We missed you. We had fun. Hope you had*

HIGH LEVEL	LOW LEVEL
Rhythmic writing.	Lack of rhythm.
I should dispatch to my sister tomorrow	*uring about another is really different.*
Lack of tangling of zones, or overlapping of letters horizontally (clear thinking).	Tangling and overlapping.
read them often for to the two of us feeling as more than just a	*as long as I as but the on a flight I'll do! Timbucktoo*

If you run your eye down the samples on the left side, the side showing high level of functioning intelligence, what do all these samples have in common?

Two things are basically the same in all the writings: *good rhythm* and *simplified stroking*. No two traits are greater indicators of high level of functioning intelligence than good rhythm and simplified stroking.

Good rhythm is the ability to maintain fairly even spacing between letters, words, and lines.

Simplified stroking, as you will recall, is the ability to write as simply and quickly as possible with the least amount of effort while maintaining legibility. Therefore the writing is devoid of unnecessary strokes and frills.

Now run your eye down the right side of the list, the side showing low level of functioning intelligence. What do all these samples have in common? What is the same about most of them is an awkwardness, a lack of rhythm, and a lack of simplified stroking.

22

EXTROVERSION vs. INTROVERSION

Extroversion-Introversion Quiz

Pick the most extroverted person, *A* or *B*, in each of the following pairs:

1.

A.

B.

[handwriting sample A]

[handwriting sample B]

2.

A.

B.

[handwriting sample A]

[handwriting sample B]

3.

A.

B.

[handwriting sample A]

[handwriting sample B]

4.

A.   B.

Francisco all the way
airport and he flew
real nice hotel called
read in the newspaper

The outro
ray have

Answers

1. A	2. A	3. B	4. B

Extroverts and Introverts

Webster's dictionary defines extroversion as, "in psychology, an attitude in which a person directs his interests to phenomena outside himself rather than to his own experiences and feelings." An extrovert is defined as "a person whose interest is more in his environment and in other people than in himself; a person who is active and expressive, or other than introspective."

Generally, the following can be said of extroverts:

- They need friends and make them more readily than introverts.
- They tend to seek out careers that allow them to interact frequently with others.
- They make their presence known more obviously than introverts in group situations.
- They tend to be expansive in their body movements, gesture often, and dress more colorfully than introverts.
- They tend to travel farther and move more often than introverts.
- They display less fear and apprehension than introverts.
- They are less inclined to suffer from migraines, ulcers, colitis, and certain types of heart diseases than are introverts.
- Most extroverts prefer to work late at night as opposed to early in the morning.

Webster's defines introversion as "a tendency to direct one's interest upon oneself rather than upon external objects or events, or a propensity for finding one's satisfactions in the inner life of thought and fantasy." An introvert is defined as "a shy person, a person characterized by concern with his own thoughts and feelings."

Generally, the following can be said of introverts:

- They prefer to be alone or in small groups and do not need or want many friends.
- They tend to seek out careers where they do not have to meet and greet the public.
- They do not seek attention in group situations.

237

- They tend to inhibit and restrict their body movements and gestures and to dress in a subdued fashion.
- They tend to limit their traveling and stay in one place for longer periods.
- They display greater fears and apprehensions than extroverts.
- They are inclined to suffer from internalizing their feelings by getting anxiety-related diseases such as migraines, ulcers, colitis, and certain heart diseases.
- Most introverts prefer to work early in the morning as opposed to late at night.

Signs of Extroversion and Introversion

Following is a list of graphological traits associated with extroversion and introversion. The traits are listed in order of significance.

EXTROVERSION	INTROVERSION
Large letters—The larger the writing, the more expansive and outgoing the writer.	*Small letters*—The smaller the writing, the more introspective and self-contained the writer.
Wide loops versus retraced loops—The mind and hand of the person are looser, freer, and more expressive when forming a wide loop.	*Retracing of loops*—Retracing results when the mind and hand of the writer are restricted and "uptight."
Garland connections—The garland is the quickest connector and one that requires a soft movement from left (the past and self) to right (the future and others) and symbolizes friendliness.	*Lack of garland connections*—This indicates a lack of friendly links to others.

EXTROVERSION	INTROVERSION
Attention-getting formations—One who seeks your attention by flamboyance in the writing wishes the approval and attention of others.	*Simple and unpretentious style*—This reveals one who does not care what others think or seek their approval or attention.
Huge or flamboyant I with huge or flamboyant signature—These are bids for ego attention by others.	*Reclined or small I with reclined or small signature*—This signals repression or diminished feelings regarding the self.
Heavy pressure—This indicates greater self-assertion.	*Light pressure*—Such a writer shows a lack of self-assertion and intensity.
The ultimate extrovert—The traits are large, loopy, garlanded letters and strokes; flamboyant style; large *I* and large signature.	*The ultimate introvert*—The traits are small, retraced writing; lack of garlands; very unassuming style; small *I* and small signature.

Knowing whether or not someone is introverted or extroverted can be very useful in a number of ways. For example, if an employer needs an aggressive, outgoing salesperson who likes to be on the road a great deal, it would be best to select an extrovert, and definitely not an introvert. Or when attempting to put troubled youngsters into appropriate activities for their temperaments, such knowledge can also be invaluable. And there are countless situations in our daily lives where such knowledge about someone could prove equally beneficial.

23
STRONG vs. WEAK WORK DRIVE

Work Drive Quiz

In each of the following pairs, please pick which writer, *A* or *B*, has the most work drive:

1.

A.   B.

Your questions of are interesting to   *Your coluemn is very*

2.

A.   B.

hit the bat   *hit the bat*

3.

A.   B.

work drive   *work drive*

240

4.

A.   B.

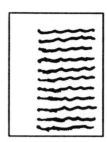   

Answers

1. A	2. B	3. B	4. A

Work Drive

The term *work drive* refers to the amount of effort a person puts forth in whatever kind of work he or she may undertake—as an executive, truck driver, receptionist, baby-sitter, gardener, homemaker, or whatever.

The person with the greatest work drive will have robust writing pressure, uphill writing, rightward tendencies, and strong horizontal movement. We have already looked at pressure, baseline, and rightward emphasis. Now we're going to address what is meant by horizontal movement.

Horizontal Movement

When we examined the universal concept of Left versus Right, we saw that a horizontal movement from left to right symbolizes moving toward the future, toward a goal. So, to assess work drive and ambition in a writing, graphologists look at all horizontal movement.

In addition to telling how much work drive you have, horizontal movement reveals whether you feel positive or negative about your work goals. Thus, horizontal movement (in combination with writing pressure, baselines, and ending strokes) is one of the best predictors of employee performance.

In general, horizontal movement is any straight line going horizontally from left to right. It could be a dash:

It could be an underline:

241

And the easiest place to see horizontal movement is on a *t* bar made with a separate stroke:

what a hit

Because it is simplest to illustrate this trait using horizontal movement made on *t* bars, we will study *t*-bar crossings. Bear in mind, though, that what you see applies to all horizontal movement, not just to *t* bars. An *H* or *A* or *F* made as follows also has a horizontal movement graphologists can analyze:

Hot Fudge Apples

And we can see horizontal movement in ending strokes and stylizing habits:

Make my day. Come on.

In assessing horizontal movement on *t* bars, it is advisable to look at several examples of horizontal movement on a page of writing in order to arrive at an average. In other words, you don't want to look at just one *t* bar and make a determination based on that one letter. Rather, you should look at several *t* bars, dashes, underlinings, and other examples of horizontal movement before arriving at a description of the horizontal movement in that writing sample.

The Four Categories of *t*-Bar Crossings

When measuring horizontal movement on *t* bars, graphologists take into account four separate aspects: the height of the crossing, the length of the crossing, the pressure of the crossing, and the angle of the crossing. In other words, we examine the following:

- How high or low did the writer cross his or her *t*?   T or +

- How long or short was the crossing?   — or +

- How heavy or light was the crossing?   + or +

- Was the line going up, down, or straight across?   + or + or +

242

Here are examples of *t*-bar crossings associated with weak, average, and strong work drive, ambition, and willpower:

WEAK	AVERAGE	STRONG
Low crossing on bar	Medium crossing on bar	High crossing on bar
Short length of crossing	Medium length of crossing	Long length of crossing
Light-pressured crossing	Medium-pressured crossing	Heavy-pressured crossing
Downward-angled crossing	Straight line across	Upward-angled crossing

So, as we see, weak *t* bars (low on the stem, short, light-pressured, and/or downward-angled) are generally associated with weak work drive or laziness. Most people have medium *t* bars in all respects and, thus, have average drive and ambition. Very strong *t*-bar crossings (high on the stem, long, heavy, and/or upward-angled) are associated with workaholics—people with incredibly strong work drive and willpower.

What if there are too many different *t*-bar shapes, sizes, angles, and/or directions in the same writing?

If, when you try to take an average of *t* bars, there are too many shapes and no average to be taken, it signifies a person who is totally undirected with regard to work drive. It's a warning sign of the potential for dangerous, antisocial behavior. This is because among convicted felons and otherwise unproductive individuals there is a high incidence of lack of consistency in their horizontal movement; they don't have any direction in life, they don't have any work goals. So they're aimless. They just hit the streets and do whatever they want.

Motivated people, on the other hand, are the most likely to be stable in their horizontal movement. They have direction and generally know what they want and what they're going after.

The longer and stronger the *t* bars on average, the greater the writer's work drive and motivation. The weaker, more frail, and lower-placed on the stem the horizontal movement is, the weaker the willpower, the weaker the drive and ambition, and the lower the writer's goals.

24

HONESTY vs. DISHONESTY

Research on Dishonesty

Dishonesty is probably the best-researched area in graphology. Studies conducted throughout Europe, South America, Israel, and the Soviet Union have produced ample data correlating a variety of traits with different types of dishonesty. With very few exceptions, the findings from each of these studies are consistent.

As noted earlier, graphology has become sophisticated enough to distinguish between one who is violent, for example, as opposed to one who is merely devious; between one who commits a crime on impulse and one who premeditates the deed.

Signs of Dishonesty

As you read through the traits that correlate with dishonest behavior, it is important to bear in mind that you will generally need to see four or more of these traits in a sample before you can say, "A-ha! This is an actively dishonest person."

There are, however, certain traits that are so strong that of and by themselves they mean active dishonesty. With these traits, which will be denoted with our dependable little guy with his thumbs down, you need not look for several other dishonesty traits to confirm that the writer is dishonest.

Most of the samples of negative traits that follow were written by convicted felons.

Overly Slow Writing

Which writer appears more dishonest?

A.

B.

The answer is *B*. You may remember seeing this before in the chapter on speed. No adult with healthy intelligence should write slowly most of the time. If he does, it means a lack of spontaneity, calculated behavior, a feeling he has something to hide.

Interestingly, when graphologists ask prisoners their names, frequently the prisoners delay a few beats before they answer. Like the overly slow writer, they're being extra cautious lest they give their real selves away.

Obviously, this conclusion does not pertain to the sort of slow writing you'll find on invitations, or in those instances where the writer is trying to be extra careful and neat.

Double or Triple Looped Ovals

Who appears more secretive (less open)?

A.   B.

The answer is *A*. Of and by themselves, double or triple looped ovals simply mean secretiveness. Remember, you can think of the oval as a mouth. When the mouth is open, it means very talkative, and when it's simply closed, it means averagely talkative. Double looped ovals do not necessarily mean the writer is not talkative, but that he is secretive. The words go through a filtering process before they come out. Too many triple looped ovals, however, are getting into the area of deceit.

Stabs in the Ovals

Who speaks with "forked tongue"?

A.   B.

The answer is *B*. Stabs in ovals are actually a fun trait because they so often work in exactly the part of the writing where someone is lying. You saw this trait earlier. It indicates one who speaks with forked tongue—a liar.

Sometimes no ovals will be stabbed until all of a sudden in one sentence several will be stabbed. When you see this, you know the writer is probably not telling the truth about whatever he is writing about at that point.

Where are the stabbed ovals in the sample above? In the *d* and the *a* of *dear*. In the word *that*, the *a* is stabbed. And in the word *what*, the *a* is stabbed.

Wedging

Which writer, *A* or *B*, is more "crooked"?

A.

who is more crooked do you think?

B.

who is more crooked, do you think

The answer is *B*, because that person's writing is wedged. *B*'s writing here and *B*'s writing in the example of stabbed ovals both contain wedged writing, which looks like bent teeth on a saw blade, or like little sailboats in the water.

Wedged writing means dangerously dishonest, criminalistic, crooked, just like the writing. Be careful of anyone with handwriting that looks like this. It is the writing of a potentially dangerous person.

The Felon's Claw

Which writer looks as though he could claw you?

A.

I am

B.

I am

The answer is *A*, the sample with the "felon's claw." This is one of the most delicious traits in all of graphology! It appears in the writing of over 80 percent of convicted felons.

Let's make sure you know what a felon's claw is. A felon's claw is when you come from a straight downstroke and immediately go into a claw shape:

It has to end like a claw.

These are *not* felon's claws:

Because the clawlike line came back to cross the *t*, *A*, *H*, or *G*, this only means tenacity. Anytime you don't want to lift the pen while making a letter, to tie the letter, it means you are feeling tenacious.

When you're making a claw shape, you are going underhand. You are coming under, reversing the natural direction you've been taught.

The felon's claw means subconscious guilt, bitterness, and bad instincts. The felon's claw maker is someone who will pretend to have your best interests at heart. He will seem to be the nicest person on earth. No one would suspect this person of having an evil bone in his body. But then, he is setting you up only to stab you in the back; he will end up clawing you. This is the most frightening because you don't know the knife is coming.

What's the personality profile of a felon's claw maker? From childhood this person has been made to feel guilty about something. Who knows what? But he feels guilty and subconsciously has developed a way to get punished: to come on like the nicest person on earth, and as soon as people treat him nicely back, to turn on them and claw them by doing something detestable—insulting them, robbing them, killing them. When he has done something horrible, we get angry and decide not to like this person, which serves as the punishment he feels he deserves.

When I first learned about this trait while studying in Germany, I balked. How could all these horrible conclusions be made based on just one shape? Well, that was in 1962, and I can tell you that since then this trait has never failed me.

Next time you're looking at graffiti, you will probably see an abundance of felon's claws. The claws are frequently ingrained in the insignias of gangs, too.

Pop Quiz

1. Let's see if you know this instinctively. One of these claws is more significant than the other. Which one's worse?

A.   B.

yes you are   yes you are

The answer is *B*, the one that came up over the baseline. The higher the claw comes, the more serious it is, and the more the writer is conscious of his guilt and criminality.

Now, some people just have a claw like *A*, in the lower zone. That's not as serious. The lower zone represents your libidinal drives. So *A* only has claws in the lower zone; he feels guilty in the sexual areas. Guilty about what? Cheating on his wife? Having sex with animals? Or guilty just thinking about sex because of a rigid parochial school upbringing? Well, answering those questions calls for pretty sophisticated graphology, which is another book in itself.

The felon's claw also frequently occurs in the lower zones of rapists. This does not mean, however, that all people with felon's claws are rapists.

2. What would it mean if your sixteen-year-old daughter always had handwriting with lower zones that looked like this:

I am so happy he's coming

And then one day she came home, and you noticed her handwriting looked like this:

We're going to be sooo happy! What a party we're planning.

What would you do now?

   Get her birth control pills.

3. What do you think it would mean if someone had a felon's claw only in his signature?

Jeff Sanders

   Because your signature represents your public self-image, someone who makes a felon's claw only in his signature feels guilty only about the image he is projecting.

4. Bill writes a thank-you note to the women in the office. What do you think this claw means?

Dear Sally, Jenny and Sandy,

   Something's going on here in the mind of Bill when it comes to Jenny. He's making the claw only on her name, in the lower zone. Hmm. What does he feel guilty about?

Omitted Letters or Pieces of Letters

Who's devious by way of omission?

A.

B.

[handwriting sample A: "ȷ one / disbandent / demostration"]

[handwriting sample B: "of one / disbandment / demonstration"]

The answer is *A*. Another delicious trait! A handwriting that's permeated with missing pieces of letters, missing letters, and missing words indicates someone who is devious by way of omission. This is being dishonest by not telling the whole truth.

What's missing in the words *of one* above? The *o* of *of*, correct? What's missing in the word *disbandment*? The *m*. Now, you have to decide whether the person can spell or not. If he can but is constantly missing parts of the writing, it means he is constantly devious by way of omission. However, if letters or words are missing only on key phrases, then the writer may be feeling deceptive only about those key words or phrases. Or he might not be able to spell at that point. To decide, you have to use common sense.

Continuous Mistakes

Who feels guilty and anxious about his writing?

A.   B.

[handwriting sample A: "California young"]

[handwriting sample B: "California going."]

The answer is *A*. A slip of the pen is highly significant. Here is where graphology gives us clues to our subconscious that our conscious may not know about. Have you ever found this happening: "Gee, every time I write his name, I make a mistake on it!"? This is your subconscious revealing that you are anxious about that person.

If a person can hardly write without making mistakes, something is wrong. It either means he's falling apart physically, mentally, or both, or it indicates he is a dishonest person. If you are looking at an employment application where the writer is constantly making mistakes on, say, his social security number and on many other factual statements, you've probably got someone who's lying.

Retouching

Who goes back and covers his tracks?

A.

I forgot to tell you,

B.

I forgot to tell you.

The answer is *B*. Now, some people will write, for example, the word *had*:

had

and then go back and think, "Whoops! My *a* isn't closed enough!" And they'll go back and do this:

had

That's called retouching. If there are no other signs of dishonesty, this just indicates someone who is overly perfectionistic about himself. This person forces himself to work toward absolute perfection. But if there are other signs of dishonesty in the writing, or if there's a great deal of retouching, then it means someone who covers his tracks, who's used to sneaking around and going back and making sure that he didn't leave any clues. This is the person who falsifies the data, making things look like what they are not.

Signature That is Quite Different from the Writing

Who isn't what she appears to be?

A.

from your loving daughter Elizabeth

B.

from your loving daughter, Elizabeth

The answer is *B*. You learned earlier that a signature different from the script means that what you see is not what you get. It's dishonest in that the person pretends somehow to be something that she is not. This isn't necessarily a liar or thief or criminal. This is someone who puts on airs, puts on an act. She doesn't behave in public the way she really is, and that's a subtle form of dishonesty, too.

Also note the retouching in sample *B*.

250

Exaggerated and Disguised Writing

Who's the con artist?

A.

I hope to see you some time

B.

How are you? I've been miraleste High School. (to Orange Coast and I' my girlfriends, Mary, : Well thats about all.*

The answer is *A*. Exaggerated and disguised handwriting always means a con artist. This is the writing of the bluffer. Intelligent, efficient, and productive people do not feel a need to puff up their handwriting. It is only the fakers, the ones putting on airs, the ones trying to dupe you who overly stylize their writing. This takes a lot of extra time, and it's nonsense. So beware!

Ovals Made Upside Down

Who's underhanded?

A.

I want to go for cake.

B.

I want to go for cake,

The answer is *A*.

Here is an upside-down *o*:

Here is an upside-down *a*:

It is important to know that we're not talking about the writing of children, who automatically want to make ovals in this direction. But when an adult makes ovals upside down, it means underhandedness. This is a trait commonly found in the writing of embezzlers and thieves.

Segmented Letters

Who doesn't let you see the whole truth?

A.

who Do you LiKE FOR GOVENOR ?

B.

OUTSIDE OT SN27 I HAVE BE: SCHOLASTIC soccer MATCHES wi iGNOMINY OVERLOOKED. VALI'n quite often. I WATCH T.V

The answer is *B*. Remember segmented letters from the chapter on printing? When someone prints so that pieces of the letters themselves don't touch each other, this is associated with hiding and deception.

Retracing

Who's inhibiting natural instincts, not telling the truth?

A.

Please go to the market at the center

B.

Please go to the market at the center.

The answer is *A*. Remember that retraced letters have lead-in strokes, but no loop; the pen goes up and down the same stem. Here is a retraced *h*:

h

If you see a perfect Palmer handwriting in all respects, then retraced *d*'s and *t*'s are normal, and you're looking at a very traditional and correct person. However, if the handwriting is not 100 percent Palmer, and if 35 percent or more of the upper zones are retraced, the writer is inhibiting natural instincts to the point of lying.

In this chapter, we have looked at a few of the graphologic traits associated with active dishonesty. Bear in mind that there are several more traits and combinations of traits associated with lack of integrity. However, you have now learned the most basic ways that graphologists deduce those behaviors identified as "dishonest" from someone's handwriting.

PART V
TRYING YOUR HAND AT IT

like the old Indian proverb SAYS
Do not judge a Man until you've walked
2 moons in his Moccosins.
Most people don't Know Me, that is why they write
such ~~other~~ things in wich Most is not True
I cry very very often Because it Hurts and I
worry About the children all my children all over the
World, I live for them.
If a Man could SAy nothing AgAiNST a
character but what he can prove, History could
NOT Be written.
Animals STRike, not from Malice, But because they
want To live, it is the same with those who
CRITisize, they desire our Blood, NOT our
pain. But STill I MUST achieve I must seek
TRuth in all things. I MUST endure for the power
I was sent forth, for the world for the children
BuTHAve Mercy, for live been Bleeding a
loNg Time Now.   MJ.

254

25

YOUR FIRST ANALYSIS

Let's see how you're progressing in your knowledge of graphology. Are you ready to try doing an analysis yourself? Here's a handwriting sample of a man in his late twenties. What would you say about this person based on his writing at this time?

Here are some questions to guide you:

1. What stands out to your eye? What do you notice right off the bat?

2. Is the sample uphill, level, or downhill?

3. How would you describe the margins?

4. What is the slant? Leftward, vertical, rightward, or unstable?

5. What is the style? Is it cursively written, printed, or a combination? Is it stable or unstable?

6. Does the size of the writing remain consistent, or does it keep changing? Is it stable or unstable?

7. Can you guess the writer's education level?

8. What can you say about the signature?

9. Look at the last six lines of writing. What words jump out, and what do you think that means?

10. What can you say about the writer's work drive (horizontal movement)?

Super Stumper
11. What does the writer's use of two different personal pronoun *I*'s mean?

like the old Indian proverb SAYS

Do not judge a man until you've walked
2 moons in his Moccosins.

Most people don't know Me, that is why they write
such ~~things~~ things in wich Most is not TRUe

I cry very very often Because it Hurts and I
wory About the children all my children all over the
World, I live for them.

If a Man could SAY nothing AgAiNST a
character but what he can prove, HiSTORY couiD
NOT Be written.

Animals STRike, not from Malice, But because they
want To live, it is the Same with those who
CRiTiSize, they desire our BLOOD, NOT our
pain. But STill I MUST achieve I must seek
TRuth in all things. I MUST endure for the power
I was sent forth, for the world for ~~my~~ the children
BuTHAVe Mercy, for I've been Bleeding a
lONg TiMe NOW.   MJ.

1. The average person says that the writing looks very downhill, childish, and disturbed.

2. This is very downhill writing. The downhill baseline, remember, is associated with depression, feeling disappointed, disillusioned, down in the dumps . . . very, very down.

3. There are no margins, which suggests a person who doesn't see himself in a normal way in relation to his environment and other people. The words are just there, without any sense of fitting into a framework. And the writing crashes into the right margin in a few lines, indicating the potential to be extremely impulsive.

4. The slant is going in all different directions, which indicates emotional instability. A person whose slant wobbles can be warm and friendly at one moment and cold and aloof the next.

5. This person uses all three styles—cursive, printing, and print-writing; one never knows what to expect. Such lack of consistency usually reveals instability in the way the writer is thinking, feeling, and behaving.

6. Again we see instability. The size goes randomly from big to small. This person can't decide how he is going to behave. The spacing is changing, the sizing is changing, the slant is changing, the style is changing— very little remains the same!

7. The writer's level of education looks low. There are many misspellings, grammatical errors, and misplaced capital letters. Now we have to decide whether the poor level of education evidenced here is due to a lack of formal education or whether it is due to the writer not caring about the rules of correct writing.

   It appears that both reasons may apply here. Spelling errors, such as "wich" for "which," would indicate ignorance or a lack of formal education.

   On the other hand, the fact that *some* of the words contain correct use of upper- and lowercase letters while others do not indicates the writer's lack of concern about whether to put a capital in the middle of a word or not. This shows the writer's disregard for grammatical correctness.

   A lack of concern for something so basic as not putting a capital letter in the middle of a word is associated with antisocial behavior, such as openly defying the norms and conventions of society. In addition, the misplaced-capital maker's lifestyle generally would not be one like a doctor or lawyer or teacher, or anybody who must fit into the mainstream of society. Thus, a person who shows so little regard for the normal conventions of society is usually not going to adhere to a nine-to-five job.

8. First of all, when you use initials to sign something, it means you don't want your real self to be seen. You're giving the reader the minimal amount of information about who you really are. And the fact that these initials are *extra* small means that the real person really doesn't want to be seen at this time.

   Perhaps now we understand why the singer Michael Jackson, whose writing we are analyzing, often wants to wear chains, gloves, sunglasses, and costumes and has had plastic surgery.

9. The largest words in the last six lines seem to be *Blood* and *bleeding*. Remember from the chapter on size that people automatically give size and stature to those thoughts and feelings that loom large in their mind? So for some reason, at this time, "bleeding" and "blood" are looming large in Michael Jackson's mind.

10. The generally long, strong, and high *t* bars reveal that Michael has consistently high personal goals and excellent work drive, willpower, and motivation. Thus, despite the instability revealed elsewhere in the writing, the work drive is exceptionally good here and serves as a balancing factor. When people are ambitious and highly motivated, they are the least likely to become dysfunctional members of society.

SUPER STUMPER ANSWER

11. The writer's use of two different personal pronoun *I*'s generally means that the writer doesn't really know who he is at this time.

    We see Michael uses the cursive pronoun *I* on lines 6 and 8, for example, and then on lines 15 and 17, he uses the printed *I*.

    Remember, the writer's personal pronoun *I* is his personal or private self-image. If you keep changing the shape of your personal pronoun *I*, it usually means you don't know who you are. The cursive and the printed *I* are produced by very different subconscious feelings, and therefore you haven't settled on one private feeling about yourself.

Now that you know this is the writing of Michael Jackson, a number of things in the writing begin to make more sense. For example, consider the poor education level. This may be because Michael did not attend school full-time and, in fact, may have received far less formal education than the average person.

Also consider Michael's unstable slant, letter size, and use of capitals and margins. His behavior includes the kind of unpredictability these handwriting traits indicate: Sometimes Michael shows up and accepts an award, and other times no one knows where he is. Sometimes he's buying the skeleton of the Elephant Man; other times he's doing benefits for people. . . .

It's also interesting to note that Michael wrote this sample to a reporter at *People* magazine during his 1987 world tour, in response to feeling maligned and misunderstood by the press. Thus, Michael's depression at this time is easier to understand.

The circumstance of this writing also illustrates the graphologist's desire to have more than one sample of a person's writing to analyze. Remember that interpretations based on only one sample of handwriting may or may not apply to other writings of that person. For example, here is a signature of Michael Jackson's written the same year as were the set of initials analyzed above. What would you say about his public image now?

And, of course, the time and circumstances under which a signature was written are significant. Was the signature written for the public, to a close personal friend, or on a contract or photograph? In this large signature, what does the cover stroke over the name *Michael* mean? Recall that such an ending stroke signifies a feeling of defensiveness and a need for self-protection.

PART VI
THE USES OF GRAPHOLOGY—
REAL-LIFE CASES
FOR YOU TO SOLVE

26

GRAPHOLOGY AND PSYCHOLOGY

In the preceding sections of this book you've learned what graphology is, how to recognize a number of handwriting traits, and what those traits or combinations of those traits can tell you about personality characteristics. Now let's take a look at some of the applications of graphology. In my experience graphology can have a profound impact in seven major areas: psychology, social work, medicine, education, business, personal uses, and crime solving.

We'll devote each of the next seven chapters to one of these areas. To illustrate how graphology is used in each area, we're going to describe some real-life situations where graphology helped to "crack the case." Many of these cases come from my personal files. But before you read how each was actually solved, I suggest you first try to solve it using what you've already learned about graphology. Now let's get down to cases!

———————

This first chapter illustrates graphology's uses in the field of psychology. By "psychology," I mean studies of the mind as practiced by psychologists, psychiatrists (who also have a medical degree), and other mental health professionals. Graphology certainly can be applied in psychology. In my opinion, every psychologist should analyze a patient's handwriting before doing anything else. In five minutes of looking at a given handwriting sample, a psychologist trained in graphology would know more about a patient than he would know after two years of twice-weekly visits to the doctor's office. He or she would know whether the patient was an introvert or an extrovert, expressive or repressive, stable or not, schizophrenic or psychotic, manic-depressive, taking drugs or alcohol, physically ill, and more.

And if a psychologist would ask his patients to write about their lives, such as their jobs and families, the psychologist would gain tremendous and instant insight into their underlying feelings in these areas that otherwise might go undetected for a long time. For example, a woman might not be consciously aware of her hostility toward her husband. But whenever she writes his name, it is mistake-laden, overly angular, illegible, or out of kilter with the rest of her writing.

Let's look at a case in the field of psychology where graphology can help.

What's Lisa's Problem?

You are recommended to the mother of a ten-year-old girl as someone who might shed some light on her daughter's problems. The mother is out of answers.

Her daughter, "Lisa," has always been a model student, has earned good grades, and is well behaved and well liked. Recently, however, Lisa seems to have fallen apart. Her grades have gone down, and she often gets into fights with classmates and her teacher. The school psychologist has decided that Lisa is so far behind that she should be held back a year and put into a class for disturbed children.

Lisa's mother is extremely distraught. A friend of hers who uses graphology to screen employees has recommended you as someone who can look at a handwriting and determine something about the writer. "I don't want my child held back a year," Lisa's mother tells you. "I don't know what's going on with her, and no one else seems to. Can you help me?"

You tell her to have the child write about school and home life. You'll analyze the writing and tell her what comes to light.

Here's a sample of Lisa's writing. What can you say about her? Do you have any idea what her problem or problems might be? (*Hint:* Does any particular part of the writing start to change in size?)

she won't let me watch any show past

9. and i want to get my ears pearced and she wont let me. My aunt Ruth come and took me shopping.

My Uncle Phil sent me mother a birthday present but he never sent me anything. I don't miss him vary much.

What's Lisa's Problem?

This is quite advanced graphology, so you should be very proud of yourself if you guessed the problem with Lisa.

First of all, would you say Lisa's problem is that she is intellectually impaired? Is this the writing of a ten-year-old child with inferior intelligence?

No. It is not. One must be familiar with the way ten-year-olds write, but I can tell you from studying the writing of thousands of children of different ages and intellectual capacities that Lisa's writing reflects normal intelligence for her age.

Emotionally, however, another picture emerges. We notice a wobbly slant, particularly in the paragraph that starts, "My Uncle Phil sent me. . . ." We also see here that the *U* in "Uncle" got way too big. What does it mean when something suddenly gets way too big? It means an overcompensation for whatever gets too big. Why would Lisa want, or need, to call such attention to the word *Uncle*? Maybe because "Uncle Phil" isn't really Lisa's uncle, and subconsciously she's overcompensating for that when she writes "Uncle."

What else looks different in this paragraph from the rest of the writing? Well, the spacing is off, meaning she stopped and started as she wrote this. The thoughts were not coming out spontaneously. She exhibits the greatest number of mistakes and misspellings, the greatest amount of slant wobble, and the greatest degree of overall instability in this particular area of the writing. So we observe many signs of anxiety associated with "Uncle Phil."

What else suddenly changes size in this area of the writing? What about the lower zone? Isn't it much longer and fuller here when writing about Uncle Phil than in other areas of the writing? What do overly long lower zones mean? They mean feeling restless in the area associated with the body and basic drives. These are unusually big lower zones to see in a girl of only ten years of age and are nearly twice as big as any other lower zones in the sample.

Some of the lower zones in this section are very angular. What can we say about the nature of these feelings then? Are they the soft emotions (like love, ease, gentleness)? Or are they the hard emotions (anger, tightness, aggressiveness)? They are the hard emotions.

So why does Lisa make a big deal about "Uncle" and get very big on her lower zones, too, when thinking about him? What would you conclude? What would you tell Lisa's mother?

Here's How the Story Actually Unfolded

I called Lisa's mother and asked whether "Uncle Phil" was Lisa's real uncle. The mother was aghast! "How did you know?" Uncle Phil, the mother explained, was a good friend of the family and not a real uncle of Lisa's. They just called him "Uncle" so he'd feel more like family.

I continued, "Has Uncle Phil ever spent much time alone with Lisa?"

The mother, beginning to sense what I was driving at, answered slowly, "Yes, after my divorce he used to pick Lisa up from school every day and baby-sit her until I got home."

I prepared a report strongly suggesting that Lisa's relationship with "Uncle Phil" be examined in greater depth, as this appeared to be the source of a tremendous amount of anxiety and repressed anger in Lisa.

Lisa's mother then took Lisa to psychology professionals, who concluded that Lisa had, in fact, been molested by "Uncle Phil." The police became involved and subsequently discovered that "Uncle Phil" had been convicted of child molestation in Alabama eleven years prior and had failed to register as a sex offender when he had come to California, where Lisa and her mother lived.

27

GRAPHOLOGY AND SOCIAL WORK

In defining the area of social work, I include people who have to make decisions on one or more of the following: whether or not other people should receive or continue to receive treatment, whether or not they stay in prison, whether or not they get welfare, whether or not their children get taken away from them, and so on. These are the kinds of decisions social workers and parole officers make.

How much more information social workers would have if they knew about graphology and were able to apply it! For example, graphology would help in deciding whether a person was ready to have his or her child back. If the person's handwriting revealed that the individual was still incompetent, unstable, or on drugs or alcohol, then he or she would not be ready to be a parent again.

Let's look at a few sociology situations where graphology could help.

YOU ARE THE GRAPHOLOGIST

Is This Man Ready for Society?

You are a probation officer in Los Angeles County. Like most people in your profession who work in the inner city, your case load is unbelievably heavy. Every day you get several new cases—before you've had a chance to review the old ones. If you get even one opportunity to meet with one of the prisoners to whom you've been assigned you feel lucky. Yet, you are eventually responsible for determining whether or not these prisoners are fit to return to society. You're supposed to evaluate their rehabilitation progress and their readiness for the outside world. You rely on reports from wardens, guards, and prison psychologists, but you are very aware that the rate of recidivism in the United States is over 80 percent. You don't want to contribute to this alarming statistic, but what can you do?

Recently, you've been asked to make a recommendation regarding a certain prisoner with whom you've spent a total of five minutes. The guards report that his behavior in prison has been good. The prison psychologist says that, based on the prisoner's perfectly normal behavior in therapy sessions, the man is probably reformed.

Following is a sample of the prisoner's handwriting, which you've requested. It was written on lined paper with a vertical left margin. Based on what you see, would you recommend parole or continued confinement? Why?

HAVING DARK BRICK, WITH A WOODEN DECK A/ WITH tHE SURROUNDING GROUNDS EXtREAM/y WELL tERRACED AND /ANDSCAPED. tHE EytE WALL/ COU/D HAVE METAL INSERt/ IN ORDER tHAt tHE HONEY5iC/E VINES MIGHt C/iMB. MARtHA'S ROOF COU/D SERUE AS A SUN-1 A/So I wou/b /iKE to SAy tHAt MARtHA COU/b ACCOMMODATE 500 INDUCtEE/ At 1 tiME. At tHE MAIN ENtRANCE tHERE COU

YOU ARE THE GRAPHOLOGIST: SOLUTION

Is This Man Ready for Society?

Well, let's look closely at his writing for some clues.

Is the right margin normal? It is difficult to see in this sample, but the right margin is crashing into the right side of the paper. This means that the writer does not plan ahead, is dangerously impulsive, and doesn't learn from his mistakes. It's as if there's a wall there at the end of the paper and the writer doesn't see it; he just crashes into it.

Is the left margin normal? No, it is abnormal too. This is equally disturbing as crashing into the right side of the paper because it's so abnormal. Remember this trait in Ollie North's writing? Why write on paper that has a left vertical margin line if you're going to ignore it? Remember that a left margin represents the line of society, and when the writer totally goes out of its bounds, he's symbolically going out of the bounds of the lines of society.

What else about the writing is abnormal? It is too controlled. Remember that overcontrolling is a compensation for an inner fear of loss of control. This man is trying to write perfectly. What we see here is a writing that has a stilted, abnormally slow quality to it, indicative of one who is one step away from cracking up. What the therapist sees, though, is an overly controlled individual who seems to have a good hold over the outward demonstration of his emotions. *He* appears normal; *his handwriting* does not.

What about the distance between the words? It is overly wide, meaning he puts an abnormal distance between himself and others; he is paranoid and suspicious of the motives and intentions of others because he himself is untrustworthy. The writing is also extremely slow and block printed, indicating a person who doesn't want to reveal his real self. And there is an abundance of clubbed strokes, meaning cruelty.

So, based on this sample of handwriting, would you conclude that this man is ready for society, or should he continue to receive professional help and remain in confinement?

266

Well, when we see a combination of traits, all of which mean a scary individual, the whole becomes greater than the sum of its parts, and it's even more frightening than each trait considered separately. Each negative trait becomes that much more negative. Anybody who ignores the line of society in such a flagrant manner and who also has as many signs of dishonesty, violence, and cruelty as we see here is not fit to be loose in society.

This is the writing of James Huberty, who, on July 18, 1984, gunned down twenty-eight innocent adults and children at a McDonald's restaurant in San Ysidro, California, the largest single mass homicide in the United States to date.

YOU ARE THE GRAPHOLOGIST

Should We Let Him Out?

Once again, you're a probation officer. A prisoner is being reviewed for parole. You've been asked for your recommendation. Should the man be released, or do you recommend continued confinement? Here's his writing:

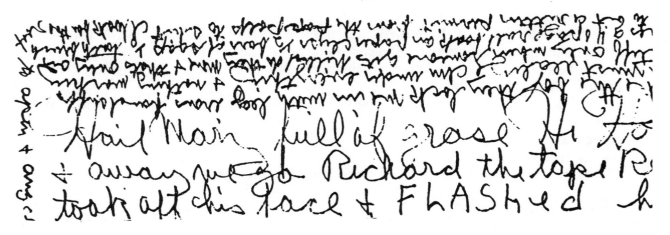

YOU ARE THE GRAPHOLOGIST: SOLUTION

Should We Let Him Out?

This decision should be all too obvious. The answer is no. And convicted mass-murderer Charles Manson (whose insane writing this is) probably won't be freed too soon.

28

GRAPHOLOGY AND MEDICINE

According to Huntington Hartford in his book *You Are What You Write*, numerous scientific studies have concluded that many deadly illnesses show up in the handwriting long before the onset of any clinical symptoms. Often the body knows it is sick before we have any conscious awareness of the problem. So if we could get to that information, just think how much earlier we could seek treatment for diseases such as cancer and heart disease, and perhaps save lives.

An interesting case was illustrated in an episode of the popular TV series "St. Elsewhere." A patient was donating his blood intravenously to his critically ill daughter in the bed next to him. To determine at what point it would be dangerous for the man to continue donating, each hour a nurse came in and made the man sign his name on a chalkboard. When suddenly he couldn't write legibly anymore, the doctor stopped the treatment.

What this show dramatized is that, if at any point you are unable to physically write anymore, then something is either physically or psychologically wrong. It's an immediate tipoff to get yourself help. If you can't write today, and yesterday you could, something's seriously wrong!

If, however, you've just played racquetball for three hours or are overly tired or anxious, don't expect yourself to be able to write well. But if there are no extenuating circumstances, and suddenly you can't write, hie thee to a doctor.

Let's look at some scenarios in the medical world where graphology might be useful.

YOU ARE THE GRAPHOLOGIST

Who's the Hypochondriac?

Two new patients are waiting in Dr. Cur-um's outer office, both of whom complain of chronic back pain, and both of whom have been to countless other specialists. None of the other specialists has been able to find anything wrong.

Before interviewing them, Dr. Cur-um is looking at a handwriting sample of each of the patients. He immediately suspects that one is a hypochondriac, and the other appears to have a physiological problem. From the two handwriting samples on the next page, can you guess which one is the hypochondriac?

Sample A

I must still be developmentally 14! Ahhargh!
Jesus and pass the mazola oil— things
have not been real easy up here in Luther
Burbank country. Number 1, our house deal
did go the way of all things headed for the
Long Beach reprocessing plant. Our roof needs
to be replaced (and guess who's doing it? My
body aches). And there's this tax initiative
which I'm sure you've heard about — Prop. 13

Sample B

4340 REDWOOD Hy.
SUITE 242,
SAN RAFAEL, CA.

YOU ARE THE GRAPHOLOGIST: SOLUTION

Who's the Hypochondriac?

The hypochondriac is *A*. In this case, it's easier to determine which person is physically sick, because there is an obvious tremor in *B*'s sample.

Tremors are never normal, and when a tremor is uniform throughout the writing, we know that it must have a physiological cause. In all other respects, *B*'s sample appears normal, balanced, and stable.

On the other hand, *A*'s handwriting is devoid of any tremor but has some of the classic components of hypochondria, which we learned about in the chapter on zones. These traits include the combination of a dominating lower zone (preoccupation with the physical) with uneven pressure (the worrier), compulsive use of space (obsessive qualities), and too many underlines and exclamation marks (tendency toward exaggeration).

Thus, on the basis of a superficial screening (naturally, Dr. Cur-um will go much further with an examination, tests, and whatever else is necessary), one person obviously has a physical problem, and the other exhibits signs of something psychologically wrong.

Who's the Drug Addict?

You're a physician. You have in front of you handwritings of two new patients. Which one of these would-be patients is a drug addict, *A* or *B*? Even though you haven't read about this, please take a guess.

Sample A

*following book who don't improve?
They are left thinking they have not
been sincere enough in attempt
& are somewhere not honest.
Hogwash! They are just as sincere.
Only a still unknown factor is
missing in their system.*

Sample B

*ready for three days, but haven't
been able to get to the postoffice
yet to mail it to you.*

YOU ARE THE GRAPHOLOGIST: SOLUTION

Who's the Drug Addict?

The answer is *A*. The clues are the splotches, the weird configurations, and the blackened areas in *A*'s sample. There's something about it that just looks drugged.

Imagine how useful graphology could be to medical doctors if they knew before any medical examination whatsoever that their next patient was a drug addict. Is a patient likely to tell a doctor right off the bat that he is a drug addict or an alcoholic?

29

GRAPHOLOGY AND EDUCATION

Education is another area where graphology's uses are plentiful and necessary. In Chapter 33, "The Future of Graphology," I'll go into more detail about ways that graphology could be applied in education. But for now let's take a brief look at one case.

YOU ARE THE GRAPHOLOGIST

Who's Got Dyslexia?

The following samples were written by children in a class for emotionally disturbed students. Which child should not have been adjudged emotionally disturbed, but really has dyslexia?

Sample A

Mom -
pleaze help Tony
de reobdx for

Sample B

dollars. See, this person already, had a gift certificate so she couldn't have two, she either got to pick a person or to give it back to Music on the Move, she gave it back to Music On the Move. Everybody wanted me to get the Gift Certificate so Music On the Move picked me, and Everybody yelled Lori, Lori, lori, she

Who's Got Dyslexia?

A is a dyslexic who was thrown into the emotionally disturbed class by error. It would be as easy for a teacher to see dyslexia in the handwriting as it is for you.

What is it about the writing that tells you this child has dyslexia? The answer is the reversal of letters, which is one of the first symptoms that something is wrong in the child's brain pattern, having nothing to do with emotional behavior by and of itself. Examples of reversals are *d*'s that look like *b*'s, *n*'s and *w*'s that are upside down, and, in a word, the third letter appearing before the second letter. It's as if you took something and made it cross-eyed; you put things on the wrong side of each other.

In many of these cases, the child isn't getting good grades: he can't read well; he can't write well; and he can't memorize well. Out of frustration, he may act up in class, and the teacher often thinks that the child's problem is a behavioral one. Unfortunately, as a result of dyslexia, the child often develops a behavior problem and is put into the emotionally disturbed children's classes. A quick view of the child's handwriting would reveal that the culprit is really dyslexia.

On the other hand, *B* should be getting psychological counseling. This child is not reversing letters. What's wrong here is that the writer is showing the signs classically associated with depression and emotional instability: the slant is wobbling, the pressure is changing, the size is going from small to huge, and everything about the writing is inconsistent and mistake-laden. These traits are evidence of a behavioral problem.

30

GRAPHOLOGY AND BUSINESS

There are countless uses for graphology in business. Let's look at these three areas:

1. Hiring
2. Firing
3. Establishing who works well with whom and whom to promote

Hiring

You've already seen how much information one handwriting sample can give you. We can often use this information to determine the right person for the right job, answering such questions as: What's this applicant's intelligence level? Is he honest? Is he hardworking? Should he work alone or with others? Should he be in sales, or is he better suited to working with small details over long periods of time?

Employers also frequently ask me to analyze whether a prospective employee's handwriting indicates he is on drugs or alcohol. We will not go into the graphological signs associated with alcoholism or drug abuse, however, for they are enormously complex. Suffice it to say that if a writing is shaky, tremorous, excessively mistake-laden, or otherwise "unhealthy" looking, then there is probably something wrong with the writer, and it would not be wise to hire someone in this condition.

The data overwhelmingly support graphology's usefulness on the front end; it saves dollars for everybody. You can tell more about an applicant in a few minutes of looking at his handwriting than you can after administering a psychology test, running a credit check, giving a medical examination, giving a battery of aptitude tests, and interviewing him for an hour in person.

YOU ARE THE GRAPHOLOGIST

Whom Would You Hire?

Look at the three men pictured on the following page. All three have applied for an accounting job in your firm. They all have the same college degree, all are likable, and they all come highly recommended. Which would you hire?

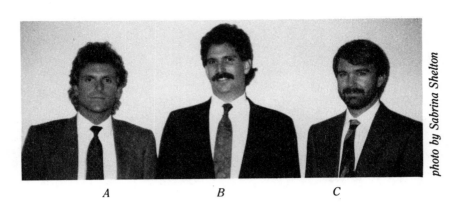

A   B   C

Based on this information alone, you couldn't possibly know which one to hire. But what if you saw their handwritten applications? Which one would you pick?

Sample A

laude from UCLA and went on to get my MBA from Loyola University. I passed my CPA exam in February.

Sincerely,

Alan Campbell

Sample B

Thank you so much for taking the time to meet with me. I was very impressed with your entire operation. The staff was cordial and helpful. I sincerely hope that I can become part of your team.

Sincerely,

Phil Doherty

Sample C

I love our interview, when I received an offer from another organization, I have until the end of the week to let them know.

Best regards,

Paul Gianini

274

Whom Would You Hire?

I hope you picked *A*. *B*'s and *C*'s writings spell trouble, for different reasons. *B*'s is totally unstable, going in every direction possible, with nothing being level or even. The writer is therefore totally unstable. *C*'s writing is so acutely angular as to look like teeth on a saw blade, and you don't need anyone in your company with such acute angularity! This is someone who's so uptight he's like a rubber band about to break, about to explode at any moment. This could make *C* a definite liability. *A* is emotionally repressed (leftward slant) but is otherwise exhibiting stability, neatness, and detail.

All three men have charming signatures, and that's what an interviewer would see: bubbly, outgoing, charming, confident, friendly exteriors. The rest of the handwriting tells the real picture, however.

FRANK AND ERNEST ©by Bob Thaves

Firing

People are fired from their jobs for many reasons, including incompetence, frequent tardiness, insubordination, lack of productivity, and difficulty in getting along with others. Where a graphologist is often instrumental is in pointing out the guilty party when a crime has been committed within the company. This often leads to the firing of the "bad guy."

This use of graphology overlaps the area of criminology, or investigative work, in several instances. We will look at several examples in the coming chapter on crime solving.

Many companies sustain substantial losses due to employee theft. Actually, employee theft is one of the leading reasons for companies going out of business. The U.S. Department of Commerce estimates that in 1988 $182 billion was lost by U.S. businesses due to crimes committed by their employees. Nearly $100 billion is spent annually on security measures designed to prevent these internal crimes.

Obviously, the thieves are being hired in the first place (the companies didn't use graphology to start!), so the problem is that someone in the department is stealing, or embezzling, or coming in late at night and emptying out the warehouse. Who's doing it?

Cartoon reprinted by permission of NEA, Inc.

A skilled graphologist can take statements written by the suspects and know when they're lying, when they're feeling stressed or anxious. Very often, without costly investigation, a quick screening of the suspects' handwriting will alert the investigators to the probable suspects in the case. The investigators can then narrow their focus and zero in on the people most likely to have perpetrated the crime.

Establishing Who Works Well with Whom

An important job of the manager is to get subordinates to work as an effective team. Graphology can provide insights into workers' character, helping managers to bring together compatible people or to understand and alleviate conflicts.

YOU ARE THE GRAPHOLOGIST

Why Isn't This Project a Success?

Two department heads have been assigned to work together on a project. Suddenly their productivity level has gone way down, and there's constant dissension between them. Let's take a look at their writing and see what might be the cause:

Sample A

- 4 hops in 2 months to avoid sentencing for breaking shored neck
- manipulative
- L.D. through school - no college / dropped out 10th gr.

Sample B

The whole family will be coming out for the holidays. I'm so excited!

Why Isn't This Project a Success?

In this instance, these two people do not get along because they are so unalike. *A* is very repressed and leftward, doesn't want to express emotional feelings. She is also introverted, with very small writing, and writes downhill and slowly, meaning she is depressed, disillusioned, and cautious. *B* is very rightward, is demonstrative, wants to operate on an emotional level. She is also extroverted, comes on big, and is very uphill, full of enthusiasm, speed, and spontaneity.

Thus, these two women spend all their time disagreeing with one another because they don't like each other. On the other hand, if one of these people were the boss and the other person had to take orders from her, their differences in character might not be a problem. They wouldn't have to work side by side; they'd be of different rank.

Establishing Whom Should Be Promoted

Graphology is also useful when promotions are at hand. Suppose you know that a certain employee is good where he is, but now you want to promote him to an area where you don't know if he'll necessarily be as skilled. Let's say he was taking orders where he is now working so efficiently, and you want to move him up to manage a department of fifty people. Is he as good a leader as he is a follower? These types of questions can be answered by a graphological screening.

31

GRAPHOLOGY AND PERSONAL USES

Is there any time in your life when knowing if someone were intelligent, hardworking, honest, healthy, and stable would be of use to you? I'll bet you said, "Yes!" Let's look at some everyday situations.

YOU ARE THE GRAPHOLOGIST

Which Person Would You Hire as Your Housekeeper?

You've had three disastrous housekeepers in a row! The first one showed up only half the time, the second one didn't understand a word you said, and the third one robbed you blind! So you've decided that this time you'll make use of handwriting analysis to assist you in hiring a good housekeeper once and for all. Whom would you hire, *A* or *B*?

Sample A

> things better. I still at times
> feel guilty over things that
> I haven't done, it keeps
> me from doing some things

Sample B

> so nice doing all the fun
> things that we had planned.
> Most of all eating all

278

Which Person Would You Hire as Your Housekeeper?

I just wanted to make sure you were paying attention! The answer is *B*.

What's wrong with *A*? What *isn't* wrong with *A*? That person's writing is permeated with felon's claws; it's overly slow, retouched, and bent. The distorted letter shapes further reveal psychosis.

So if you want to hire a housekeeper who is a thoroughly corrupt nut case—go with *A*!

There are endless other uses for graphology in your daily life. Here are just a few:

- With whom should you go into business?
- Whom should you date?
- Whom should you hire as your baby-sitter? your contractor?
- Who would make the best bookkeeper, accountant, gardener, auto mechanic, house-sitter, etc.?

32

GRAPHOLOGY AND CRIME SOLVING

Crime solving is probably one of the most exciting areas for the graphologist. Why? Because if an employer hires someone a graphologist advised against, it may take a long time before the employer realizes the graphologist was right, for negative traits don't always surface right away. But in crime solving the information the graphologist provides can often help catch the culprit quickly, so in many instances the graphologist sees the results of his work right away.

In crime solving, the number one way that graphology is useful is in discernment of falsehoods in written statements. When a crime is committed and I am brought in to help, my standard procedure is to ask the company or investigating firm to have all possible suspects write statements on unlined paper describing where they were on the day in question, everything they did, and everything they know about the crime, and to finish the statement with a declaration that they did, or did not, commit the crime and do, or do not, have any knowledge about it.

YOU ARE THE GRAPHOLOGIST

Who's Setting Fire to the Plastic Surgeon's Office?

You're sitting in your office one day when you get a call from Chester, the head of a security firm. Chester has been retained by the owner of a large medical office building to solve a series of mysterious fires that have broken out over the past four months. Clearly arson, each fire was set late at night in the seventh-floor office of Dr. Re-does-em, a plastic surgeon.

The possible suspects are numerous, as Dr. Re-does-em has had trouble with three former employees and is currently being sued by several patients. Apparently, some of these patients thought they were going to come out looking like Liz Taylor and ended up looking like one of Liz's husbands instead! So maybe one of these disgruntled patients has decided to do a little "de-facing" of her own, starting with the doctor's offices!

Chester explains that he's calling you on the recommendation of a friend and wants to know if you can look at the handwriting of the suspects in the arson fires and find the guilty party. You explain that you will find out what personality traits are common to arsonists. Then you can look at the handwriting of the suspects to see if any of them have those characteristics. Chester agrees to secure the handwriting of the suspects while you seek out a member of the psychology teaching staff at the local university to learn what traits are common to arsonists.

You find out that, in general, arsonists are severe introverts (small writing size), and unlike most criminals, they have no desire for public recognition (small signature). Arsonists are frequently repressed people (leftward slant) with deep-seated sexual deviation or sexual problems (abnormal lower zones), obviously aren't very stable (unstable writing), and are usually angry (tics, tightness, angularity).

Chester later gives you the writing of fifteen suspects, but none of the samples matches the description of the arsonist. You tell Chester, and ask him if there are any other suspects.

"Well," the chief of security admits, "seems like every time we turn around, we have more suspects. It seems there's no shortage of people who have it in for Dr. Re-does-em. Everyone hates him! Even his wife and kids! Even his mistress! The parking lot attendants in the building curse him out in Spanish! And to top it off, Dr. Re-does-em informed me that he's started having problems with some of his colleagues in the building, and some of *their* staff, too! Anyhow, we've pretty much ruled out members of his personal life, because the arsonist obviously has access to the building. We're fairly certain whoever's doing this is someone who works in the building."

"Can you get me those people's handwritings?" you ask.

"I can't figure out how I can because I'm under strict orders to make sure no one knows they're being investigated. The building owner is terrified of being sued. Those first writings I just got you out of the doctor's file cabinets. I don't know how I could get the others, though. I guess we're at the end of the road with graphology. . . ."

OK, Super Graphologist, what would *you* do at this point?

I had to think of a way to get the samples of these people without their knowing about it. I asked Chester if there was anyone who went into these offices from the outside, so that maybe we could secure handwritings from the trash cans, drawers, or tabletops of these other suspects.

Chester said, "No. No one else, other than the cleaning crew that comes in at night."

Aha! Next thing I knew, I found myself dressed in a little pink cleaning woman's uniform entering the building where the fires took place. I had been told to ask for Marjorie, the head of the floor crew for the seventh floor, who had been alerted that I was coming.

As I scrounged through wastebaskets and desks collecting writing samples, I remember being suddenly struck with a thought: What if the arsonist shows up right now? What if he decides to torch the place while I'm foraging in a back office?

I found several samples I wanted to examine, and was loading my apron, when suddenly I was interrupted by a very large, very mean-looking, very, very ugly cleaning woman who wanted to know what the hell I was doing there!

I nervously explained that I was new and was part of the cleaning crew assigned to this suite of offices.

"No, you ain't!" she accused, her eyes narrowing.

"Yes! Marjorie assigned me here. I'm supposed to handle this suite of offices," I exclaimed.

She stared menacingly at me. "No one told *me* about you! I'm head of cleaning for the building, and I never seen you before! You don't look right! You don't belong here, and you got no cause to be here!" She grabbed a broom off a cart, and held it with both hands like a baseball bat, ready to attack if necessary.

I made a sudden decision to get the hell out of there! As I dashed out the door and down the hall toward the stairs, the monster cleaning woman was right on my tail, screaming obscenities at me, waving the broom . . .

Below are four of the writings I gathered from the offices. Do you think anyone would match the arsonist profile of (1) severe introversion, (2) instability, (3) repression, (4) anger, (5) deviant sexuality, and (6) no desire for public recognition?

Sample A

Dr. Gray called regarding
meeting for lunch on Wednesday.
Call him after 5 pm.

Joe

Sample B

Mrs. Connally called again, wanting to
know if X-ray has any Report,

Sidney

Sample C

Mary, I will be away all thursday morning in surgery.
please reschedule any and all appointments.

Norman

Corey!
I'm Leaving early on Tuesday,
My Parents are flying in.
I hope that's okay!

Shelly.

YOU ARE THE GRAPHOLOGIST: SOLUTION

Who's Setting Fire to the Plastic Surgeon's Office?

Did you guess correctly that the arsonist was *B*? If you did, you probably saw each of the six qualities. Let's take a look at each one:

1. *Severe introversion*—Small writing is associated with introversion. And since we're after the "severe" introvert, we're looking for *very* small writing. Suspects *B* and *C* have very small writing.
2. *Instability*—To determine instability, we look to see if a writing keeps a reasonably stable quality in regard to such traits as slant, sizing, baseline, margins, and spacing. *A* seems the most unstable, but *B*'s writing has some elements of instability, too, such as misplaced capitals and abnormal letter shapes.
3. *Repression*—*B*'s and *C*'s samples both have leftward slants, meaning they hold back their real emotional feelings.
4. *Anger.* *A*'s and *B*'s samples both have excessive temper tics, tightness, and angularity, which means the writer is angry, frustrated, uptight, ready to explode.
5. *Deviant sexuality*—This clinches it for *B*. The lower zone shapes are bizarre and reversed, meaning abnormal libidinal drives. The lower zones in the other three samples are normal.
6. *Shrinks from the public*—Did you notice that *B* also has the smallest signature in comparison to the rest of his writing, meaning that he does not want public attention?

Here's How the Story Actually Unfolded

I called Chester and told him I'd found someone who was an angry person with criminal tendencies and who definitely fit the profile of an arsonist.

Chester had the man put under surveillance. One evening some weeks later, the suspect was caught red-handed trying to enter the building with an incendiary device in his briefcase.

283

Who Murdered the Secretary's Boss?

A secretary who was responsible for throwing a surprise party for her boss drove to work the night before the party to secretly decorate his office.

She used her key to enter the building. As she approached her desk, she heard the voices of two men engaged in a heated argument inside her boss's office farther down the hall. She recognized her boss's voice but not the other man's. She stopped and decided she should probably leave and come back later.

Just then the argument grew louder and more furious, and the unidentified man began screaming and threatening her boss, saying, "You used to tell me you love me. You used to give me compliments and show me your feelings! And now you don't, and I can't stand it! I sit at home alone, day after day. And now you're spending all your time with Boomer! Don't lie to me! I know you are! And, I'm going to get rid of him. Boomer is history tonight!" Frozen, the secretary listened to the man grow angrier and angrier, until suddenly a gunshot rang out!

Shocked and not wanting to be seen when the killer emerged from the office, the secretary dove under a desk. She watched a man's feet dash past her and out the door. Paralyzed for a few moments, she finally got up and slowly entered her boss's office. She found his bloody, lifeless body slumped over his desk. She called 911.

At about 11:00 P.M., you receive a phone call, and a police detective tells you he is calling because you were recommended by another detective who you helped on a case similar to the one they have right now. It seems that you can look at handwritings and tell who's homicidal, right? Frequently you can, you tell him.

The detective tells you about the secretary and the murder of her boss. There is urgency now because of what the secretary overheard—that the killer is going to kill someone else tonight, and they want to prevent that, if possible.

From what the secretary overheard, the police have surmised the killer was a disgruntled former employee who may have been having a homosexual affair with the boss. He apparently didn't mind not having his job, or even sitting alone waiting for the boss to call, but he really minded that the boss never called anymore. The killer accused the boss of using his power to hire men he wanted to seduce, and the killer said he "knew" about the boss and another man he called "Boomer." Just before the killer pulled the trigger, he screamed that neither the boss nor "Boomer" would be coming into Comtrex Industries ever again!

You tell the detective you will be right down, and that he should have someone at the company pull out the files of all employees who have quit or been fired within the past twelve months.

When you arrive, they have pulled sixty-four applications of men who had quit or been fired during that time. This is a huge company with thousands of employees. You split the applications into two piles: stable and highly unstable.

On the following page are four of the applications that made it into the "highly unstable" pile. Can you figure out who the murderer is from these samples?

And, by the way, if you can, you might also be able to find out who his next victim is and prevent *his* murder!

Sample A

IF RELATED TO ANYONE IN OUR EMPLOY
STATE NAME AND DEPARTMENT
(OMIT NAME OF SPOUSE)

(ACCOUNTING)
SUSAN LITTLE

REFERRED BY SUSAN

FIRST

EMPLOYMENT DESIRED

POSITION SYSTEMS ENGINEER

DATE YOU CAN START Now

SALARY DESIRED 30,000

ARE YOU EMPLOYED NOW? YES

IF SO MAY WE INQUIRE OF YOUR PRESENT EMPLOYER? IT'S OKAY

MIDDLE

Sample B

IF RELATED TO ANYONE IN OUR EMPLOY
STATE NAME AND DEPARTMENT
(OMIT NAME OF SPOUSE)

Nobody

REFERRED BY Jerry

FIRST

EMPLOYMENT DESIRED

POSITION Computer operating

DATE YOU CAN START May 1, 1986

SALARY DESIRED 2400/month

ARE YOU EMPLOYED NOW? yes

IF SO MAY WE INQUIRE OF YOUR PRESENT EMPLOYER? NO. I don't want them to...

MIDDLE

Sample C

IF RELATED TO ANYONE IN OUR EMPLOY
STATE NAME AND DEPARTMENT
(OMIT NAME OF SPOUSE)

No

REFERRED BY Sandra Lisbon

FIRST

EMPLOYMENT DESIRED

POSITION Data Entry

DATE YOU CAN START July

SALARY DESIRED 25,000 a year

ARE YOU EMPLOYED NOW? Yes I am

IF SO MAY WE INQUIRE OF YOUR PRESENT EMPLOYER? I would rather you didn't

MIDDLE

Sample D

IF RELATED TO ANYONE IN OUR EMPLOY
STATE NAME AND DEPARTMENT
(OMIT NAME OF SPOUSE)

Fred Conrad

REFERRED BY

FIRST

EMPLOYMENT DESIRED

POSITION Regional Sales

DATE YOU CAN START Now

SALARY DESIRED #32,500 00

ARE YOU EMPLOYED NOW? Yes

IF SO MAY WE INQUIRE OF YOUR PRESENT EMPLOYER? NO

MIDDLE

Who Murdered the Secretary's Boss?

Did you find the killer and figure out who he's going to kill next? Let's take it step by step. What personality traits are you looking for?

Are you looking for an introvert or an extrovert? Well, you know you're looking for a man who "sits alone day after day," so you're probably looking for an introvert and thus *small handwriting*.

What else are you looking for? Remember, the secretary also overheard the killer saying that he missed being praised and told that he was loved. This sounds like someone who is highly emotional. Remember, repressive people bend over backward to avoid emotional situations; they aren't looking for someone to tell them that they're loved. So you're looking for a *rightward to far rightward slant*.

You're also looking for a homosexual, so you're looking for "versatile" sexuality, or *"abnormal" lower zones*.

It also sounds very much like the killer does things on impulse. He pulls a gun out and kills a man. Can you recall a trait that indicates that someone is impulsive? It's where the writing *crashes into the right margin* again and again.

And most likely you're looking for someone who is uptight and angry. Therefore, you are not looking for roundness, but *angularity*.

Finally, someone who takes a gun and goes to kill people is obviously unstable. So you're looking for *unstable writing*.

In summary, you're looking for small writing, a rightward slant, abnormal lower zones, a crashing right margin, acute angularity, and unstable writing. Suspects *B* and *C* both have these elements present in their writing. What do you conclude?

Here's How the Story Actually Unfolded

When I saw these writings by *B* and *C*, I was struck by something in the "Referred by" portions of the samples. Suspect *C* had been referred by a woman ("Sandra Lisbon"), while Suspect *B* had simply written "Jerry" in the same space. "Jerry" was written very large, showing he was given high regard by the writer, and the lower zone on the *J* was overly long, bloated, and twisted, showing a "deviant" physical or libidinal feeling toward Jerry. Suddenly I had a flash! Could "Jerry" be "Boomer," the man who "would not be coming into Comtrex" ever again?

I told the detective of my strong feeling that Suspect *B* was the killer, and that whoever "Jerry" was could well be "Boomer" and, therefore, the next victim.

After dispatching some men to try to find Suspect *B*, the detective asked, "Well, who the hell is 'Jerry'? We've got to get to him. It may already be too late!" With the help of the boss's secretary, they figured out who Jerry was.

Suspect *B* was not at his home, and two officers staked out his house. When Jerry couldn't be reached by phone, and when no one answered his door, the police staked out his house as well.

A man matching the description of Suspect *B* arrived at Jerry's home and knocked on Jerry's door. The police on stakeout approached the man as he attempted to break into Jerry's house, and the man fled. He was apprehended and did, in fact, turn out to be Suspect *B*. He was carrying a gun, which later was found to be the gun used in the murder of the boss.

Who Stole the Diamonds?

One afternoon you get a call from the operations manager of a chain of jewelry stores, who tells you that they have just discovered $30,000 in raw diamonds missing from the safe of one of their stores.

"It has to be one of the seven employees who work in the store. Can you help us?"

So you tell the manager the procedure and you get the statements. You narrow the suspects down to the following two people. Here are their statements. Who do you think stole the diamonds?

Sample A

I would never do anything like this. I shouldn't even be a suspect! I have no knowledge of the theft and did not participate in any way.

Larry Chappel

Sample B

before, and I left at 5:00 p.m. I don't know anymore than this.

Paul Morris

YOU ARE THE GRAPHOLOGIST: SOLUTION

Who Stole the Diamonds?

If you guessed A, you got the bad guy! What is the major difference between the two samples? Both contain many traits associated with dishonesty. But A's signature is huge and adorned with swirls and swishes. What does that mean?

Remember that the signature represents one's public self-image. When it's huge, it means the writer wants to stand out in the crowd, be rich, successful, noticed, a somebody of great social standing. And when the writer decorates the letters it means he wants to be seen as flamboyant. He wants to put all kinds of frills and decorations on himself, just as he does on his letters. Someone with a simplified signature with simple strokes, like *B*'s, is not the type to want to wear a lot of jewelry or want to be looked at in that same material manner.

So *A*'s signature is huge, looks as though it is wearing jewelry, with huge letters, and is as dishonest as they come.

Here's How the Story Actually Unfolded

I told the operations manager of the jewelry store, "I believe Harry is your man." The manager took this information and relayed it to the team of private investigators he had hired to work on the case. The investigators then zeroed in on this particular suspect and intensified their investigation. As a result, they uncovered additional evidence that left no doubt as to this suspect's guilt.

The jewelry store owners just wanted their diamonds back. They approached Harry and offered him a deal whereby if he gave back all the jewels, the store would not press charges. He then confessed, returned the diamonds, and everyone lived happily ever after . . . well—I hope.

YOU ARE THE GRAPHOLOGIST

Which Employee Is Giving Away Trade Secrets?

You are contacted by a company that develops highly sophisticated, classified computer software for a national defense system in England. They tell you that they suspect their technology is being delivered into enemy hands by one of their employees. Specifically, the company fears that some sensitive secrets have been falling into the hands of Eastern European bloc operatives and/or other communist countries.

In all, there are twenty possible suspects. All of them have passed extensive security scrutiny, and all are supposed to be British to the core.

You are asked to analyze the writings of the twenty suspects to help determine which employees look capable of doing something like this. Which ones look particularly dishonest and capable of committing treason?

Here are five of their writings:

Nigel McAllister

Department. Would you please consider this request at your earliest convenience.

288

Constance Masters

WE HAVE A MEETING ALL SET
FOR a month FROM now. Okay?

Margaret McShane

I am looking forward to meeting
you - at the reception on September 9.

Ian Gilroy

Carlisle, Cumberland, England
28 years of age and 1.

Spencer Wadsworth

in London. Assuming we can produce
this kind of volume, I have every confidence

YOU ARE THE GRAPHOLOGIST: SOLUTION

Which Employee Is Giving Away Trade Secrets?

The most suspicious sample is that of Margaret McShane.

Here's How the Story Actually Unfolded

It was easier than I thought, because I was prepared to do a full dishonesty test on each writing, to rank them 1 through 20, from the most dishonest to the least dishonest. But lo and behold, I came across Margaret McShane's sample. "What's wrong with this picture?" I asked myself. "What doesn't look the same about her writing that we see in that of the other four English people?"

Do you see why the answer is immediately apparent? Someone with a name like

289

"McShane" should not be writing like someone from an Eastern or Central European country. McShane's writing contains several indicators associated with handwriting taught, not in Britain, but in Eastern and Central Europe (as well as South America)!

Here are three letters and how they are made in Western Europe and North America, and how they are made in Eastern Europe and South America:

	WESTERN EUROPE AND NORTH AMERICA	EASTERN/CENTRAL EUROPE AND SOUTH AMERICA
Personal pronoun *I*		
Lowercase *a*		
m's and *n*'s		

The company took it from there and soon discovered that Margaret McShane was actually Ludmilla Katchamakov . . .

YOU ARE THE GRAPHOLOGIST

Suicide or Murder?

One morning you're sitting at your breakfast table reading the paper, when your eyes are drawn to a photo of a piece of handwriting next to an article. According to the caption, the handwriting is a suicide note written by a man who was found dead, hanging from a tree outside a BART subway station in the Northern California area.

Here's a copy of the suicide note. Does it look like the author of this note was feeling suicidal?

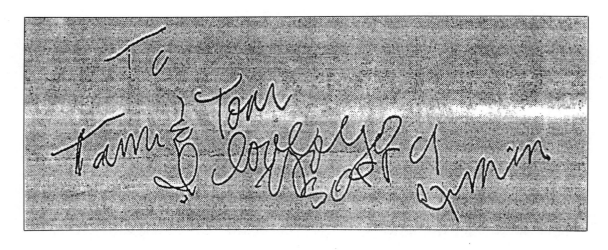

Suicide or Murder?

Look at it a moment; then ask yourself the following questions:

- Is a suicidal person feeling full of mental energy, or lacking in it? Therefore, would you expect the writing to be uphill or downhill?
- Is a suicidal person feeling motivated or unmotivated? Therefore, would you expect the writing pressure to be light or heavy? Would you expect the horizontal movement to be weak or strong?
- Would you expect a suicidal person to be feeling happy and communicating well or not? Is the writing legible or illegible?

Answering these questions shows how every handwriting aspect associated with depression and giving up are missing from this "suicide" note. The writing is up instead of down. The horizontal movement is strong instead of weak. The writing is powerful and heavy instead of feeble and light. Something doesn't compute.

Additionally, when you read the article, you discover that the name of the dead man's sister, to whom the note was addressed, isn't spelled correctly. Also, the pen used by the deceased to write the note was never found. Now why would a man take the time to hide a pen he used to write with before killing himself? The police have also said that no fingerprints whatsoever were found on the note. You read further that the NAACP was unwilling to accept that the man, who was black, committed suicide.

What would you do now, Grapho-Detective?

Here's How the Story Actually Unfolded

The article mentioned the name of a woman at the NAACP. I decided to write a letter to her, offering my services free of charge.

I later examined the alleged suicide note and compared it with the writing of the deceased, and it was clearly a forgery. In fact, four other independent graphologists later came up with the same results. Consequently, the case was reopened, but to date nothing has been resolved.

One of the interesting issues that was brought to light here is: How many such suicide notes that are just presumed to be authentic in fact are not? Authorities often assume that if there's a note a death is truly a suicide. Yet it's so easy to make a hanging or a fall out a window look like a suicide when it isn't. How many of these notes are assessed inaccurately? How many homicides have gone down as suicides?

How Do You Tell Your Client That He's the Bad Guy?

At times, a graphologist also has to be more than just a handwriting expert. For example, you get a call from Tom, the president of a large auto dealership in Southern California, who says he is suffering a loss of nearly a million dollars a year in stolen parts. Tom is certain that someone within his organization is behind the crime, and he asks you to help.

You explain the procedure of collecting statements, and Tom says he is leaving town for a few weeks and is going to have his second-in-command, Arnie, the vice president, call you and take it from there.

When Arnie later calls, you explain how to get all the suspects together and have them write what they do or do not know about the thefts, what sort of measures they would recommend to minimize the thefts, and to furnish a statement that they did, or did not, have anything to do with the crime, then sign and date their statements.

It becomes quite apparent that Arnie has little faith that some handwriting person is going to be of any use, and he has a condescending tone in his voice. He makes it clear he is just doing this to humor Tom, the boss.

A huge package of statements soon arrives, and with it is a patronizing handwritten cover letter from Arnie. Jumping out at you from his writing are blatant deception and active dishonesty!

What do you do, Super Graphologist?

YOU ARE THE GRAPHOLOGIST: SOLUTION

How Do You Tell Your Client That He's *the Bad Guy?*

Here's How the Story Actually Unfolded

I knew I had a major bad guy in Arnie right then and there. And he was the VP! So I went through all the statements to try to piece together what was going on. By looking at the content where each writer felt guilty, I was able to ascertain the scheme. It involved certain employees conspiring with an outside supplier. A certain number of parts were ordered, the purchase orders approved, a lesser amount of parts delivered (although all were logged in), and those involved were pocketing the cash difference.

I immediately put in a call to Tom, the president of the company, and was told that he was on vacation in Mexico and wouldn't return for another week, but he might call in for messages. I told the secretary that I wanted to leave a message for Tom to call me at his earliest convenience. I told her the message was confidential and not to mention it to anyone else.

Within two minutes, my phone rang. It was Arnie, the vice president. "I understand you have the results, Ms. McNichol. What did you find out?" My heart started pounding! I hemmed and hawed and stammered, "Gee, I'm sorry, Arnie. I put that file at the bottom of the pile, and I don't have the paperwork anymore, and I'm just leaving the office, and I'll have to get back to you—I'm just dashing out the door right now! I'll call you later!"

I hung up the phone and sat there, very shaky. What was I going to do? Tell the guy, "Hey, *you* did it . . ."? No way! This guy scared me to death! His immediate call back to me told me just how desperate and anxious he was, despite any outward skepticism he may have shown initially.

Ultimately, I contacted a friend who was able to use law enforcement contacts and obtain Tom's home phone number. I eventually reached Tom at his vacation hotel room in Mexico and told him the startling findings. After a great deal of resistance to

292

believing such a thing, he decided to hire an outside security firm to see whether an investigation of these people would yield anything.

The security firm he retained, starting with the leads provided, managed to catch Arnie and the other culprits red-handed in this stolen-parts scheme. Several of the participants were subsequently convicted.

YOU ARE THE GRAPHOLOGIST

Did the Aunt Sign the Will Under Duress?

You are hired by a probate attorney named Collins. Collins is representing the nephew of a dead woman who had amassed and saved nearly $2 million during her lifetime. The nephew was shocked to learn that his aunt had changed her will shortly before her death and had named a neighbor, of whom she had never been terribly fond, as one of the heirs to her estate. The attorney of the dead aunt, who had prepared her will, had been named executor of a trust fund that would revert to the nephew's control in ten years.

Collins tells you the nephew feels his aunt must have signed the will under duress because she never would have done something like this. Collins wants you to look at the dead woman's signature and determine whether she wrote it of her own free will.

You ask what the woman's medical condition was at the time she signed the will. You're told she was eighty-three, had been recently hospitalized with her second stroke in ten years, and was suffering from renal and heart failure. She was known to be taking seven different medications.

Here's the dead woman's authentic signature in a 1967 will, and here it is in the 1989 will in question. What would you tell the nephew?

A.

Mayme Jenkins

1967

B.

Mayme Jenkins

1989

YOU ARE THE GRAPHOLOGIST: SOLUTION

Did the Aunt Sign the Will Under Duress?

The signature on the 1989 questioned will was not written under duress but is, in fact, a blatant forgery. This is definitely *not* the writing of an eighty-three-year-old woman who had suffered two strokes along with other debilitating illnesses. This 1989 signature is too smooth and was obviously written by someone much younger and in good health.

So what do you do now, Super Graphologist?

293

Here's How the Story Actually Unfolded

My first thought was to try to discover who the forger might be. I asked the nephew and his attorney to provide me with the particulars of the case. I was given copies of all the files. I soon became acquainted with the handwriting of the attorney who had drawn up the aunt's will and was named executor of it. Lo and behold, as I was poring over documents, I came across the handwritten hospital release form that the old woman had allegedly written three weeks before her death. In it, she asked to be let out of the hospital and released her doctor as her physician. The handwriting, however, was not that of the old woman, but of her attorney!

We theorized that the dishonest attorney forged the old woman out of the hospital so that when she allegedly signed her new will, no one could claim that she was hospitalized at the time and therefore not of sound mind and body. Now the question became: if you forge someone out of the hospital, and then she dies as a result, isn't this murder?

Apparently, the forger had not anticipated that the nephew would hire a lawyer and a graphologist. In fact, police records revealed that this same attorney had been charged in the past in Nevada with gaining the confidence of aged, wealthy people and swindling their heirs out of their rightful inheritances.

I couldn't prove that this dishonest attorney forged Mayme Jenkins's name on the will, but I could prove it was his handwriting on the hospital release form. Unfortunately, I was not allowed to testify at the trial because the nephew's attorney had not disclosed me as a witness during the discovery phase. At that time, he and the nephew had no real knowledge of any foul play and had not yet retained my services. Thus, I'm afraid that this is a case where someone literally got away with murder—on a technicality.

Subsequently, the nephew tried to interest the district attorney's office in his case, but to no avail.

YOU ARE THE GRAPHOLOGIST

Was Patty Hearst Really Brainwashed?

You may recall the infamous Patty Hearst case. Patty was kidnapped by the Symbionese Liberation Army in the early seventies. Later, when she was finally apprehended and charged with robbery, attempted murder, and a host of other crimes, her defense was that she had been brainwashed by her kidnappers.

Here is a look at Patty's writing during her captivity:

We had b' smash the dependencies created by monogomous sexual relationships, and to do this we had to destroy monogomy in the cell. Monogomy only serves to reinforce male supremacy and the oppression of women. Monogomy means that "The men wear the pants." We had to destroy all the attitudes that make people think that they have to be monogomous; fear and passivity, false sense of security, power-trips,

Before Patty was kidnapped, her writing was large, rightward, rounded, cursively connected, and loopy. If you had to decide whether Patty was brainwashed or not, based on what you know about her writing before being kidnapped and what you see here, what would you conclude?

YOU ARE THE GRAPHOLOGIST: SOLUTION

Was Patty Hearst Really Brainwashed?

In my opinion, Patty had definitely been psychologically altered between the time she was a happy high schooler and the time she was writing death threats to her parents.

I was struck by how dramatically Patty's writing changed after she was kidnapped. It went from round, rightward, large, Palmer-style writing to being small, printed, and leftward, all of which are graphological traits associated with withdrawing into a world of her own and disassociating herself from life around her. The smallness means she grew introverted. The leftward slant means she did not want to feel, or to show any feelings. And the printing signifies not wanting to reveal her real personality to others.

It's inconceivable that Patty plotted to change her handwriting at the time she was in captivity so that she could later argue that she had been brainwashed. How could she have known which traits meant what?

Had anybody seen the difference in Patty's writing, I think it would have been an immediate demonstration of her innocence. It certainly convinced me that she had been brainwashed.

It's interesting to note that Patty Hearst's original attorney had three graphologists set to testify in her defense. The judge in the case had ruled that such testimony would be admissible, provided the graphologists established their expertise.

At the last minute, however, for some unknown reason, Patty's attorney canceled the graphologists, and I believe that this was the reason he lost the case. Had the attorney shown graphically how Patty Hearst's handwriting had changed, I think it would have been visual, hands-on proof that she had been brainwashed. A picture is worth a thousand words.

Death Threats

Death threats are a very big problem for people who have a lot of money and are known to the public, people such as celebrities, politicians, and heads of major corporations. They are particularly susceptible to extortion, blackmail, and other such crimes.

Nearly every movie star receives a daily bunch of such threats. Some people think that the last character an actor played in a movie is really the actor, and if he happened to play a bad guy these people want to blow him away. Or they want his money. The same is true of politicians: "You made a bad law, and I lost my job! You're gonna be a dead man!"

If the note is handwritten, a graphologist can play an invaluable role in helping to determine whether the threat should be taken seriously, or whether it was written by someone who simply likes to hear himself talk. If it should be taken seriously, a graphologist frequently can ascertain additional useful information about the writer, including the writer's ethnic origin, education level, background, handedness, what type of job he might have, and whether he appears young or old, is physically ill, is an alcoholic or drug addict, or is violent.

Jody Foster received many letters from John Hinkley before his attempt to kill President Reagan. A more recent case is that of Rebecca Schaeffer, the twenty-one-year-old actress who had been a co-star of "My Sister Sam" and had recently been featured in movies. Schaeffer had apparently received a great deal of correspondence from her assailant over a two-year period. I recently saw the handwriting of the man charged with killing Schaeffer. In a letter to his sister, he outlined how he was obsessed with somebody and had to eliminate her so he could eliminate his obsession. The handwriting was absolutely deranged. Thus, here's another case where the knowledge of what is normal versus abnormal in writing might have saved a person's life.

Celebrated Cases Where Handwriting Identification Has Played a Role

Graphology has played a role in a number of other celebrated cases.

Serial-Killer Case

Ted Bundy, a celebrated killer, a master of disguise who was recently executed, ensnared many young women, often using a simple approach. He would pick up a woman in a bar or disco by using a waitress to send the woman a drink accompanied by a note inviting her to join him. If the young woman approached, she would most likely become his next victim.

In addition to changing his physical appearance, Bundy used very different methods in his killings, so that the authorities in several states thought they were looking for several different murderers.

An investigator in one state, going over the facts of a murder case he was looking into, recalled that he'd read about a similar case in another state where a handwritten note was found on the victim. This investigator contacted the other state's authorities and obtained a copy of the note in that case. When the two notes were compared and the handwriting matched, officials in several states suddenly realized they were looking for one serial killer, not a series of killers. Thus, Bundy's handwriting became one of many factors leading to his eventual capture.

Billionaire Boys' Club Murder

Do you remember the Billionaire Boys' Club case, which, like the Ted Bundy murders, was also dramatized in a television miniseries? In this case, a young man named Joe Hunt was initially swindled out of a great deal of money by a man named Ron Levin. Hunt wanted revenge and plotted Levin's death.

With his bodyguard, Hunt went to Levin's Beverly Hills home and forced Levin to write him a check for a million dollars. Then Hunt and his bodyguard chloroformed Levin, stuffed him into the trunk of their car, drove him out to a desolate place, and killed him. Levin's body was never found.

Hunt and his bodyguard took great pains to leave no fingerprints or other clues at the scene. It was the perfect crime—almost! The imperfection was that Hunt had left, by the front door, a crumpled, handwritten "hit" list of things to do while in Levin's apartment.

Had it not been for this handwritten list, Levin's disappearance might never have been solved. Instead, Hunt was found guilty of first-degree murder and sentenced to life in prison without the possibility of parole. The bodyguard was sentenced to three years. And, by the way, the million-dollar check Hunt forced Levin to write? It bounced!

Here is the note Hunt inadvertently left by the victim's front door.

AT LEVINS
TO DO

4   5. CLOSE BLINDS

5   4. SCAN FOR TAPE RECORDER

1   1. TAPE MOUTH.

2   2 HAND CUFF — ③ PUT GLOVES ON

6   3. Explain Situation

✓   4. ~~Leave Him Initialed~~ Xerox

8   5. Put Answering Service on 668 1ST Ring

9   6. Get Alarm Access Code and Arm Code

10   7. Date STAMP DOCUMENTS

     8. Date STAMP LETTERS

11   9. Make File of Letters (TAKE Holes WITH YOU) and other Material

14   10. Kill DOG. (EMPHASIS) ~~~~

14   11 Xerox Authorizations (if Any)

12   12. USE CORPORATE SEAL

   13. HAVE LEVIN SIGN AGREEMENTS and Fill in BLANKS

13   14. Xerox everything So he has a Copy Initialed Copies

Note the wobbly slant, the clubbed strokes, the misplaced capital letters, and the mixing of handwriting styles in this most revealing sample. Also note how the largest words on the pages are *Kill DOG*, *TAPE MOUTH*, and *HAND CUFF*.

Nazi War Criminal Josef Mengele

The Mengele case displays another fascinating aspect of police work where handwriting played a key role in crime solving. If you will recall, Mengele, the Nazi war criminal, took on the identity of another German man and lived happily ever after in Brazil. It wasn't until after his death that it was discovered that the handwriting of this man matched the handwriting of Mengele.

Soon thereafter, authorities exhumed the man's body, and forensic experts provided further incredible information. For example, from one tooth, a forensic dentist was able to determine where this person had been raised; his race, sex, age, and height; and what type of food he'd eaten all his life.

It is most interesting to note that here was a man who tried to change everything about himself—his appearance, his fingerprints, his name, his profession, his history—but the one thing he couldn't change was his handwriting. That remained Mengele, even forty years later. He couldn't change his brain prints!

Italian Terrorist Case

Some years back, a man who was kidnapped by an Italian terrorist organization wrote a note to his wife, which was included with a note from the kidnappers describing their demands.

The wife sought the help of the authorities. The authorities brought in a graphologist to look at the note from the husband to see if it was really his writing. If it was, the graphologist was to determine whether he wrote it under duress and to provide any other information about him. The graphologist was also then asked to look at the ransom note written by the kidnappers.

The graphologist confirmed that the alleged husband's note was indeed written by the woman's husband. Further, the graphologist determined that the note from the Italian terrorist organization had been written by somebody who had been educated in Arabic as a first language—a language that is written from right to left—and not in a language that goes from left to right. This was apparent because the writing had many indicators of someone who originally had been taught to write from right to left, as in the Semitic languages, because the pressure pattern was reversed. There were other characteristics of Arabic in particular as well.

The revelation that the kidnappers might, in fact, be Arabs posing as Italian terrorists in order to throw everyone off was sufficient information for the authorities to find the kidnappers and free the victim.

The Hitler Diaries and the Salamander Papers

Two more celebrated cases that involved handwriting to a great degree were the Hitler diaries and the salamander papers. Surfacing in the early 1980s, the Hitler diaries were of worldwide interest until they were found to be forgeries.

Similarly, the salamander papers were a series of letters purported to have been written by Joseph Smith, the founder of the Mormon religion. According to the letters, Smith had actually received his inspiration from a "mystical salamander" instead of a divine angel. This revelation shook the very foundations of the Mormon religion and led to theft, corruption, and eventually murder.

No one knew who had committed these crimes until two handwriting experts proved that the salamander papers and many other documents were clever forgeries done by the young man who claimed to have discovered them—Mark Hofmann. In 1987, Hofmann was convicted of theft by deception and second-degree murder.

PART VII
GRAPHOLOGY AND YOUR LIFE

33

THE FUTURE OF GRAPHOLOGY

Since graphology involves the study of handwriting, its future necessarily depends on the future of handwriting itself. In this chapter, we examine the current state of handwriting in the United States, discuss the beneficial role that handwriting plays in our lives, and explore the handwriting-behavior connection. We also look at the status of the discipline of graphology and suggest ways to make it more widely accepted and utilized in the future.

Do We Even Need Handwriting?

Yes. Have you ever tried to go a complete day without handwriting anything? Think of all the times you sign your name or jot down a reminder note, a phone number, or other information—do you reach for a keyboard or a pen or pencil? Even in this age of word processors and supercomputers, the vast majority of us would be unable to go even one day if our pens and pencils were taken away from us.

What Is the State of Handwriting in the United States Today?

Yet handwriting is deteriorating to the point where the U.S. population may well be on the way to losing the ability to write altogether. I am increasingly alarmed by the number of young people who can barely handwrite. Ask most high school teachers how kids write these days, and they'll tell you they can hardly read their students' writing. Based on my own research, I would estimate that today close to 75 percent of high-school-age children have never developed the ability to write in a coherent, fluid, natural cursive style. The standard for handwriting thirty years ago was far superior.

Why Has Handwriting Deteriorated in Our Society?

Let's face it—teachers are overworked, and it takes less time to grade multiple-choice tests than to decipher handwritten essays. Besides, many teachers think the need for skilled handwriting is being eliminated by sophisticated typewriters and word processors. It's no wonder then that the teacher's attitude toward handwriting has become, "We'll get to handwriting later . . . if we have time."

But more is being undervalued here than the importance of handwriting. At the root is the fact that our society is fixated on the tangible—numbers and machines and things we can actually touch and see. Anything to do with the mind or emotions doesn't seem to count for much. A student in the United States can go through elementary, junior high, and senior high schools and earn a college degree without ever taking a course in psychology. Can it be more important to learn about the War of 1812, for example, than it is to learn the psychological fact that violence begets violence?

Thus, while the United States is the most technologically advanced country in the world, it also leads the world in violent crimes and murders per capita. And as a nation we are virtually helpless when it comes to dealing with drug abuse and violence against one another. Yet daily more and more scientific evidence points to the profound role that the mind plays in every facet of life. For example, doctors are learning that many physical illnesses appear to be influenced to a great degree by our attitudes and states of mind. And, ironically, the U.S. judicial system appears to be the only authoritative institution in the nation that does recognize the role of the mind and emotions in our lives; some of the largest court awards have been for "emotional distress."

What Are the Advantages of Being Able to Handwrite?

You've learned that when we handwrite, the brain directs the hand to move. This movement not only enables us to express our thoughts; it also reveals our underlying emotions and even the physical state of our bodies. These are the aspects that graphologists analyze, but the ability to handwrite provides a number of other unique benefits:

- *Communication with others*—No other species has the ability to communicate thoughts and feelings through written symbols at any point in time, from any place on earth.
- *Communication with self*—To date, handwriting is the fastest and most practical method of jotting down notes, reminders, messages, recipes, directions, phone numbers, and the like.
- *Identification*—Each person's handwriting is unique. Your handwriting and signature can identify you without your needing to be present (or needing to be alive, for that matter).
- *Memory*—Handwriting improves your ability to recall information. Studies have shown that when a person physically writes something down by hand, his or her ability to recall it increases dramatically. Seeing the words while thinking them and writing them cements that information into the memory better than any other method.
- *Achievement of goals*—Handwriting enables you to focus on your goals more effectively. A study of Harvard University graduates showed that the 3 percent who regularly wrote out their goals earned an average of ten times more income than the 97 percent of graduates who did not.
- *Physiology*—Handwriting enhances fine motor skills. Studies all over the world have shown repeatedly that those who can handwrite with facility have greater fine motor skills overall than those who have never learned to write. Handwriting exercises that are practiced in elementary schools are the only regular activities requiring fine motor skills that we teach our children.
- *Autographs*—Handwriting enables us to acquire and cherish a unique part of our heroes. This is something humans have done throughout history.

- *Graffiti*—Though graffiti is often unsightly and offensive and defaces public property, it has existed throughout the ages in every corner of the world. And without it, public bathrooms would be dull.

To take full advantage of the benefits of handwriting, we need to put more emphasis on the teaching of handwriting in our schools. Writing should be fun. Children love art classes, and there's no reason they shouldn't also love handwriting. However, we make it difficult to love handwriting when we give our children oversized pencils with no erasers and paper with extra-wide lines. These unwieldy tools make the writing process awkward, cumbersome, and definitely not fun. There's no reason children shouldn't learn to write using normal-sized pencils with erasers on normally lined paper.

American educators have thought so little about handwriting over the years that U.S. schools have barely changed from the Palmer method, invented over a hundred years ago. There is another system taught today, called the D'Nealian system, but it is only a slight modification of the Palmer system.

The Palmer method has been used widely in U.S. public schools since the late 1800s. It came into vogue during the Victorian era, a time when everything had frills and decorations. A woman's hat might have had birds and nests and all kinds of flowers attached to it; furniture had doilies; pianos had little coverings; everything had an additional little adornment that served no purpose besides decoration. So, too, are Palmer method letters adorned with curlicues, wavy frills, and whatnot.

Do you remember how the Palmer capitals *F*, *Q*, and *H* are made? Here's what you were taught:

$$\mathcal{F} \qquad \mathcal{Q} \qquad \mathcal{H}$$

Now, why do we need all these curlicues? They serve no purpose; they don't make our handwriting easier to read, help us write faster, or help us communicate better. So let's get rid of them. In fact, I propose a major overhaul of our writing system, a real streamlining.

The goal of a writing system is to enable us to communicate quickly, easily, and legibly. The Palmer method definitely fails in quickness and ease. So, we need to choose from the many available handwriting traits and graphological movements in order to devise a writing system that is fast and easy and results in quick comprehension by the reader.

But before we actually make any decisions about our new system, something else should be considered: Is there a connection between the way you behave and the way you were taught to write? There is evidence that the answer is yes.

Writing Systems and Behavior

Recently a number of fascinating studies by researchers from the University of California and Harvard University have shown that when a person is forced to do a specific physical activity, a chemical change occurs in his brain and there is a subsequent psychological consequence. One study found that when subjects were asked to smile for certain periods of time, endorphins and other hormones were released in the body and the subjects experienced mood lifts and were more relaxed, their immune systems stronger.

Therefore, could a country's writing system, which young children practice every day, affect that country's behavior as a nation? Could the very act of making certain graphological movements be a key to passing on these traits within a society? It might be interesting to look at some writing systems and their possible connections to national behavior.

Handwriting and Great Britain

The British have always taught their children to write in a slightly more vertical manner than have the Americans. And, as a stereotype, are not the British a bit more reserved, a bit less inclined to reveal their real emotions to other people? Are not the Americans more open about the way they think and feel? Could there be a connection? The British are encouraging their children to hold themselves upright, to practice self-control in their writing exercises, while the American system lets us lean right into the feeling.

Handwriting and Germany

The old German system of writing, which was in vogue there until the forties, was nearly 100 percent angular in style. Here are two samples:

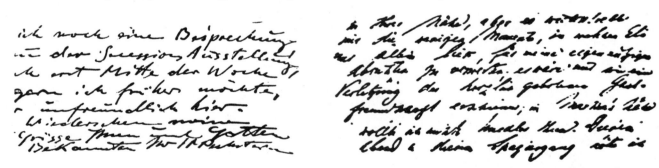

The movements that were taught to German children were abrupt, angular, and sharp, much like the Nazi goose-step marching style.

If you were taught to make only abrupt or angular hand and arm movements in your handwriting, would you not become a more aggressive, angry, unyielding person? Remember when you tried to write in an angular style earlier? The traditional German stereotype is of a dour, unemotional, no-nonsense, unyielding personality. Is there a connection between what you practice doing physically in your writing and what you become?

After Hitler's demise, Germany completely changed its writing style. It adopted the Western, round style of writing and discarded the predominantly angular style. The first generation to learn the new writing system recently tore down the Berlin Wall.

Now that we've examined the role of handwriting in our lives, let's take a look at the past, present, and future state of graphology in our society.

Where Has Graphology Been?

As long as there has been handwriting there have been great men and women who believe that the manner in which we write is connected to who and what we are. Aristotle said, "Spoken words are the symbols of mental experience, and written words the symbol of spoken words. Just as all men have not the same speech sounds, so all men have not the same writing."

Roman historian Suetonius Tranquillus found handwriting indicative enough of character to make this observation about Emperor Augustus: "I have above all remarked . . . [that] he does not separate his words, nor does he carry over to the next line any excess letters; instead, he places them under the final word and ties them to it with a stroke."

The artist Thomas Gainsborough refused to paint a portrait unless the subject had an example of his handwriting sitting next to him.

In his novel *Dr. Jekyll and Mr. Hyde*, Robert Louis Stevenson includes this line by Mr. Guest, the head clerk, speaking to Mr. Utterson, the lawyer: "There's a rather singular resemblance; the two hands are in many points identical: only differently sloped." He was referring to Jekyll's and Hyde's handwritings.

Other graphology proponents were Aesop, Julius Caesar, Cicero, Sir Walter Scott, Disraeli, Elizabeth Barrett and Robert Browning, Balzac, Goethe, Edgar Allan Poe, George Sand, Thomas Mann, Alexandre Dumas, and Emile Zola.

In recent history, Sigmund Freud wrote several technical works demonstrating graphology's validity and uses. Alfred Binet, who developed the modern IQ test, conducted many years of exhaustive research on graphology. He called graphology "the science of the future."

Where Is Graphology Today?

Graphology may be the science of the future, but its overall acceptance is greatly affected by its status in the academic world. Throughout Europe, the Soviet Union, South America, and Israel, universities offer formal training and, in some instances, doctorate degrees in graphology. In these parts of the world it is very difficult to get a job of any significant responsibility without first having one's handwriting analyzed. Israel, considered the leader in the field, even trains its border guards in the science to help them detect undesirables trying to enter the country.

While nations and businesses around the world have been making use of graphology for decades, its use has only recently begun to spread in the United States. Part of the reason for this lag is that very few schools in the United States offer any type of formal training in graphology. There is virtually no place to actually earn academic credits in the subject from an accredited university. Because U.S. universities do not consider graphology worthy of academic consideration, the American public has generally followed suit and ignored the field.

Since there are no degree programs or licensing requirements for graphologists in the United States, anyone can simply declare himself an "expert" without having the slightest idea what he is doing. Many gross oversimplifications, contradictions, and inaccurate statements have been made by these self-styled authorities. Consequently, graphology is often perceived as an art form belonging in the realm of the occult.

Despite the unavailability of formal education in graphology in the United States, more than one thousand major U.S. companies have sought trained professionals and today use graphology for hiring and crime-solving matters. Countless small businesses and individuals have also begun to use graphology.

Where Does Graphology Go from Here?

Once we get the schools to put more emphasis on handwriting, we need to train teachers in the rudiments of graphology. In education alone, a knowledge of the basics could aid in solving countless problems and perhaps even save lives.

Test for Handedness

Most elementary school teachers in the United States are unaware that a simple test exists for handedness. Instead, the average teacher automatically sticks the pencil in every child's right hand, even though approximately 10–20 percent of the children should be writing with their left hands.

Sit a child at a table and put candy or a colorful toy in the middle of the table, just out of reach. Which hand does the child use to reach for the desirable item? Ask a child to throw a ball and to kick a ball. Ask him to eat. Ask him to pick up a pen. Repeat these procedures several times, and it should become evident which hand the child prefers.

In rare instances, a child will keep switching hands, which most likely means that the child is ambidextrous. In such circumstances, ask the child to choose which hand feels best for writing.

Spot Physical Problems

Teachers should be trained to recognize certain types of disabilities from handwriting. Graphologists can often use certain patterns that develop in a child's handwriting to distinguish one type of learning disability from another and learning disabilities from physical illnesses, such as dyslexia from epilepsy. Learning-impaired children are often incorrectly lumped together in what are commonly called "educationally handicapped" classes. By knowing the specific problem of a child early on, we can get him the right help sooner.

Teachers should also be trained to spot visual and hearing problems as manifested in handwriting.

Spot Psychological Problems

Teachers can learn how to identify emotional problems in handwriting. For example, a child whose writing suddenly becomes microscopic is retreating into his own small world at the expense of reality. A child who suddenly cannot write without trembling or making numerous mistakes is also in need of professional help.

Junior and senior high school teachers should be able to recognize a troubled student from his handwriting. The biggest tip-off to a child's use of drugs or alcohol is a marked change in his handwriting. Drugs and alcohol have an immediate effect on handwriting, and teachers can be trained to spot this so the child can be helped at once.

These are just some of the ways graphology can be useful in education. But the science of graphology can tell us even more about ourselves and can even help us change.

If You Change Your Handwriting, Can You Change Your Personality?

Yes. If you have found something in your handwriting that you don't like, you can try to change or get rid of it and thereby change or get rid of the trait. This process is called *graphotherapy.*

There is ample evidence from documented case histories throughout the world that graphotherapy really works. Earlier we learned that the physical act of smiling seems to cause elevated moods and a healthier immune system. Graphotherapy works on the same principle. By a physical act alone, you can effect psychological changes. Forcing yourself to write uphill, for instance, will actually help you start to feel more "up" emotionally.

Let's say that you have a problem with finishing what you start. Maybe you keep thinking you won't succeed and therefore wonder why you should keep going. Maybe you fear making a sales call or find you are reluctant to make plans for the future. You can come up with all kinds of reasons and excuses to prevent yourself from taking action: it won't work; you're not really qualified; it will cost too much; you really don't have the time.

You could take your problem to a traditional psychotherapist, who would try to help you solve it through dialogue and psychological counseling. Or you could go to a qualified graphologist, who would analyze your handwriting to find the graphological traits that correspond to your problem. In this instance, it is likely that the graphologist would find traits such as stopping too short of the right margin and a falling baseline. You will recall that these traits indicate putting up imaginary barriers to how far you can get in life (right-margin avoidance) and a tendency to give up before finishing (falling baseline).

The graphologist would then instruct you to think of several phrases that express your desire to change and to write these phrases, taking care to go out to the right margin and to keep your baseline from falling. He would ask you to write this assignment twice in the morning and twice in the evening every day and to try to be conscious of your handwriting whenever you take pen in hand.

After practicing graphotherapy techniques for about three months, most people report that they can write in the new, prescribed manner without consciously thinking about it. If this happened to you, you would know that your subconscious had gotten the message—not only in your handwriting, but in your life as well. And you would find yourself making those dreaded sales calls without trepidation, planning to do more than you ever dreamed, and having energy to burn.

A final note: graphotherapy, because it requires only pen, paper, and a couple of visits to a graphotherapist, is one of the most inexpensive and practical means of self-improvement.

Giving Graphology Its Due

As its applications suggest, graphology belongs first and foremost in the field of psychiatry. Why psychiatry as opposed to psychology? The field of psychology deals with the emotional and intellectual aspects of an individual, while the psychiatric field encompasses the physical as well. It is for this reason that a psychiatrist must have a medical degree in addition to a Ph.D. Thus, graphology belongs in the same field as psychiatry because it concerns itself with the same three issues: the physical, intellectual, and emotional states of individuals.

It is only through the rigorous standards of formal science that graphology will be able to assume its rightful place as a serious field of study and a part of our everyday lives. Not only should there be degree programs in graphology, but standards and testing requirements must be established to separate the dilettantes from the professionals. Committees of recognized and established graphological experts should set the standards and procedures for determining what constitutes competence in this field.

These measures would lead to the application of graphology in areas where it is now ignored—at a great cost. A case in point: Many professional examiners of questioned documents go out of their way to disassociate themselves from handwriting analysts so that no one will question their scientific ability. But, in fact, if they had more knowledge of graphology, they could do a better job.

I have seen document examiners who, because they don't know the effects of aging, medicine, and drugs on handwriting, will declare a signature inauthentic when in fact it is valid. Many document examiners cannot discern whether a writer was sick or intoxicated at the time he wrote his name, or whether the writer had aged thirty years between the comparison samples. As a consequence, certain signatures and handwriting samples are erroneously declared inauthentic because they look so different.

Therefore, lack of knowledge of graphology limits the abilities of these document examiners. They would be better examiners of questioned documents if they knew how handwriting is affected by insanity, mental breakdowns, alcoholism or drug addiction, Parkinson's disease, old age, and other conditions. Instead, they pooh-pooh graphology and often make grave mistakes in the courtroom because of their ignorance.

Seeing Is Believing

The only logical explanation for why so many people continue to spurn graphology is that they are just plain ignorant about the subject. I don't want to believe that people are simply narrow-minded and won't recognize the truth when it's staring them in the face. I prefer to think that most Americans must have been exposed, if at all, to the wrong display of graphology by people who've only read a book or taken a class or who perform at fairs and sideshows and don't really know what they're doing. No rational person who sees how graphic movement relates to personality could possibly say that it is any less worthy of academic attention than is body language, psychology, or Pavlovian theory.

I hope this book has convinced you that graphology is a valid science and has tremendously beneficial uses in society. My fervent hope is that there will be a huge clamor by the public to put this subject into our schools, deem it worthy of academic research, and establish it once and for all as a credible field of study.

34

THOSE LAST FEW TIDBITS

Tidbit #1

How a person reacts to your instructions to write two paragraphs about anything he wants, sign his name, and date it tells you a lot about him before you even look at his writing.

Tidbit #2

Let's say the person from whom you have requested a writing sample has a lot of trouble getting started or doesn't want to think of something spontaneous. The person says something like, "Well, what should I write? Can I quote a poem? Can I copy something? I don't know what to write."

What such people are already telling you is that they don't really want to reveal much about themselves. They're telling you they're not spontaneous and everything has to be premeasured, calculated, because they don't want to give themselves away.

Other people just get going! They jump right in and write, revealing their lack of trouble getting started on new projects.

Tidbit #3

Ninety-nine percent of people, when they find out I'm a professional graphologist, want me to analyze their writing immediately.

People who are very reluctant, however, or even refuse to give a handwriting sample are usually either illiterate or dishonest. Illiterate people don't want you to see that they can't spell, or don't know when to capitalize, or can't make a correct sentence. More often than not, however, the reason for the reluctance is that the person is afraid you're going to uncover his dishonesty. He has something to hide!

Tidbit #4

Suppose you ask someone for a handwriting sample and he says, "Which handwriting? I have several." What does that mean?

Paranoia. It means this individual doesn't think that any *one* of his personalities will be good enough, so therefore he gives you a choice, hoping one of them will please you. It's not a good sign.

Tidbit #5

More women than men enroll in graphology courses. In the fifteen years I have taught at six University of California campuses, my classes usually have been 80 percent women and 20 percent men. And when I've asked the psychology professors about the ratio in their classes it was about the same.

In the professional world, however, there are more male psychologists than female psychologists, and there are *far* more male psychiatrists than women. But when talking about extracurricular courses, it would appear women far outnumber men in their desire to know about emotions and other people.

Tidbit #6

If you want to be the most scientific about taking samples, give people the same directions and have them write with the same type of pen and blank paper while sitting comfortably at a desk. Be as uniform as possible in all aspects, and then you will have a uniform basis for comparison.

Tidbit #7

Graphologists have studied the handwritings of people who live to ripe old ages to see what they have in common in their handwriting. The results show a great deal of stubbornness, followed by tenacity and mental intensity.

Tidbit #8

Studies of the writings of highly successful people in any area of life—whether it's the top janitor or the top corporate president—show they share a high degree of mental intensity (uphill writing), followed by a high degree of tenacity, emotional stability, and people skills. Once again, we see that a high IQ alone is not a factor in success. Someone with a high IQ who is emotionally unstable is not going to be successful.

Tidbit #9

In studies of the writings of mass murderers, graphologists find a preponderance of bizarre drawings or doodles. This means defiance and a desperate need for attention in an antisocial manner. These people can't just write and express themselves in a normal way. They always have to do their own thing, too.

In addition, these writers frequently use small letters with huge, flamboyant signatures, meaning they are severely introverted with a desperate need to be noticed by the public. But they don't know how to get noticed in a normal manner.

Finally, most mass murderers have irregular spacing or bizarre margins (or both), which means a lack of proper adjustment to their environment and aberrant relationships with other people. And, as expected, we find great instability in most aspects of the writing.

Tidbit #10

When I studied three thousand of the attendees of my graphology classes over ten years, I found that 90 percent were rightward slanters, 5 percent were vertical, and about 5 percent were leftward.

This leads me to believe that people who *express* their feelings are more likely to take an interest in learning about feelings and what they mean. Leftward writers—repressed people—lean over backward to avoid emotional situations and therefore are not as "inclined" to take classes that deal with their emotions.

Tidbit #11

I'm often asked how I give people the "bad news." What do I say, for example, when given a sample that shows the writer to be a liar, pervert, or general scumbucket?

Well, if it's strictly professional I'll call it as I see it and say something like, "The individual under assessment is not always truthful. There appears to be deviant sexuality . . . and the writer often engages in activities associated with con artists."

On the other hand, if someone shows me his handwriting at a cocktail party and the handwriting reveals him to be a liar, pervert, or general scumbucket, then I might say something like, "Well . . . you would make a great detective [and therefore a great criminal, too!]," and "My, oh, my—what versatility in the sexual areas! And charming and persuasive? Wow!"

35

ANALYZING YOUR OWN HANDWRITING

Now it's your turn to analyze yourself!

Before you get out the sample you wrote at the beginning of the book, let's see how well you know what your own writing looks like without looking at it:

- What is your writing slant—left, vertical, right, or wobbling?
- What is your baseline—uphill, level, downhill, or up and down?
- What are your zones like? Balanced? Does one of your zones dominate?
- What is the overall size of your writing? Small, medium, large? All sizes at once?
- What is the speed of your writing? Fast, slow, moderate, or all speeds?

Now get your sample out, and get ready to find out all about yourself. Maybe you'd better be sitting down!

Have you got it in front of you? What do you think? Do you see more now than you did before?

Even though you can probably see a whole lot of things right off the bat, start by looking at the basic traits in order.

Legibility

Is your writing legible or illegible? You may not be a good judge of that. You may have to ask someone, "Can you read this?" If he says he can, then your writing is legible. If he says he can't, then it's illegible. If he can read only parts of it, then it's partly legible and partly illegible.

What does legibility mean? It means a desire to communicate. The more legible your writing, the better you are at communicating with others. The more illegible your writing, the more you are a poor communicator of your thoughts and feelings and shouldn't be in a job where your assignment is to communicate clearly with others.

Slant

What is your slant? Does your writing lean to the left, point straight up and down, lean to the right, or go in all directions? If it's leaning to the left, is it leaning slightly to the left or greatly to the left? If it's leaning to the right, is it strongly to the right or only mildly to the right? Or is it wobbling in all directions?

Based on your answers, are you repressed or expressive of your real emotions with other people? Or are you all these things and emotionally a basket case?

Now that you've determined to what degree you reveal your true feelings to others, consider whether your slant changed on just a particular word or phrase. What does that mean? If you suddenly reared straight up or went to the left, then you've suddenly taken out the feeling or you are lying. Do you recall? And if you suddenly went rightward, you felt particularly emotional at that thought. Do you have Maniac *d*'s?

Baseline

What does your baseline look like? Of course you wrote on blank paper, as you were instructed, right? If you insisted on using lined paper, you don't follow rules and you need guidelines (or maybe you just don't own any blank paper!). If you did write on blank paper, you should now have a baseline. So hold the page straight up in front of you and look to see whether the writing goes uphill, stays level, goes downhill, or goes in all directions.

Recall that the most positive direction in which to write is uphill, that it is most difficult to keep a perfectly level baseline, and that a downhill baseline indicates depression, disappointment, disillusionment, and fatalism.

Did the baseline of your writing go up or down on any particular words or phrases? What does that mean?

Margins

What are your margins like? Hold the paper away. Do you have any margins? Where do you have margins? Where are they the biggest or smallest? Did you leave too much space on the top or bottom or right side or left side? Are the margins even all around? You know what that means, right?

Spacing

Now look at the spacing between your letters, words, and lines. Is it wide, narrow, or normally spaced? Is it changing? Is it extra-anything? Does it change between certain words or phrases? You know what that means.

Pressure

What about your writing pressure? Turn the paper over and feel the writing from the back. Is it heavy, medium, or light pressure? If it's heavy, were you feeling intense? If it's light, were you not feeling intense? Did you feel particularly intense during a particular passage?

315

Size

Is the overall size of your writing small, medium, or large? Are you an extrovert? An introvert? An extrovert *and* an introvert? Do any words, phrases, or spacing get bigger or smaller in particular places? What does that mean?

Speed

Was your writing fast or slow? Or was it a combination? Do you remember how to tell that? Did it slow down in any place? (Ahem!) Was there any place in particular where you wanted to be very cautious? How would your describe yourself ordinarily? Are you usually a fast, average, or slow writer?

Zones

Do the zones in your sample look like your normal zone pattern? Were your zones balanced? Were your upper and lower zones the same size, and was the middle zone about one-half or three-quarters the size of the upper and lower zones?

Were your upper or lower zones balanced within any given word? Or are you top-heavy? Do you have a dominating upper zone? Do you live in a fantasy world at the expense of reality? Are you theoretical over practical?

Do you have a dominating middle zone? Remember, that means you're self-centered and overly concerned with outward appearances and the immediate moment.

Does your lower zone dominate? If so, are you overly oriented toward the physical, libidinal, and material aspects of life?

Did your lower zone dominate on just a particular word or phrase? What does that mean? Did your upper zone dominate on just one word or phrase?

Style

Now look at the style of your writing. Are you a connected writer, a print-writer, or a combination thereof? Or are you a printer? If you are a print-writer (you do a little of each), are you the efficient type of print-writer, or are you the inefficient type? Are you a combination of both? If some of your connections are efficient and some are inefficient, are you efficient or inefficient? Can you be an efficient person if half the time you're inefficient?

Do you cursively write some words, then at random print some others? What does that mean? (*Hint:* Nothing good!)

Are there any words you suddenly printed? Do you remember what that means?

Do you have a conventional writing style or an unconventional one? Are you traditional, or do you have an "artistic" temperament?

Connecting Strokes

What are your connecting strokes? Do you remember what a desirable balance of connecting strokes is? Do you primarily make garlands, arcades, angles, or threads? What do these mean?

Signature

Now look at your signature. Is it the same as the rest of the writing? Is that just one of many signatures you have? Or is it the same signature you always use? Is one of your names bigger than the other name? Is one of your names going uphill or downhill?

Is one of your names illegible? Is part of your name illegible? Is it the last part of the last name? The part that says "berg," "stein," "gonzalez," or "oshowitzelov"?

Are you going to change your signature now? Are you easy to forge?

Do you like your public self-image? Do you not like it? Are you the real thing? Are you a bluffer? Are you comfortable with yourself?

Do you write like most famous men and women who have reached the top? They write with highly legible signatures as large as or slightly larger than the rest of the writing.

Horizontal Movement

What is your horizontal movement like? Do you have strong, medium, or weakly made *t* bars, for example? Are you a workaholic, directed, or lazy? Are you a little of everything?

Honesty vs. Dishonesty

Are you honest? Do you write too slowly, or do you have stabbed ovals, too much retracing or arcading, upside-down letters, constant mistakes and touch-ups? Finally, do you have the infamous and dreaded felon's claws?

Now let's zoom in on the lie. The first thing to do when discerning falsehoods in written statements is to hold the paper away and look at the paper as a whole—especially the left margin. If a certain line or paragraph juts out farther to the left than the preceding lines, then you lost spontaneity at that point. And if in the same section the spacing suddenly gets too wide or too narrow, then you know for sure something odd is going on there!

Now look at several aspects of the writing in depth. Did the slant of any of the writing suddenly change? Did the words fly above the line or fall below? Did the writing suddenly get very narrow or overly wide? Did it suddenly get overly slow? Did something change, and was it more than one thing? Very often when someone is writing a lie, or is about to, the person makes a mistake. Did you make a mistake right before, during, or after you wrote the lie?

OK, is it all more obvious to you? Now get out that love letter!

By the way, don't forget that you *can* change your handwriting—and thereby diminish your negative traits (see page 309).

36

WHERE DO YOU GO FROM HERE?

If you've fallen in love with graphology, as I sincerely hope you have, the best way I know to become good at this is to practice. Go over and over what you've learned in this book until you know the concepts by heart. Then have your friends and family members bring you handwriting samples of people they know and you don't, and see how close you come to analyzing them correctly.

Keep up your graphology studies; I promise graphology won't let you down.

318

PART VIII
A BIT ABOUT DOODLES

37
DOODLES

Doodle Quiz

Before you start reading about doodles, let's see how much you may already know about them without realizing it.

Please answer the following questions with "true" or "false."

1. The most common reason for doodling is boredom.

2. Children who doodle frequently on their school papers are usually not doing well in class.

3. People who think they have no artistic talent usually don't doodle.

4. We cannot analyze random doodling, only conscious drawings.

Answers

1. True	2. True	3. False	4. False

Doodle Challenge

Now, please take a sheet of paper and trace the box and circle within the box seen below. Draw in the box the first thing that comes to your mind. The explanation for this assignment will be given at the end of this chapter.

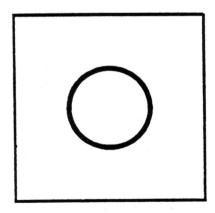

Explanation of Doodles

The dictionary defines a doodle as aimless scribbling, especially when the attention of the doodler is elsewhere.

A graphologist defines a doodle as an expressive movement, made consciously or unconsciously, from which insight into the personality and mood of its originator can be gained.

Consciously Drawn Doodles

Consciously drawn doodles are those we intentionally draw, where our minds are focused on our doodles and we are aware of what we are doing.

They provide insight into our attitudes, interests, moods, creativity, imagination, and areas of concern. These doodles give us a great deal of information about the psychological state of the doodler who may not be able to put his or her true thoughts or feelings into words but feels free to put them into drawings.

Consciously drawn doodles often reveal valuable information which might otherwise go undetected. For example, I have seen many cases of the "model prisoner" who says that he is completely cured (and usually claims to have found Jesus, too) but whose doodles indicate otherwise by depicting violent and antisocial things such as guns, knives, people bleeding, and people being robbed. Psychologists and social workers can tell you how many mental patients reveal their real thoughts and feelings not in what they write but in what they draw and doodle.

Analysis of consciously drawn doodles is also helpful for gaining insight into the young child who cannot yet speak well or write. For example, children who continually slash at the paper, producing only rigid, angular movements devoid of any attempt at roundness, are statistically more likely to become aggressive and angry types who get frustrated easily and for long periods of time.

Unconsciously Drawn Doodles

Unconsciously drawn doodles are those made while our conscious minds are focused on something else and our hands are scribbling, drawing, or doodling at the same time.

They provide insight into our subconscious mind, which is often of great help when we are uncertain, confused, angry, or anxious but consciously do not know what we are really feeling. For example, imagine a man who keeps avoiding setting a date to get married to the woman to whom he has been engaged for several years. Even he is not sure why he keeps stalling. Then one day he notices that he often doodles a spiderweb while talking to his fiance on the telephone. At other times while talking to her he draws a race car. He seems to draw these two things—spiderwebs and race cars—only when talking to his fiance. What could this mean? Well, it means that he feels trapped, caught in a web, and eager to get away in a hurry. With this knowledge, both he and his fiance can begin to deal with the problem realistically.

Unconscious doodling often points out areas of conflict between our conscious thoughts and feelings and those of our unconscious. For example, let's say that when asked by someone how he is feeling a man says, "Just fine, thanks," but while talking about this he is doodling a haphazard and hideous face with a huge frown on it. How do you think this person is really feeling?

Why Do People Doodle?

As with handwriting, *Homo sapiens* is the only species on earth that can doodle. But, unlike with handwriting, people can communicate with all other humans on earth through their drawings and doodles regardless of the language they speak. Pictures are universal. People were drawing and doodling long before writing existed, and all peoples everywhere, in every corner of the earth, doodle. Young and old doodle; smart and dumb doodle; artists and nonartists doodle. The human being has a desire and a need to express himself using visual symbols released through drawings or doodles.

Doodles are fun to make and allow the person complete freedom of expression with no preset rules or restrictions. Anything goes.

People usually start doodling when their minds start to wander from whatever activity they are engaged in. The majority of doodlers report that they doodle the most when talking on the telephone, listening to a teacher or speaker, attending a boring meeting, or waiting for something.

Why Do Some People Doodle All the Time but Others Only Rarely?

There is no definitive answer to why some people doodle all the time and others don't. There are, however, some interesting statistics:

- People who have artistic ability, or believe they do, tend to doodle far more than those who say they can't draw a straight line.
- Children who frequently doodle on their school papers are usually doing poorly in school, feeling bored and apathetic about learning, and are more likely to be delinquents than those students who do not doodle on their schoolwork or class notes. If a student is always doodling in only one specific class, then he probably does not like that particular class and is not likely to be doing well in it.
- Among young children who frequently doodle or add little drawings to their schoolwork we find a high incidence of learning disabilities and problems with spelling and reading. A child may have dyslexia or other learning problems or deficiencies that he does not have to worry about when doodling, when he is free to express himself as he sees fit.
- Adults who have superior literary skills doodle the least, probably because they feel more comfortable expressing themselves in words rather than in pictures.
- Adults involved in creative pursuits such as poetry, painting, sculpting, photography, design, engineering, construction, mechanics, and fashion are more frequent doodlers than those engaged in highly structured careers such as accounting, bookkeeping, computer operating, etc.

How Doodles Are Analyzed

Doodles are analyzed the same way handwriting is because both are forms of graphic movement. Thus, like handwriting, doodles are interpreted in the following five ways:

1. *Physiological deductions*—Are the strokes in the doodle made smoothly or do there appear to be breaks, uneven pressure, shakiness, and the like associated with physical illness and/or the use of alcohol or drugs?

2. *Commonsense deductions*—If someone is always doodling the same thing, common sense tells us that the person has a fixation on the particular subject he is always doodling. If a person doodles happy, active, smiling, and "normal" looking people or objects, then we know that he is likely to be healthier than someone who doodles hideous figures, violent acts, trapped animals or people, and the like.

3. *Deductions using universal concepts*—Here we look to see if the doodles are big or small, symmetrical or asymmetrical, light or heavy in pressure, neat or sloppy, left or right, organized or disorganized, traditional or nontraditional, round or angular, narrow or wide, fast or slow, complex or simple, detailed or lacking in detail, pleasing to look at or hideous, etc. Then we apply the universal interpretations for these traits as discussed in Chapter 7.

4. *Simple psychological interpretations*—Once again, we must have some psychological acumen to make many interpretations. For example, if one person draws snails and another draws racehorses, which person is likely to be in a greater hurry? Which person is more competitive? Which person has greater patience? The racehorse doodler is in a greater hurry and is more competitive. The snail doodler would be feeling more patient.

5. *The scientific method*—Many interpretations of doodles are based on scientific interpretations derived from studying thousands of samples and case histories gathered from around the world. An example of a scientific doodle interpretation would be one where a child is asked to doodle a house and draws it with round windows instead of the usual square ones. Scientific data show that this is often how children who have been sexually molested draw windows.

How Doodles Are Categorized

Doodle types are divided into two major categories:

1. *Abstract doodles*—Abstract doodles have no immediately recognizable meaning. For example, a person may doodle triangles inside boxes spiraling downward over and over again. Probably no two people will have the same interpretation for this doodle. Abstract doodles may be consciously or unconsciously made, but their interpretation is the same. For example, suppose someone doodles a knife dripping with blood. Whether that doodle was drawn consciously or unconsciously, the interpretation is the same: The person was emotionally disturbed and felt violent and extremely antisocial at the time the doodle was drawn.

2. *Recognizable doodles*—There are unlimited recognizable doodles that people may draw. Everything in our universe is possible to see and doodle, and there are infinite ways these things can be depicted in doodles. Hence, it is impossible to list the meaning of all types of recognizable doodles. However, a large number of commonly drawn doodles which have been studied around the world for meaning will be discussed below. As with abstract doodles, recognizable doodles may be consciously or unconsciously made, but their interpretation is the same.

Interpretation of Commonly Made Doodles

- *Boxes*—The most common doodles, universally, are boxes made in endless sizes, dimensions, and numbers. Boxes indicate a desire to be constructive. If the boxes are three dimensional, they indicate an ability to see all sides of an issue.
- *Triangles*—Triangles are the second most common doodles seen universally. They reveal a rationalistic state of mind and a desire to see things come to a head.
- *Arrows*—Arrows indicate feelings of ambitiousness, drive, and motivation.
- *Haphazard lines*—Aimless lines that do not form any particular shape or that go in all directions with no rhyme or reason indicate that the doodler is feeling undirected, fragmented, without structure or purpose, irritated, and frustrated.
- *Stars*—Stars indicate a feeling of hopefulness, a looking forward or up to things, and optimism.
- *Circles*—Circles are made with round movements and automatically indicate a more passive feeling than angles. They are associated with feeling sociable, talkative, and friendly and with a desire to be flexible and loving.
- *Hearts*—The doodler has love on his mind, in most cases.
- *Flowers*—Flowers represent the feminine side of ourselves, a desire to see growth, nature, and reproduction. If the flowers are in an arrangement, the doodle denotes a sense of family and togetherness. Noted psychologist Carl Jung states that people who dream of flowers frequently have a need to release emotion that they feel unable to express openly at the moment.
- *Food*—Drawing things to eat or drink indicates a need for love, a desire to be filled up. Of course, it may indicate thirst or hunger too.
- *Animals*—Doodling animals usually means that the person is sensitive to living creatures. The type of animal doodled says a great deal about the mood of the doodler and often the type of person she would like to be. Doodles of weak, passive, or small animals indicate slowness, a lack of self-confidence, and more introverted tendencies. Doodles of aggressive animals like tigers and lions represent feelings of assertiveness. Doodles of fun-loving animals like otters and monkeys indicate a playful doodler. Doodles of animals that move very quickly usually represent a desire to get away quickly.
- *Transportation methods*—Doodles of cars, boats, trains, wagons, buses, and the like represent a desire to get away or to reach a goal. The faster the type of vehicle doodled, the greater the haste to make a point or speed away. We often find people who are bored with their jobs doodling vehicles.
- *Houses or buildings*—Doodles of houses and buildings represent the doodler's attitude about his home life. Houses should definitely have doors and windows which indicate that there is a way for the resident to see out and for others to see into him. A warm and inviting house that looks lived-in, with smoke coming from the chimney and the like, indicates the doodler has a happy and positive attitude toward his home life. A stark, unadorned, or haphazard house indicates that the doodler has an unhappy association with his home life.
- *Trees*—The tree represents our egos and our ambitions. A healthy tree is one that is large, robust, sturdy, balanced in the size of the trunk in relation to the top portion, full, and alive. A tree that has leaves and fruit on it indicates that the doodler associates love, sex, and children together. Bare, drooping branches indicate depression and lack of fighting spirit. The doodler is looking down, not

up. A tree drawn without roots indicates that the doodler feels himself without roots (or it may indicate that the doodler is not good at drawing).

- *People*—Doodlers who draw only profiles of people often don't like the way they look, or they feel they cannot draw well. A full figure should be drawn with hands and feet (a face would help, too) and should be in proportion. Not drawing hands on one's doodle indicates a feeling of being unable to do things, of not having a hand in things; not drawing feet indicates a feeling of not belonging anywhere, not having roots. The face is all-important, especially the expression on it. A smile is desirable and a frown is not. All parts of a face should be present. Missing parts of the face indicate a person who feels fragmented, not whole, and faceless. Accentuating eyes, or drawing only eyes, indicates that the doodler feels cautious, suspicious, and as if he has to have eyes on all sides of his head. Doodling ears usually means that the doodler feels he has to listen too much to someone.

Doodle Tidbits

Tidbit #1

People who have artistic talent, or who think they have artistic talent, tend to doodle a greater variety of things, and to doodle more often, than people who feel they are not artistic.

Tidbit #2

People who doodle scribbles are not feeling good about themselves, are confused, and often have a lot of problems. Scribbling with angularity is a sign of a potentially violent person who is in a state of acute frustration, is nondirected, and is feeling very angry.

Tidbit #3

Doodling anything ugly, hideous, tormented, ghoulish, monstrous, or representing evil or death indicates a tormented person who is very unhappy and capable of committing antisocial acts.

Tidbit #4

Doodling on anything within reach, especially if it is something inappropriate such as newspapers, magazines, schoolwork, walls, buildings, or books, indicates antisocial feelings and behavior and a desperate need to be seen and heard.

Tidbit #5

Doodling on one's body and getting tattoos is an expression of not wanting to be mainstream, of needing to flaunt one's individuality. If it is overdone, it indicates a desire to self-destruct.

Tidbit #6

People who like to doodle in their spare time usually have artistic inclinations.

Tidbit #7

People who get bored very easily often start doodling on whatever paper happens to be around.

Tidbit #8

People who tend to doodle the same things over and over again usually feel they don't have artistic talent. These people tend to doodle those few things they think they can draw adequately.

Tidbit #9

People who shade in their doodle shapes tend to be sensual; those who shade in existing letters or shapes unconsciously are revealing unexpressed sensuality. People who fill in letters or shapes consciously are usually feeling like staying within a structure or setting limits on themselves at the moment as opposed to feeling adventurous and creative.

Tidbit #10

Doodles that are detailed, symmetrical, and balanced reveal that the doodler is feeling constructive, organized, and law-abiding.

Tidbit #11

Doodles that are made with random lines or designs and lack balance and symmetry are made by people feeling out of sorts, disorganized, aimless, careless, and possibly wayward.

Tidbit #12

People who rarely, if ever, doodle, are usually those who limit their creative expression and feel much more comfortable expressing themselves in words than in pictures.

Pop Quiz

What does it mean if you doodle on a letter you write to someone? What can you say about the person who wrote the letter seen below?

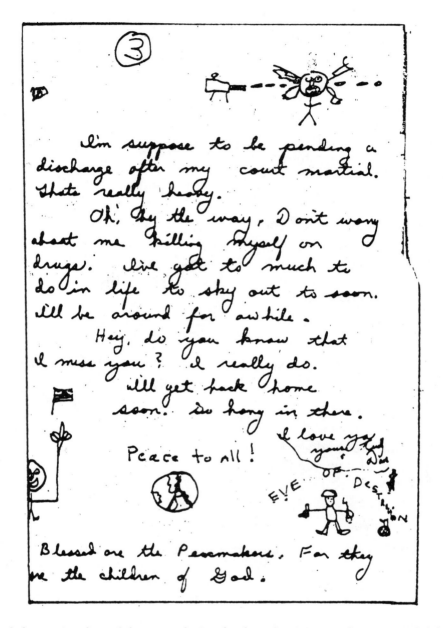

One of the traits found frequently in the handwritings of convicted felons is the desire to doodle on their written messages to other people. The person is not content to simply handwrite his message but feels compelled to flaunt his antisocial tendencies by doodling and drawing on his letters. The letter seen above was written in 1972 by David Berkowitz while he was in the army stationed in Korea. Berkowitz is known as "Son of Sam," which is how he signed notes left beside the six people he murdered over a few-month period in New York in 1976 and 1977. As of this date, Berkowitz is still in prison.

Here are a few more examples of some notorious felons who have doodled on their letters to other people:

The Zodiac Killer
How would you like to get the following letter in the mail?!!

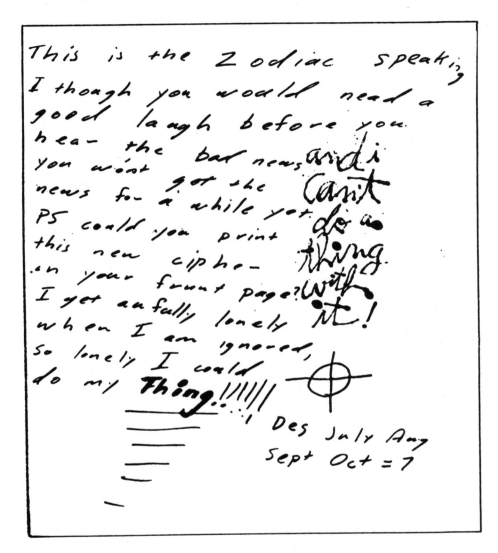

We've seen the Zodiac's writing before on page 89 when we talked about Maniac D's. Recall that the Zodiac killed more than sixty people in the late 1960s and early 1970s in the San Francisco Bay area. To date, he has not been caught. The letter seen above was the inside page of a greeting card sent to the *San Francisco Chronicle* on November 8, 1969. Wow! This is as scary as it gets! A young child would know there's something wrong with this letter.

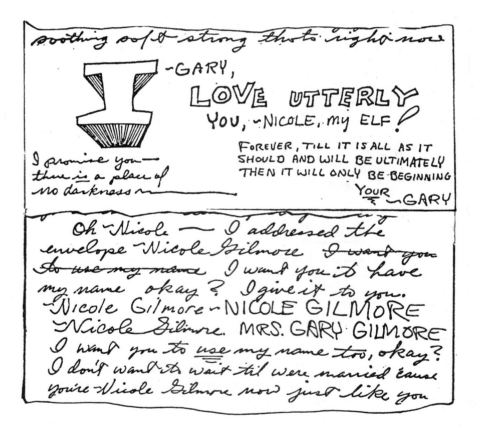

Gary Gilmore, 35 at the time, murdered two innocent strangers in 1976 in Utah during a murderous rage brought on by a quarrel with his lover, 20-year-old Nicole Barrett. He was sentenced to die, and his demands for a swift execution brought him the title of the "right-to-die killer." He was executed a year later. While in prison he had written Barrett more than one hundred letters with doodled drawings all over them, such as the one seen here.

Fromme attempted to assassinate President Ford and was a member of the Charles Manson Family. Here we see her own brand of doodling where she puts squiggly lines here and there, makes strange attachments to various letters, and draws attention to her writing with various types of doodled formations.

Byron Stanley

Stanley admitted to shooting three men to death in a church in Milwaukee in 1985. He was known as the "Priest Killer," and he claimed that he was following God's orders. He had been angry at the church for allowing women to give scripture readings. He claimed to hear voices, and several psychologists testified that they thought he was legally insane at the time of the killings. The court found him sane, however, and had him committed to a state department of social services. Here we see Stanley has written in all directions, added his own weird shapes, retraced letters sporadically, and drawn a large, distorted question mark.

Aleister Crowley

Aleister Crowley (signature)

Crowley was known as the most evil man in England during the 1930s. It is reported that he practiced witchcraft and was brought to trial many times but somehow avoided being locked up. He was addicted to drugs and was a high priest of sadistic rituals. Several of his many wives died mysteriously, and it was thought that Crowley drove them insane. He had many mistresses as well, several of whom committed suicide. Now, if that isn't a pair of treacherous scissors and an abnormal preoccupation with the lower zone in his signature, I don't know what is! I'd like to see the handwriting and doodles of the women who kept falling in love with this sadist!

Charles Manson

Charles Manson
Box B33920
Represa Calif
95671 (envelope address)

Here we see an envelope from the infamous leader of the Manson Family, responsible for at least seven deaths of innocent people in the Los Angeles area in 1969. Manson has remained in prison since his conviction in 1970. Although the zip code on the envelope doesn't really look like a traditional doodle, it qualifies as a conscious doodle because it is a form of free graphic expression that is not traditional. We do not put zip codes on at an angle, nor do we underline them twice at an angle. This highly individual way of putting down the zip code is all the graphologist needs to see to know that we have an extremely hostile, antisocial individual who goes out of his way to flaunt his defiance. Here we see that Manson demands attention for his antisocial behavior. The zip code screams out at the reader.

Doodle Challenge Explanation

Okay, now it's time to analyze the doodle that you were asked to do at the beginning of this chapter. Recall that you were instructed to copy the box with the circle in the center and draw in it the first thing that came to mind. This is a conscious doodle.

This box is one of twelve boxes of an internationally acclaimed "doodle test." Each box has a geometric shape within it, and each represents an aspect of our personalities. The box with the circle in it is the first one of the twelve. It represents the self-image.

Below is a reduced picture of the twelve squares that make up the "doodle test." This test originated in Europe, and it has been widely used throughout the world as a diagnostic tool of human behavior. The interpretations made of the responses to each box have been systematically categorized and related to each doodler's life story. In this manner, analyzers have been able to develop a system for determining what is considered a normal or an abnormal response.

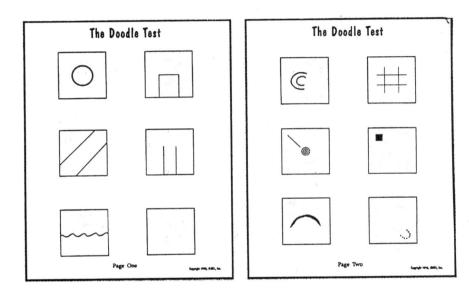

Once again, here is a picture of the Doodle Challenge box you were asked to fill in with the first thing that came to your mind:

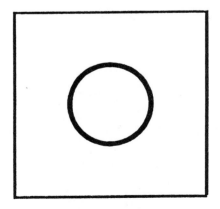

The most common responses to this box are to make the center circle into a sun, a moon, a flower, or a face. It is common to make a face in a sun or a moon or a flower. For a happy doodler, the face is smiling. A frowning or scowling face indicates unhappiness or anger. If there are lines radiating from the sun, we look to see if they are symmetrical. Symmetry represents balance, sound reasoning, perfectionism, detail-minded qualities, and an innate sense of order and logic. Asymmetrical lines in this box indicate that the doodler is out of sync, not balanced, feeling lopsided, and a bit disordered.

In this box, a healthy ego is expressed by making the circle the focal point of the doodle. Ignoring the circle or deforming it signifies a person in trouble and in need of professional help.

Okay. Now, let's see how well you can do analyzing responses to this box.

Doodler A

What is this doodler's self-image? Well, there's a face, which is what we want to see, and it's got all of its parts. The self-image seems to be a rugged, macho, burly, manly kind of guy who is very serious, stern, and gruff. Too bad it was drawn by a woman . . . no, just kidding. But what if a woman had doodled this box? Methinks we'd have a bit of a sexual identity crisis. Men rarely draw a female figure in this box, and women almost never draw a male figure here. In reality, this doodle was drawn by a male in his late 30s who is a sculptor and builds log cabins. He looks very similar to the guy he drew.

Doodler B

This doodle was drawn by a nine-year-old girl. We see the smiling face, the long hair, and the teeth in her mouth. There are birds flying in the background and some sort of picture with a person wearing a hat in the upper-left corner. This child was doing average in school at the time, was seeing a dentist regularly, and was already strongly interested in the arts. She was constantly doodling and drawing in

334

her spare time and made up cartoons for people as gifts. Today, this girl is twenty-one and is graduating college with a B.A. in graphic arts. She wears hats all the time. She is also beautiful, a gifted actress, very popular with her peers and professors, the recipient of several educational grants, and surely a future world leader who will be revered by everyone. This is my daughter, Ariel. What was your first clue?

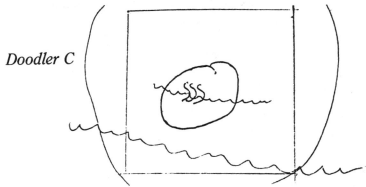

Doodler C

This is not a healthy response. This doodle was drawn by an eighteen-year-old boy who chain-smoked, was heavily into marijuana use, was not doing well in school, and wanted to be an actor. He's twenty-one years old today and is doing even more drugs and is trying to get into the army. Notice that he drew outside of the box which indicates rebelliousness. There is no recognizable drawing in this box as there should be.

Below are the doodle responses of two seventeen-year-old girls. Which girl, Doodler D or Doodler E, is a good student who works part-time? Which girl, Doodler D or Doodler E, is a juvenile delinquent who is cheerful but never really tries very hard and has been arrested for prostitution several times?

Doodler D   *Doodler E*

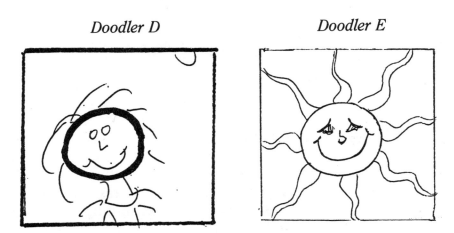

Doodle D was drawn by the juvenile delinquent. The lines are sloppy and asymmetrical, and there is not much effort exhibited here. One might not know that this doodler was a delinquent but it would be obvious that there is a lack of real effort, a lack of precision, a lazy quality, and definitely a looseness. But at least she's a happy hooker . . . oh dear, just kidding.

Doodle E was drawn by the good student. Here we see symmetry in the lines, a concerted effort, balance, and a sense of purpose along with the cheerful attitude.

335

This doodler was twenty-five at the time he doodled this response. When he was asked if there was anything else that came to his mind when he looked at the box with the circle in it, he said, "nope." He committed suicide three years later leaving his parents a note that said, "Goodbye. Hope you have a good life. It ain't worth it."

Doodler G

Uh-oh! This is the doodle of a thirty-nine-year-old male. What do you think? He made the main circle, in the middle, into one of a pair of eyes which each becomes a face unto itself. Then these two faces become the eyes of the big face he made out of the box. This is not a normal or healthy response. I obtained this sample from this man while he was in prison for distributing pornographic films, pandering, grand theft, and a number of other felonies. The psychologist assigned to him at this time described him as a dangerous schizophrenic. This description fits his doubling of the main circle. He is showing split personalities right here in this doodle.

This is the doodle of a thirty-year-old man. What do you think? Is the circle the focal part of the doodle? Yes, it is. Although nothing is drawn in the inner circle, it becomes the moon and is definitely the spot where the eye is directed. Here we see the wolf baying at the moon. This is the doodle of a highly successful artist whose artwork is shown all over the world. We see his artistic talent, which his handwriting alone would not have revealed, here in this doodle. Notice the patience he demonstrated, the balanced design, and the great amount of detail.

Below are the doodles of two nine-year-old boys who are now both twenty-three years old. Can you tell which boy is receiving a National Science Foundation Fellowship and is getting his doctorate in social sciences at University of California, Berkeley? Can you tell which boy is a high school dropout and has been in trouble with the law?

Doodler I   *Doodler J*

Doodler I is the studious graduate student. There's no way to know from his doodle how exceptionally bright he is, but we can see that he appears well-adjusted with his self-image, has a smile on his face, and has buttons on his shirt. Those two little buttons say a whole lot. They denote orderliness, conservatism, and neatness in outward appearance. There is no explanation for the fact that one shoulder is colored in and the other isn't. Perhaps this boy was feeling a bit lopsided, or different from his peers, at the time. Guess who? Yep, this author is one proud mama. This doodler is my son, Jason.

Doodler J is the high school dropout. His doodle is not what a parent wants to see. He's all mouth with his tongue sticking out, which about says it all.

This is the doodle of a forty-three-year-old woman. What do you think? Is it normal? Yes, it is. This lady has a tremendous sense of humor and doesn't take herself too seriously. It's interesting that she doesn't put a nose on her rabbit because she's always saying that she thinks hers is too big.

What do you think of the two fifteen-year-old Doodlers L and M seen below?

Doodler L   *Doodler M*

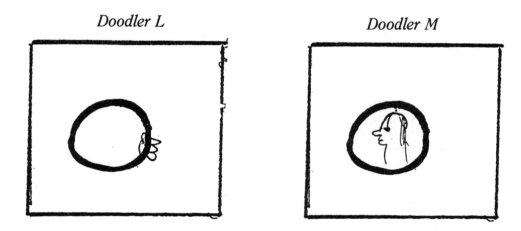

Doodler L is a fifteen-year-old boy who is a drug addict, a runaway, and a delinquent now under the care of the state. His doodle response is not normal. It is an unrecognizable shape with no meaning to it. He has made no effort here, and he feels off to the side and deformed, maladjusted, and like a blob without purpose.

Doodler M is a fifteen-year-old girl and like Doodler L is a drug addict, a runaway, and a delinquent now under the care of the state. We want to see a face in this box but not the way this doodler drew it. Her response is terribly abnormal. The main circle is not the basis for the face as it should be but looks something like a porthole through which we can see a strange person's profile. This girl doesn't have a good sense of herself but rather feels like she's looking at herself from the outside. She is not on her center.

Final Doodle Comments

Well, I hope you've begun to see how much fun and how interesting doodle interpretations can be. What people draw, and often what they draw on, can tell you a lot about them.

After you've seen a great many responses to a specific doodle task, such as the box with the circle in it that we've just finished discussing, you'll readily see which responses are normal and which are not. You'll see how closely people's real-life stories match their responses.

Most exciting of all is the fact that even in young children we can often identify those who are in trouble or who soon will be just from their doodles. With that advance information, we may be able to get that child help right away and ward off impending problems.

BIBLIOGRAPHY

Allport, Gordon Willard, and Vernon, Philip E. *Studies in Expressive Movements*. New York: The Macmillan Co., 1933.

Battan, David. *Handwriting Analysis: A Guide to Personality*. San Luis Obispo, CA: Padre Productions, 1938.

De Sainte Colombe, Paul. *Grapho-Therapeutics: Pen and Pencil Therapy*. Hollywood, CA: Laurida Books Publishing Company, 1966.

Downey, June E. *Graphology and the Psychology of Handwriting*. Baltimore: Warwick & York, Inc., 1919.

Falcon, Hal. *How to Analyze Handwriting*. New York: Cornerstone Library, 1974.

French, William Leslie. *The Psychology of Handwriting*. New York and London: G. P. Putnam's Sons, 1922.

Hamilton, Charles. *The Book of Autographs*. New York: Simon and Schuster, 1978.

————. *Collecting Autographs and Manuscripts*. Norman, OK: University of Oklahoma Press, 1961.

————. *The Illustrated Letter*. New York: Universe Books, 1987.

Hartford, Huntington. *You Are What You Write*. New York: Macmillan Publishing Co., Inc., 1973.

Hill, Barbara. *Handwriting Analysis*. London: Arrow Books, 1985.

Holder, Robert. *You Can Analyze Handwriting*. Englewood Cliffs, NJ: Prentice Hall, Inc., 1958.

Jacoby, H. J. *Analysis of Handwriting*. London: George Allen and Unwin Ltd., 1939.

————. *Self-Knowledge Through Handwriting*. London: J. M. Dent and Sons, Ltd., 1941.

Kanfer, Alfred. *A Guide to Handwriting Analysis*. New York: Dell, 1962.

Lewinson, Thea Stein, and Zubin, Joseph. *Handwriting Analysis*. New York: King's Crown Press, 1942.

Marcuse, Irene. *Guide to Personality Through Your Handwriting*. New York: ARC Books, Inc., Second Edition, 1967.

————. *The Key to Handwriting Analysis*. New York: The McBride Company, 1955.

Marley, John. *Handwriting Analysis Made Easy*. North Hollywood, CA: Wilshire Book Company, 1967.

Marne, Patricia. *Crime and Sex in Handwriting*. London: The Trinity Press, 1981.

Myer, Oscar N. *The Language of Handwriting and How to Read It*. New York: Stephen Daye Press, 1951.

Olyanova, Nadya. *Handwriting Tells*. Indianapolis: The Bobbs-Merrill Company, 1936, latest revised edition 1969, North Hollywood, CA: Melvin Powers, Wilshire Book Company.

————. *The Psychology of Handwriting: Secrets of Handwriting Analysis*. New York: Sterling Publishing Company, Inc., 1960, North Hollywood, CA: Melvin Powers, Wilshire Book Company.

Rawlings, Ray. *The Stein and Day Book of World Autographs*. New York: Stein and Day, 1978.

Rice, Louise. *Character Reading from Handwriting*. New York: Frederick A. Stokes, Company, 1927.

Roman, Klara G. *Encyclopedia of the Written Word*. New York: Frederick Ungar Publishing Company, 1968.

——. *Handwriting: A Key to Personality*. New York: Pantheon Books, Inc., 1952.

——. "Tension and Release: Studies of Handwriting with the Use of the Graphodyne." Personality-Symposium, No. 2, New York, 1950.

Sara, Dorothy. *Handwriting Analysis for the Millions*. New York: Bell Publishing Company, 1967.

Saudek, Robert. *Experiments with Handwriting*. New York: William Morrow & Co., 1928.

Singer, Eric. *Personality in Handwriting*. Westport, CT: Associated Booksellers, 1954.

Solomon, Shirl. *How to Really Know Yourself Through Your Handwriting*. New York: Bantam Books, 1973.

Sonnemann, Ulrich. *Handwriting Analysis*. London: Allen & Unwin Ltd., 1950.

Steiger, Brad, and Howard, William. *Handwriting Analysis*. New York: Ace Publishing Corporation, 1970.

Teltscher, Herry O. *Handwriting—A Key to Personality*. New York: G. P. Putnam & Sons, 1942.

Wolff, Werner. *Diagrams of the Unconscious*. New York: Grune & Stratton, 1948.

ABOUT THE AUTHORS

Andrea McNichol

Andrea McNichol is one of the leading graphologists in the United States and a highly respected researcher in the field.

McNichol studied graphology at the Sorbonne and at the University of Heidelberg. After receiving a bachelor's degree and teaching credentials from the University of California, Berkeley, she undertook an eight-year study in conjunction with psychiatrists and other medical doctors, correlating graphological characteristics with mental and physical conditions. With the cooperation of Alcoholics Anonymous, the National Association of Educators, four California penal institutions, and a variety of business groups, McNichol investigated the relationship between handwriting and such characteristics as alcohol and drug use, intelligence, criminal tendencies, and success in business. She has also conducted numerous studies under the auspices of the University of California, exploring the relationship between handwriting and personality.

In 1975, McNichol designed the first college-level graphology course at an accredited U.S. university, the University of California, Los Angeles. Since that time she has taught courses on graphology at six campuses of the University of California, where she has consistently received the highest student ratings.

McNichol has been featured in such publications as the *New York Times*, the *Los Angeles Times*, *U.S. News and World Report*, and *Time*, and she has appeared on numerous national television programs, including all the major network news shows and the "Tonight Show." The author of *Advanced Studies in Graphology*, McNichol has been published in a wide variety of books, magazines, and trade journals. She has been consulted on such celebrated cases as the Hitler diaries, the Josef Mengele case, and the Billionaire Boys' Club murder.

In 1980 McNichol founded the Los Angeles-based firm Graphology Consultants International, which specializes in the examination of questioned documents and personality assessment for business and law enforcement agencies. She regularly consults with several Fortune 500 companies and other corporations in the United States, Mexico, and Canada. McNichol conducts training seminars throughout the world in the use of graphology. She is one of the most sought-after speakers and teachers of the science in the United States today.

Jeffrey A. Nelson

Writer/producer Jeff Nelson studied English at Yale and Stanford universities, receiving his bachelor of arts degree from the latter in 1979. Starting out producing commercials, he has gone on to produce network and cable movies and miniseries.

His writing credits include both episodic and documentary television.

INDEX

More Praise for Andrea McNichol's
Handwriting Analysis: Putting It to Work for You

"I recently read your book and found it to be utterly fascinating. I have been interested in graphology since my youth and had always considered it to be a mysterious and difficult skill. Your book cleared away the mystery leading me to realize that it was not as difficult a subject as I had imagined and left me with pure intrigue and a desire to learn more. It has become part of my routine assessment of patients. I feel as if I have gained a powerful insight on some very volatile situations. This experience has been invaluable to me both professionally and personally." —Nyla J. Snyder
Registered Nurse, Fort Wayne, IN

"I recently had the opportunity to read your book and found it absolutely fascinating! Every other book I've encountered on this topic has treated it as little more than a parlor game. I knew there had to be more to it, but until your book I could never locate a reliable source of information.
—Rita Monaco
Essex Falls, NJ

"For the past seven years, I have been studying handwriting analysis. I have read several books on the subject but have found your book to be the most logical and easy to understand."
—Mary Pat Hyland
Endwell, NY

"I have purchased several books on handwriting analysis over the years. Your book is the best of its kind that I have ever found."
—Ed Ryder
Upland, PA

"Your book is excellent, an unexpected pleasure, and the best I've read."
—Jim Kreider
Newton, MA

"I have now personally purchased and distributed 72 copies of your book. From those clients to whom I have provided a copy, I have had nothing but very favorable comments. Thanks again for taking the time to write the book so the novice can have some feel for some of the benefits to be derived from this most exciting and challenging profession."
—Gerald R. Brown, G. Brown & Associates
Wilsonville, OR

"I found your text to be very complete and integrated in its view and approach."
—Marc K. Davis
Ft. Myers, FL

"I have recently read your book. In fact, more than read it, I've studied it. I have always loved psychology and found the correlation between the two subjects to be fascinating. As you said in your book, I will never look at anyone's handwriting the same way again!" —Diane L. Fleming
Jersey City, NJ

"I am writing to say how much I enjoyed your book. It is one of the books on graphology I have most enjoyed and is very different in approach from anything else I have read on the subject."
—Clare Hanson
Diamondhead, MS

"I found your book to be prepared so logically that remembering facts is just plain fun!"
—Pavel Heger
Newton, MA

"Bravo! I just read your book and I loved it. I loved your treatment of margins and spacing, and until now I've never been able to analyze printed writing. The quizzes are great and I love the 'who-dun-its.' For me, the study of handwriting is now divided into 'before-your-book' and 'after-your book.'"
—Jake Van Scherick
Meriden, CT

"Thank you so much for what I have learned from you. It has truly changed my life."
—Teresa J. Hee
Honolulu, HI

"I just finished your book and enjoyed it immensely and am busy analyzing my friends' handwriting samples. Before I read your book, I had tried some books from the library and found them so dull and uninspiring that I returned them promptly. Strangely, upon rereading your book I find I am enjoying it even more the second time around."
—D. Hofheimer
Long Beach, NY

"Thank you for your years of research and also for your masterful structuring of the information. I have never been so charmingly drawn into a body of information."
—Yolande S. Hilpisch
Belmont, CA

"I really think you've done an excellent job on your book. The material is well presented and the handwriting samples are great."
—Pat Peterson
Naperville, IL

"I found your book a delight to read! Thank you for making the subject so interesting."
—Jeanne Fellow
Lodi, CA

"I am 12 years old and have bought your book. I have found it most interesting and fun."
—Catherine Reaves
Inwood, WY

"Of all the graphology books in my library and of all those in the Denver Public Library, your book is the most current, accurate, and useful. Thank you for an excellent book!"
—Richard Sweeny
Certified Master Graphoanalyst, Denver CO

"I am an English citizen and have just moved over to the United States. Recently I had the good fortune to read your book, which I feel sets out very clearly the basics of the science and is extremely 'user-friendly.' "
—Kathryn Casside
Laguna Beach, CA

"I am 22 years old and during the summer I signed out your book and was astounded by the nonhoroscope accuracy of the book's revelations . . . and now I think graphology is my calling."
—Jason Hotte
LaSalle, Ontario, Canada

Learn More About Graphology
A Special Offer for Readers

If you would like to continue studying handwriting analysis with Andrea McNichol, you can send for any of the following products from the McNichol-Nelson Graphology Institute, Inc.:

Handwriting Analysis with Andrea McNichol:
8-Hour Video Course and Workbook—$89.95 (plus shipping and handling)

Based on Andrea McNichol's popular University of California course and filmed in a classroom setting, these videotapes let you follow along as McNichol demonstrates and explains handwriting traits related to intelligence, creativity, emotional stability, aptitudes, sexuality, and much more. These videos are not only informative but lots of fun, too, and you can proceed at your own pace and convenience. A teacher since 1975, McNichol has consistently received the highest student evaluations.

You'll receive two high-quality, 4-hour VHS videotapes plus a special 60-page workbook designed for you to follow along in as you view the tapes.

The Doodle Test: Video Program and Workbook—$29.95 (plus shipping and handling)

A way to learn how to instantly analyze many key personality elements, such as your confidence level, self-image, competitiveness, feelings about your parents, feelings about sex, and much more, the Doodle Test video program is fun and easy. Simply doodle the first thing that comes to mind in each of the boxes on the two test sheets that are included (no artistic talent is required) and then watch the 1-hour-long VHS videotape to interpret your test. You'll soon discover why your doodles reveal oodles.

In addition to explaining how to analyze the Doodle Test, McNichol shows you how to interpret a wide variety of your favorite everyday doodles, including doodles of boxes, spider webs, triangles, houses, and people. The Doodle Test video program comes with extra test sheets, because after taking the test yourself you'll want to give it to everyone you know.

Hidden Messages in Your Children's Writing—$14.95 (plus shipping and handling)

Andrea McNichol has just written a very special and important book for understanding your children, *Hidden Messages in Your Children's Writing*. Designed for analyzing the drawings, doodles, and handwriting of children ages 2 through 17, this illustrated 64-page book will show you how to use graphology to learn what your children are really feeling but may not be saying.

You'll learn ways to determine how your child is doing compared with other children his or her age, what his or her hidden talents and abilities are, and whether he or she is happy, intelligent, well-adjusted, stable, and in good health. McNichol also shows how to notice important warning signs indicating that it's time to get your child professional help, including tips on spotting drug and alcohol use. If you have children or are a teacher, this book is an absolute must.

Dishonesty in Handwriting:
Video Program and Workbook—$29.95 (plus shipping and handling)

Use graphology to spot thieves, liars, rogues, and your average, everyday "bad guys"!

In this 2-hour VHS video program, the same one Andrea McNichol uses to train FBI and security agents throughout the United States, you will learn how to use handwriting to get honest people into your life—in your business, home, or personal relationships.

McNichol gives many samples of the handwriting of infamous criminals and also devotes a section to spotting the signs associated with the potential for violence, including special warnings that indicate when it's time to take action.

Your Handwriting Analyzed at the Institute—$19.95 (plus shipping and handling)

What does your handwriting reveal? Are you a leader or a follower? Do you have untapped potential? Are you eager to face the future or do you cling to the past? Are you a go-getter or do you put up imaginary barriers for yourself? What kind of job would best suit you? Do you have the number-one handwriting trait associated with successful people?

You can receive a personalized, individual 10-page analysis of your handwriting analyzed with the same techniques Andrea McNichol uses when working for such clients as the FBI, Scotland Yard, the Justice Department, the Department of Defense, and a wide range of Fortune 500 companies.

What to do to receive your analysis: Using a ballpoint pen on a blank, unlined sheet of 8½-by-11-inch paper, write a two-paragraph letter to yourself about anything you want. Include your *full signature*, and on the back of the sheet, *print* your full name, address, and phone number.

Order Form

Delivery Info

Name _____

Address _____

Suite or Apt. _____

City _____ State _____ ZIP _____

Day phone number (_____) _____

Evening phone number (_____) _____

Method of Payment

☐ Check or money order enclosed

☐ Bill my credit card:

    ☐ Amex ☐ MasterCard ☐ VISA ☐ Discover

Acct# _____ Exp. date ____ /____

Name on credit card _____

Cardholder signature _____

	Quantity	Price Each	Total Item
8-Hour Video Course		$89.95	
Doodle Test Video		$29.95	
Hidden Messages		$14.95	
Dishonesty in Handwriting Video		$29.95	
Your Handwriting Analyzed		$19.95	
SUBTOTAL			
+ Shipping			
CA residents add 8.25% sales tax			
TOTAL			

Shipping and Handling Charges

1 item	$5.95
2 items	$6.95
3 items	$7.95
4 or more	$8.95
Your Handwriting Analyzed s&h	$3.50

Canadian and non-continental U.S. residents: Add $4.00 to all s&h prices.

Mail your order and payment to:
MNGI, Inc.
10573 West Pico Blvd., Ste. 820
Los Angeles, CA 90064

To order by phone
with your credit card,
call toll free **(800) 927-4540**.
Non-U.S. residents call **(310) 441-4540**.

For fastest service, **fax** your order: **(310) 441-4540**.
Please do not send samples for analysis by fax.
